be free... and set others free

John: This is a book about leading. Without vision and leadership, people perish . . .

SHANE: . . . or at least run around in circles.

John: There are a few good leaders, and lots of books on leadership. But one of the biggest problems today is an abundance of ineffective or bad leaders.

SHANE: We've gotten really good at busting on bad leaders . . . which has made us suspicious followers. This book is also about following. And there aren't many books on *followership.*

John: I like that: a book about leading *and* following.

SHANE: When we started The Simple Way community, we had an anarchistic saying: "A strong people need no leader," and we determined that we would *not* have a leader . . .

John: . . . Hmmm.

SHANE: It worked pretty well—*for about a week*. A lot of folks today have serious hesitations about following others. Can you blame them? They've seen so many immoral teachers, bad presidents, crooked CEOs, scary preachers and pretentious mean people on the Left and on the Right . . . it's no wonder there is a distrust of authority.

John: I remember hearing the saying in the 1960s, "Don't trust anyone over 30." And as African-Americans, distrust of authority is common. But Shane is right. Especially in the church and in politics—but also everywhere else—a lack of confidence in leaders has grown. In fact, it is rampant. I don't like that. But the answer to bad leadership is not *no leadership*; rather, it is *good leadership*.

SHANE: So where do we begin?

John: We begin by following Jesus. What does it mean when He asks us to deny ourselves, take up His cross and *follow Him*?[1] One thing it means is that we all begin as followers; and to be good leaders, we have to know how to be good followers.

SHANE: We have to rediscover the endangered art of apprenticeship, of finding people in whose steps we can trust and follow.

John: We have to find people who will come along with us as we lead and who will carry on the vision after us. After all, if you only have a vision with nobody on board, you aren't a leader . . . just somebody with a good idea. A leader without followers won't go far.

SHANE: And followers without a leader just wander.

John: In the end, all the footsteps of good leaders and good followers must lead to Christ and to the freedom found in His cross.

SHANE: But sometimes the path is hard to find on our own. It's time to reimagine leadership and followership together. Walk with us . . .

Note
1. See Mark 8:34.

FOLLOW ME TO FREEDOM

LEADING AND FOLLOWING AS AN ORDINARY RADICAL

SHANE CLAIBORNE
& John M. Perkins

Regal

From Gospel Light
Ventura, California, U.S.A.

Published by Regal
From Gospel Light
Ventura, California, U.S.A.
www.regalbooks.com
Printed in the U.S.A.

Interior Design: Rob Williams
Transcription: Marcia Zimmermann
Editorial Support: Katie Jo Brotherton, Deena Davis, Andrew Koch,
Steven Lawson, Alanna Swanson, Pamela Toussaint and Mark Weising
Theological Editor: Dr. Gary Greig

This book is printed on 30 percent post-consumer waste, which is certified
by credible, thorough environmental agencies.

Library of Congress Cataloging-in-Publication Data
Perkins, John.
Follow me to freedom : leading as an ordinary radical / John Perkins,
Shane Claiborne.
p. cm.
ISBN 978-0-8307-5120-4 (trade paper)
1. Leadership—Religious aspects—Christianity. 2. Christian life.
3. Liberty—Religious aspects—Christianity. I. Claiborne, Shane, 1975- II. Title.
BV4597.53.L43P46 2009
248.4—dc22
2009029753

2 3 4 5 6 7 8 9 10 / 15 14 13 12 11 10 09

Rights for publishing this book outside the U.S.A. or in non-English languages are
administered by Gospel Light Worldwide, an international not-for-profit ministry.
For additional information, please visit www.glww.org, email info@glww.org, or write
to Gospel Light Worldwide, 1957 Eastman Avenue, Ventura, CA 93003, U.S.A.

CONTENTS

AN INTRODUCTION

SHANE: I was introduced to John Perkins when I read his book *Let Justice Roll Down*. He opened my eyes and set my heart on fire as he told how he had responded to extreme racism and hatred with forgiveness and love.

John showed no fear as a civil rights leader in the Deep South in the late 1960s, when everything, including his life, was on the line. He modeled being an ordinary radical before I even knew the term. Not even halfway through the book, I knew John Perkins was a leader I wanted to follow.

Not so long after that, John and I met. He came down to visit our little experiment in community on the north side of Philadelphia. I remember wanting to give John an impressive tour of our nonprofit organization, but all he wanted to do was sit on the steps in front of our building and eat ice cream with the kids. He had been on plenty of snazzy tours of ministries that were going to "transform the world" and just wanted to meet our friends here in the neighborhood.

I remember later that day whining to John about how we had been working so hard and hadn't seen much of anything get better. There were still gunshots all the time—there was still heroine, there was still prostitution, there was still poverty, there was still pain. I remember complaining, "It's been over three years and there aren't many signs of change." John looked me dead in the eye and, with the gentleness of a father, plainly and so sincerely explained the way things work: "Oh, Shane, you'll start to see some things change. You'll start to see signs of transformation—in about 10 years. Or maybe 12." And he didn't flinch. That was his promise: We'd see change *in 10 or 12 years*. I gulped. That was nearly half my life up to that moment, yet somehow I knew he spoke the truth, and it gave me hope.

John's was (and is) the voice of someone who has committed his life to a movement that requires deep faith and revolutionary patience, who has set his hand to the plow and hasn't looked back. That's someone I want to rub off on me . . . so I followed.

John soon invited me to join up with the Christian Community Development Association (CCDA),[1] one of the few organizations that crosses the generational divide with a relentless conviction that the old and young must dream together. It's an incredible family that has been practicing resurrection and paving the way to freedom in some of the toughest corners of our world.

John: A few years back, I started hearing rumors about Shane. You might have heard some too. Word was going around that a group of mostly young white middle-class Christians, led by a guy who dressed like a monk, had stirred up things on the north side of Philadelphia. All the fuss started when the Roman Catholic Archdiocese threatened to evict some homeless families from a boarded-up church building where they had taken refuge. Shane and his college buddies were rightly outraged, became squatters with the families and risked arrest. Once better housing was found for the families, instead of retreating back to the suburbs, Shane and his friends stayed on. They could have swept into the struggling neighborhood, offered a cure to the immediate crisis, left some boxes of food and departed with smiles on their faces. They could have returned to their college campuses, written papers on their inner-city triumph and been heroes. Instead, Shane and some of his friends did the unthinkable by joining in with the people: they felt the pain, saw the need for more and made North Philly their home too.[2] I admit it: I liked what I had heard, and I was curious.

So, I arranged a trip to Philadelphia to see things firsthand. By then, Shane and his friends had created The Simple Way—an intentional community that is part of what is now being called the new monastic movement.[3] They pooled their resources and committed themselves to doing life together. In a small way they remind me of myself when, decades earlier, I moved my family from the suburbs of Southern California back to my native Mississippi, at the height of the civil rights movement.

Sure enough, Shane and I sat on the stoop in front of his building on Potter Street, eating ice cream with the kids. You can learn a lot about a person when you watch him in his environment, and you can learn even more when you observe him interact with the children. You know what I saw? In Shane, I sensed the most humble, sensible, kind radical you will ever meet. His unusual dress and quiet manner disarm you. But you immediately know there is more going on inside.

He actually listens—tenderly listens, not just to your words, but also to your heart. He asks probing questions and wants real answers too.

There on the stoop, my ice cream melting, I could see concern and love pour out from Shane for the folks in his neighborhood—a deep love—and I could see his neighbors respond with respect for him. He reminded me a little of my oldest son, Spencer, who like Shane had so much hope that things could be better for the poor. Spencer led a little community in Jackson, Mississippi, but a few years ago he suffered cardiac arrest. I really think he died of a broken heart—shattered because he saw the need and had the passion but was unable to do more. Spencer would have found Shane's revolution irresistible. It would have given him hope, and he would have joined in.

Right away, I could see that Shane was not a crazy cult leader but a prophetic voice—and I knew he was someone we needed to join in with us. At CCDA, we had talked a lot about how to keep the vision of reconciliation and community development moving forward, how to pass it along to the younger generation. We invited Shane to be on the CCDA board of directors, and we have become stronger, richer, deeper people because of his involvement. Now the demands of his travel schedule make it hard for him to attend board meetings, but we still need his presence and his voice, so he is on our board of advisors.

Not only has CCDA grown from Shane's example, but people respond to him at the Urbana missions conference, Westmont College, the National Pastor's Conference, and pretty much wherever he goes. They get excited about his story and embrace his challenges; after all, Shane is cool. He is real. But he really connects with people when they see that he doesn't just do things *for* the poor; rather, he has a charisma *with* the poor.

Shane and his friends went to North Philly, not saying, "Here we are to lift you up," but saying, "Here we are to become one with you." Historically, a big divide has separated blacks and whites—and there hasn't been a deep enough commitment to fill the gap. Whites typically come alongside blacks for a little while and then leave. Shane and The Simple Way are there to stay. They also do life a little different. No one can ever accuse them of being a typical nonprofit, dependent upon a denomination, foundation or church for funding. Because of their simple lifestyle and because they have not presented themselves as a source of material goods in North Philly, they do not have the same interdependencies as some others. They are free to be more radical and lean on Jesus.

I know Shane will not want me saying all of this about him.

SHANE: Amen to that.

John: But this is my part of this book, so I get to do some talking. One time, Shane surprised and challenged folks at Willow Creek Community Church. Without any advance warning—so that people would have their best footwear on—he invited everyone to the altar to take off their shoes. And as you can imagine, at Willow Creek that meant a pretty big pile. The next week they gave the shoes out to people who needed them. Another time, at a CCDA board meeting in Atlanta, we discovered he wasn't staying at the nice hotel with the rest of us—by choice. At night, he quietly slipped away and camped out under a bridge with some homeless folks. That was a real wake-up call. He doesn't do these things to impress anyone, but he makes an impression. I am struck most by Shane's humility.

Today, we need humble and creative leaders—people who lead out of who they are. This new generation has not been infected so much by the historical racism and prejudices that have contaminated my own generation and the boomers—both blacks and whites. Shane is one of a new breed. He is an emerging leader that I am comfortable following. I don't know what the future will look like, but I know I want to tag along.

SHANE: You probably have already noticed that John and I are a little different from each other . . . *I have more hair.* Honestly, I am a recovering redneck from Eastern Tennessee; he is an elder statesman of the evangelical church from Mississippi. He was born before World War II was fought. I was born the year Saigon fell and the Vietnam War ended. He wears a suit and tie. I only wear a tie to hold my hair back . . . and since John busted me on my clothes a few pages back, let me say, my clothes are a little different because I make them with my momma each winter. I'm still working up to sewing the suit—you can call me an apprentice seamstress . . . or "tailor" I reckon (I think my mom wanted a girl, but a boy who sews will have to suffice). John is married and has seven living adult children. I am still single (at least at the writing of this book!). He has counseled three presidents and has already been invited to the White House by Barack Obama. I had a different little campaign this last election: "Jesus for President" (more on that later). And so it goes. You'd be hard-fetched to find a more unlikely duo. While our pasts are about as different as you can get, the future that we invite you to imagine with us is almost identical.

John: The temptations faced, the stories told and the physical abilities at 30 years old are a little different from those we meet at 70-plus years, but that's part of the fun of this conversation.

SHANE: We have each made our share of mistakes and, hopefully, learned from them; but at the end of the day, even if by default, we have chosen to be leaders—or leadership has chosen us. It seems that the stuff we put our hands to bears fruit, and that people are following . . . or at least buying our books. Heck, someone even created a "fake Shane Claiborne" on Twitter that some people follow . . . and the funny thing is some people think that's actually me! And John probably has a Facebook fan club.

John: Funny, I really do have a Facebook page! My daughter Elizabeth put it up and keeps it going. But seriously, Shane is right. We are different. And I think that's part of what reconciliation is all about. If we cannot be reconciled with people that look different than we look, then what is reconciliation? And there will be no true freedom for any of us unless we are first reconciled to each other and to God.

SHANE: Most books on leadership have best-practice models, seven secrets to success or "amazing new" paradigms (and a fair amount of fluff, too, though I won't mention any specific titles). We certainly can learn from Maxwell, Blanchard, Stanley and others about leadership, but John and I cannot write a book that way. We speak not as consultants, but as friends in the struggle. We speak out of our lives in the trenches, from the broken streets of Jackson and North Philly, from the abandoned places of the empire in which we find ourselves. Don't get me wrong: John could give you a list of "10 Ways to Transform Your Leadership" (and he probably will, and they will be magical). I, however, am just not that linear. So this will be fun.

It's also true that we wanted to write this together but have pretty wild lives (heck, we barely have time to read, much less write a book together), so our friends had a great idea: Rather than recycle material or try to physically sit down and write together, let's just get John and me together for a few hours here and a few more hours there and have some honest, raw conversations on "followership" and on leadership . . . and then turn our thoughts into a book. So here it is.

Most books by two authors are written in one voice. Nope. We decided that combining our voices would not only be difficult but would also be just plain odd (like mixing smooth jazz and punk rock and trying to dance to it). So we have chosen a unique format, trying to preserve both voices, doing a little harmonizing without homogenizing, and hoping it makes you dance. We each will tell our part of the story in our own voice, sometimes commenting on what the other says, sometimes not. Sometimes John will give a long teaching (because it is so good!), and other times (like right now) I will be carrying on. Like I said, this will be fun.

We have even sprinkled in a few blank places and numbers . . .

1. _____

2. _____

3. _____

. . . so that those of you who just have to have outlines can create your own as you go along.

We both recognize that there are no easy answers, and books can only go so far . . . but this book is more about taking you on a journey than trying to get you to a destination. We do not offer a new theory or prescription, nor do we attempt a comprehensive study. Rather, we submit our experiences, our lessons learned and our unresolved questions, in a day and time that needs leaders and followers of integrity and action.

We hope that what you read feels like a conversation you'd have in rocking chairs on the porch, sipping sweet tea (perhaps not a bad place to read it either). John and I once sat on that stoop in Philadelphia eating ice cream and just being part of the neighborhood. He listened to my dreams, my hopes and my questions. In Mississippi, I visited John's home where he and Vera Mae have a historic Southern farmhouse they have renovated. On warm, humid summer nights, John likes to sit in a rocking chair, watch the sun set and tell stories of the past and the future.

John: *Follow Me to Freedom* is not just for leaders. It is for anyone who has ever led or followed, and for everyone who wants to. So join us now. Bring along your youthful dreams . . .

SHANE: . . . and your age-old wisdom. Let's sit together on the stoop on Potter Street in Philly, and on the porch of the farmhouse in Mississippi. No anecdotes or formulas . . . just a beautiful conversation. Come on.

Notes

1. For more information about CCDA, visit www.ccda.org.
2. For more of the story, see Shane Claiborne, *The Irresistible Revolution: Living as an Ordinary Radical* (Grand Rapids, MI: Zondervan, 2006).
3. To learn more about intentional communities, see Jonathan Wilson-Hartgrove, *New Monasticism: What It Has to Say to Today's Church* (Grand Rapids, MI: Brazos Press, 2008).

*We dedicate these conversations to
the young who see great visions
and the old who dream new dreams
(see Acts 2:17)*

And who is he who will harm you if you become
followers of what is good?

1 PETER 3:13

THE PROMISE

(Raising the Next Generation of Just Leaders)

John: We all like promises, especially when the promise is for something good that will happen in the future. So God had Abraham's attention when He made a big promise. On the surface, the idea looked impossible, even outrageous. God pledged to *bless* the entire world through Abraham—everyone alive at the time and everyone who would ever be born. Every single person! Abraham, no doubt, trusted God, but he also knew that, being just one person, he could not "bless" that many people; so God's big plan must have seemed daunting. And there was one other small issue . . .

SHANE: . . . Abraham didn't even get the promise until he was about 80 years old. And it was another 20 years before his son was born. (Hey, John's almost 80, so he *could* just be getting started!)

John: What seemed unfeasible to man was quite doable for God. He kept His promise by blessing one man (Abraham), then another (Abraham's son Isaac), then a household, then a community, then a region and now, you and me. You can read the entire story in Genesis 11–21. As the promise was passed forward, God blessed each new generation.

When God blesses, the blessing is not stagnant: it moves and multiplies. The idea is to plant a seed, then water it and grow it—and then give it to the next generation. The blessing is not for one person (it is not just for you or me alone). Rather, it was given to Abraham and is now given to us so that we might be a blessing to others. That's the real purpose of ministry. Abraham blessed Isaac. Isaac blessed Jacob. Jacob blessed his 12 sons, which became the tribes of Israel. The blessing followed each person's faithfulness.

SHANE: These forefathers (and mothers!) were willing to leave everything they had for the promise of something better—even when the promise seemed impossible, or laughable, like a barren woman giving birth at 90 years old. (That's how old Sarah was when Isaac was born.) Believing in the promise meant they held everything lightly, and when God said move—they trusted and moved. It all started with an 80-year-old man who dared to listen to God!

> WHAT WE PASS ALONG IS
> HOPE AND A VISION THAT CAN
> BE CARRIED FORTH.

John: The promise is hope for something in the future, but what is the blessing? Some may equate blessing with material possessions—a big house, a car, lots of toys. Others may assume blessing means happiness, kindness and security. We say a blessing before a meal, and our children bless us, but God's promise of a blessing to Abraham was something more.

Follow me closely here. This passing on of the promise *is* the blessing, and the act of passing the blessing along is therefore as important as the promise, because it becomes the fulfillment of the promise. If a blessing is complete or finished, there is nothing to pass along except a memory. A blessing supersedes individual achievement and movements. It goes beyond a particular moment in time or spot on the map. A blessing is like a living organism, not some kind of plaque we hang on a wall or meal we eat at the end of the day. The promise contains hope, but there is always an element of it that goes unfulfilled. Sure, we might make progress and see some of the promise come about, but what we pass along is hope and a vision that can be carried forth, and a little bit more of it will be fulfilled by the next generation, and then the next.

I call this "continued leadership." My daughter Elizabeth calls it "passing the baton." This sets the stage for what it means to be a follower and a leader today.

SHANE: Hey, we could call this *sustainable* leadership—a leadership that reproduces itself.

John: That reminds me of the story of a guy named Moses.

SHANE: The basketball player?

John: Ha-ha. No, Moses the Liberator. He exemplifies reproducible leadership at its best. I've been using him as a model for the past 50 years, and he has everything to say to us today.

Let me tell you about his journey out of Pharaoh's land of captivity. Although Pharaoh had decreed that babies born to Hebrew slaves were to be killed, when Moses was born, by faith his parents hid him for three months because they saw he was a beautiful or proper child; and they were not afraid of the king's commandment. Hebrews tells the whole story best:

> By faith Moses, when he had grown up, refused to be called the son of Pharaoh's daughter, choosing rather to endure ill-treatment with the people of God than to enjoy the passing pleasures of sin, considering the reproach of Christ greater riches than the treasures of Egypt; for he was looking to the reward. By faith he left Egypt, not fearing the wrath of the king; for he endured, as seeing Him who is unseen. By faith he kept the Passover and the sprinkling of the blood, so that he who destroyed the firstborn would not touch them. By faith they passed through the Red Sea as though they were passing through dry land; and the Egyptians, when they attempted it, were drowned (Heb. 11:24-29).

Here we have both what made Moses into this great person as well as the task that he was to undertake. Moses became what I call a "just leader"—a man who heard the cry of his people and led them to freedom.

Make no excuses. First, when we look at Moses and the circumstances of his birth, none of us today have an excuse to be less than what *God says we are.* Moses was born in poverty, as a slave. He was conceived to be aborted. That's right, he was not supposed to survive outside his mother's womb. He was born in the most difficult situation, when a decree had gone out that all baby boys must be killed. What kind of psychological damage does that cause to a child?

Moses' success proves that we shouldn't attribute our present failings to an unfortunate past!

We black folks need to hear that. We can't blame slavery for everything—especially when we understand it. We poor folks need to hear that. We can't constantly mope on and on about what we don't have and yet not try to get a job or some skills and do something about it, no matter how unjustly we have been treated. We have to stop playing the victim.

We undereducated folks need to hear that. We can't forever waste time griping about how life would be, oh, so different if we just had a good education. We need to pick up a book and start reading, find a mentor, and start asking questions.

We preachers need to hear that. We can't recoil from the gospel because our culture doesn't like some of it. We need to love even more.

Moses could have remained a victim. He could have spent his life crying, "I was a slave! I was supposed to be aborted!" He could have used it as a reason to waver and fail. Instead, Moses went on to become the greatest leader, outside of Jesus Christ, that ever walked on earth.

SHANE: I like this idea of a just leader. And it makes good sense that we cannot remain victims if we are ever to see freedom—we cannot forget the past, but the past does not hold us captive. We may have scars but scars remind us that we survived. So how did Moses rise above his circumstances?

John: Moses was born into a tough environment—one of tension and suffering and pain. (Jot down the word "pain"; it will come up many times in this book.) Rather than moan and complain, we are to count it all joy when we fall into suffering, that our faith is precious like gold.[1] It's that refining fire that shapes our life for the task God has called us to.

One of the first things we learn about Moses' life is that when he was born, his parents hid him for three months. Moses' parents, in the midst of a horrible decree to kill all baby boys, protected him! He had a family, and they put his safety ahead of their own survival. You can't be a great leader if you can't guide your own family with love and honor. The basis for leadership and the greatest environment in which to develop leaders is the family. (Jot down "family," as Shane and I will talk much about it. You will see how family and community are intertwined.) Leaders will mature and develop better if they come from an intact family that passes on love and instills a strong identity with dignity.

> YOU CAN'T BE A GREAT LEADER IF
> YOU CAN'T GUIDE YOUR OWN
> FAMILY WITH LOVE AND HONOR.

Our God is a God who loves the family. That's how we end up with the concept of the Trinity. At first, it seems that God is talking to Himself in Genesis when He says, "Let Us make man" (Gen. 1:26). A good theological study shows that Jesus is the eternal Son and the Holy Spirit is the Comforter. All three were present from the beginning and make up the Family of God—the Godhead. From this we see that from the beginning, God the Father did not lead alone; He did so from within the context of family.

That's what makes what we face today in the breakdown of the family structure so tragic. Have you noticed that most of our immorality today is of a sexual variety? It's sex gone wild in our society. Why? Because the family is broken.

Let me go on a little sidetrack. I just heard about something hideous—a grandmother molesting her own grandchild. That . . . went all over my bones, and it made me appreciate my own precious granddaughter, Varah, and our family. We are not perfect . . . not by a long shot. Just ask my sons and daughters. They will tell you. But I think we get some things right. Yet, as a leader it is a constant challenge of priorities.

One day, before an important meeting with some important people who had come to Jackson to see me, my wife, Vera Mae, came over with Varah and her bicycle, which had two flats. Varah softly asked, "Grandpa, will you fix my bike?" I'm thinking, *I ain't got time.* "Will you fix my bike?" I thought about it a few seconds, looked into her eyes that were calling out to me and then said, "Sure. The people here to meet with me can wait. I'm going to do this right now."

I got my pump going and I fixed her flat. It only took me a few minutes. I put her on her bike and pushed her. I had taught her how to ride the bike. I had put her first training wheels on and was with her the first time she ever went without them. There was no way I could leave her with two flats. When she learned how to swim, I was in the swimming pool and taught her. She thinks her granddaddy can do everything. (Don't tell her otherwise!) And when I fixed her flats, I said, "You know, you're the most important person in my life right now." With her little smile, she said, "I knew it, but I wouldn't say it."

Oh, man! She *knew* it! What if I had blown that chance to affirm her? Children (and grandchildren) need to know they are important. Varah knew it, and Moses knew it . . . what would you do if your grandchild asked you to stop reading this book and fix the flats on his bike?

SHANE: Interruptions are a theme in Scripture. We have a God who is continually interrupting us—interrupting our routines, our patterns of inequity, the status quo. Abraham's life was interrupted. Moses' life was interrupted. John's life and my life were interrupted by the Spirit.

The gospels are stories of interruption after interruption. Jesus was at a wedding in Cana when His mother interrupted Him and said, "They have no more wine."[2] He had just stepped ashore in a region called the Gerasenes when He was interrupted by the cries of a demon-possessed man.[3] He was on His way to visit a sick child when a touch on His sleeve interrupted Him and He felt the power go out from Him.[4] The incredible thing is that Jesus was always available and attentive to the interruptions and surprises, like someone who stops to fix a flat tire for a stranded motorist.

Jesus was never so fixed on His vision for the Kingdom that He missed the needs of folks right next to Him. Sometimes Jesus even gets yelled at for stopping to hang out with the kids. These days, He'd get in trouble in most churches for wasting time with washing feet and drawing in the dirt; after all, there's so much "meaningful" work to be done . . . like attending board meetings, raising funds for buildings and sitting in on conference calls (wink). Most days, our life in Philly feels like one interruption after another.[5] It is packed with surprises: a knock at the door, an emergency or a kid who wants to show us the first sunflower bud.

It seems that these are the very things so many of us try to squeeze out of our lives. We love predictability. We don't want anything to alter our course, even if we know there is something beautiful on the other end of the interruption. We'd rather just keep to the daily grind and the meaningless toil that is familiar and humdrum, rather than have our rhythms broken. Yet we have a God who is all about interrupting us. What if we missed the "interruption"? (Oh, sorry for interrupting your story about Moses, John.)

John: That's quite all right. I think I interrupted myself, and I will probably interrupt you before too long. That happens when we are passionate. Even good leaders and good followers interrupt each other, yet somehow pause to listen to each other too—and that is the key. Count on it.

Now, back to Moses. When God saw His people in misery (in slavery under Pharaoh) and wanted a leader to get them out of captivity, He found a Levitical family, a priestly family, a family that did life "by faith," to put Moses into so they could nurture him. The family's faith created an environment for Moses to also have faith. Moses' parents shared with him all that they knew about God, and told him what their great-great-great-grandfather, Abraham, had said. Faith is passed down like this in a family, and by the Word of God. It's biblical: "Faith comes by hearing, and hearing by the word of God" (Rom. 10:17). Each one of us has the responsibility to put the Word of God out (speaking it and living it), so people—our children and other people's children—will come to faith. That's biblical, too: "Without faith it is impossible to please Him" (Heb. 11:6). As leaders, we should keep this core responsibility in mind, for without it we put our vision at risk.

The Bible contains God's words and what others who knew Him said about Him. That's why it is called "the Word" and why we obey it. The Old Testament practice was to display these words in places around the house—most often on doorposts—so that the Word of

God would be visible and remind the family of His work in their past.[6] By remembering what God had already done, the Jewish people knew that God would be trustworthy in the future, and their faith was strengthened.

SHANE: Before we can lead we need to have confidence in God. We like stories today, and these stories show us what God has done in the past and what we can expect God to do now. What a great story!

John: Moses was "a beautiful child." What does this mean . . . just that he was cute? No. It means that his parents saw that God had given them this child. They weren't going to let him die. They were going to save him and nurture him for a noble purpose.

A particular young woman worked in our ministry for a while, and she had this deep inferiority complex. She was always as neat as a pin when she was a little girl, but she still had this unshakable sense that everybody else was better than her. There was always someone else who got more attention, was the most liked and was the smartest. Once she said, "I watched Reverend Perkins and Sister Perkins, and it looked like they cared for all of us about the same." What she was actually saying was, "They loved me, and they cared for me." And so that sense of purpose in her was nurtured.

I was recently at a Think Tank in Santa Cruz, California, with some good friends, and we were talking about community development. Honestly, I cared just as much about the multimillionaire businessman whose name you would recognize as I did about the unemployed ministry worker you have never heard of, both of whom were at the gathering. In fact, the ministry worker needed nurturing more than the multimillionaire did. What we've got to do is create an environment so that the purpose in people can be realized. That's what Moses' parents and the midwives did for him. They weren't troubled by the king's command. They said, "We're going to do what is necessary to save this child. We're not afraid." We need to see ourselves not only as leaders, but also as nurturers, and we must develop the same attitude toward those we nurture as Moses' parents had about him.

Despite being nurtured by a good family, Moses refused to be called the son of Pharaoh's daughter. Isn't that strange? He was raised in the best schools in Egypt. He was trained to be an Egyptian. He talked like an Egyptian. He ate the food of an Egyptian. He dressed like an Egyptian. He was being cultivated to be the next prince. Then he was running away (read the entire story in Exodus 2 for the context). Even on the run, his would-be wife said: "The Egyptian helped us." But deep down in Moses' heart he knew who he was—a Jew.

IN AFFIRMING WHO PEOPLE ARE,

YOU HELP RECLAIM THEIR

INHERENT DIGNITY.

Deep down, each of us knows who we are, and that is why self-identity is so important. What was the greatest damage done to black people during the civil rights movement? It was not discrimination, separation or even physical beatings. It was self-hatred. Those who sought to keep us down tried to make niggers out of us . . . and we almost believed that we were nobodies. As long as we accepted the idea that we were nobodies, we stayed in segregation. We wouldn't think any differently until somebody like Malcolm X or Stokely Carmichael stood up and said: "Black is beautiful!"

In affirming who people are, you help reclaim their inherent dignity. You are not *giving* people dignity, that's exploitation. You are affirming the dignity that was created in people by God. Our job as leaders is to go to the people, affirm them and help them with their motivation. Our task is to educate them and help them attain the skills they need to manage their own affairs. Affirmation does not stop at saying you are beautiful or cheering for the basketball team with black superstars; it has to have action behind it that will truly help all of the people.

Moses was a Jew, and he needed to be affirmed as a Jew, because nothing could change who he was. There's nothing more deadly than one losing his identity or one trying to pretend that he is somebody else. Mordecai confronted Esther with the truth of her identity.[7] She was in the palace, and the king didn't know she was a Jew. Everyone thought she was a regular Persian girl. Mordecai tried everything he could to bring forth the truth. Finally, she had to come to the place where she would declare her willingness to die with her people: "If I perish, I perish" (Esther 4:16).

Before we can lead anyone, we have to know, accept and embrace who we are—how God created us. God wants whites to be white, not un-white. The same is true for all ethnicities. I didn't just happen to be black. My mother was black, my grandmother was black, my great-grandfather was black. I'm intentionally black. The same is true for gender, age and calling. God knew what He was doing when He created each of us. To think otherwise is to question God's ability as creator and sovereignty as Lord. *God intended you to be who you are.*

I'm not going to oppress you because you're different than me. I am going to accept you and love you. I am going to try to identify with your pain, whether you look like me or completely different. I am going to try to identify with who God intended you to be, whether or not this represents who you are or what you are doing right now. I remember being abused. I remember being slapped in the face by police officers.[8] I remember being beaten. I know what it means to be tortured—completely helpless and so close to death without actually dying. Forgiving those who tortured me released me from the burden of hatred. I was forgiven by God, and because of that, I am called to forgive those who persecuted me. Jesus made it clear, "For if you forgive men their trespasses, your heavenly Father will also forgive you. But if you do not forgive men their trespasses, neither will your Father forgive your trespasses" (Matt. 6:14-15).

Moses was also willing to identify with his people in suffering. We will talk more about the role of pain later, but let's get an initial handle on this concept. Martin Luther King, Jr., said, "Unearned suffering is redemptive." To me, that means, "I haven't had the problem, but I'll go and suffer with you." When my brother hurts or is hungry, I'll go without food too. In this way we identify with another person's circumstances. It's vicarious.

I believe that indigenous leadership development—raising up leaders from within a particular community who have a heart for and an identity in that neighborhood—was inherent in the Great Commission. Jesus said, "Go into all the world and preach the gospel to every ethnic group, every tribal group, wherever you find them."[9] He meant that we bring good news to them and then teach them how to teach others. We are not to subjugate and carry the weaker nations (or any nation) back to our strong nation. Jesus told us to take the good news to the people and tell them they've been created in the image of God. We're to notify them that their Savior has arrived and that He's concerned for them to manage their own community for the highest good of all of the people within their land and nation.

This did not always happen in the past. In centuries gone by, European nations sent men and ships to far-away places in search of tea, gold, riches . . . and slaves. We have read the stories in our history books about how Africa, the Americas, Asia, the Pacific Islands and other destinations were colonized. All too often the settlers found the treasures they sought but at the expense of the indigenous people, whom the settlers left out, oppressed and even debilitated.

There is a new type of colonization and enslavement in our day— we call it outsourcing. We let the poor of developing nations make our goods without educating or training them to get out of poverty. We also "in-source" by culling for the brightest minds of other countries, bringing them here to educate them, and keeping them here to work—to make our nation a better place. While that helps us and the individuals who immigrate to the United States, it drains the native country. The whole world would benefit if we actually trained those who live in poverty and impoverished communities and helped them create jobs in their own lands. That would truly be the Good News.

In all fairness, we are making great progress, and we can celebrate that fact. In my lifetime, I have seen most of Africa, with few exceptions, be decolonized. Now we've got to finish the decolonization as we move in and carry the gospel to them so the people can stand on their own feet. We need to invest in them and teach them how to manage their own resources so they are able to make equal exchanges with the other peoples of the world. We need to give them dignity and recognize who God has made them to be. That is their identity.

SHANE: When I was in South Africa, I learned of a saying that was common during the days of apartheid: "When the colonialists came, they had the Bible and we had the land. Now we have the Bible and they have the land." That broke my heart. Christ have mercy on us! Despite the injustice of racial segregation, the people there tell many stories of courageous leaders from among the indigenous Africans and from among the Europeans who rejected the world they had created *and* the sick theology that helped support it. (Yes, some actually twisted Bible verses to make it appear that God condoned apartheid!).

> TRUE LEADERS WILL NOT WAIT
> ON OTHERS TO STEP UP TO
> RIGHT THE WRONGS.

Many visionaries went to jail and risked their lives exposing the atrocities of colonialism. Before apartheid could fall in South Africa, there had to be people who could imagine a world without it. There is a community we stayed with in Johannesburg, just outside Soweto, where many of the riots and massacres took place. Despite the violence, something beautiful happened. At the height of apartheid, a group of white South Africans and black South Africans got together and decided they would not conform to the patterns of the world they lived in. They bought a bunch of land and began raising their families in community. Their lives were threatened, and they all risked arrest. This act of reconciliation was illegal! To this day, dozens of those courageous heroes continue to live together.

John: It is similar to what my son Spencer did at his community, called Antioch.

SHANE: Exactly. It looks a lot like what Spencer and Chris Rice did down there in Jackson as they built a family across the racial divide, and what Clarence Jordan and Millard Fuller formed at Koinonia Farm in Georgia.[10] They led with creativity and persistence.

In order for the world to change, as it did in South Africa, there must first be leaders who can imagine a different world from the one in which they live. That's not so easy. I'm sure it took effort for Moses to believe in the Promised Land, especially when his eyes had never seen it—and never would. I'm sure the folks in South Africa had to look beyond their pain to picture a world without it. It's not easy for the kids in my neighborhood to imagine a world without guns. And it's hard for folks in the Pentagon to imagine a world without nuclear weapons. But true leaders will lead, not wait on, others to step up to right the wrongs.

In Isaiah 2:4 and Micah 4:1-4, the prophets speak about people beating their swords into plowshares and their spears into pruning hooks. It's about turning things that have brought death into things that cultivate life. And these passages end by declaring that nation will not rise up against nation and the world will study (or *learn*) war no more. Something interesting jumps out at me here. The peace the prophets speak of does not begin with the nations—it begins with the people. In Isaiah 2:3, the people come to "the mountain of the LORD" to *learn* God's ways. As they walk in God's way, the people begin to beat their swords into plows. It's not the nations and their kings that lead the way to peace; it's the people of God who refuse to continue the bloodshed and it's the people who lead the nations, the kings, the presidents to peace.

These prophetic acts have changed history over and over again. It all begins with people who can imagine a world different from the one around them. It starts with a people who are so committed to that vision that they will begin to enact it . . . immediately. In the stage play *Back to Methuselah*, George Bernard Shaw wrote, "You see things; and you say, 'Why?' But I dream things that never were; and I say, 'Why not?'"[11] Robert Kennedy later quoted Shaw and challenged a nation. I pick it up now as a maxim for ordinary radicals.

John: Dreaming big is not just having a good idea. Look closely and you will discover that people who have dreams that will change the world are usually people who are well grounded. When I study what makes a great twenty-first-century leader, I'm always going to look more at content of character than about financial development or fame. Character develops the kind of passion that attracts followers and resources. We don't have to pull the trigger. We don't have to wave a banner or grandstand. We need to quietly make friends with people; steadfastly stay the course. Jesus said, in training His disciples, "Go out, and take nothing with you. Go out and make friends! If they don't make friends with you, go onto the next house and make friends with those people!"[12] (Jot down the word "friends." God is our friend, and we are His friend. A leader needs friends, and followers need a leader who is also a friend.)

People know the difference between selfish greed and true passion. They know the difference between self-promotion and God promotion. When they see passion arise in men and women of character, they want to join in. When the vision of our ministry matches what God has called people to do, they will help us carry out the work.

SHANE: When Jesus sent the disciples out with nothing at all—just like with Abraham, Sarah and Moses, it put them in a vulnerable place—where they were completely dependent on God. They could not trust in their own security or providence, but only in God. What's beautiful with the early Christians is that they were not just to wait around on God to rain down manna from heaven but, as John said, they were also to make friends and trust that people along the way would take care of them and welcome them into their homes. It put the early Christians in a position where not only were they to practice hospitality, but they were also to be dependent upon receiving it. As one of the early Christians said, "We have no house, but we have homes everywhere we go."[13] I don't know about John, but even though I don't own a car, I have a dozen on my block that folks will let me use when I need one. Jesus, too, was always borrowing stuff. He borrowed a donkey, a house, a boat—He even borrowed the tomb in which He was buried. From that we can learn that vulnerability is a value, not a threat. It's something that good leaders know well: they need other people.

John: I have made and kept friends over the past 50 years of ministry because I believe in people's potential. Every person is created in the image of God and made to be creative. I have so little secular education, and so many ideas, but I don't have the skills to pull them off. I've had a clear vision during my years of ministry, and people have wanted to work alongside me. When people join with me, I want them to bring their creativity to the project I'm working on. When everyone invests resources, then everyone can see the development of people or a project that shows results! Some of these friends of mine have been committed for up to 50 years and, believe it or not, they all still like me! The content of your character will determine the caliber of your relationships.

SHANE: That's what we call a "theology of enough." There are enough resources. God did not create an economy of scarcity. God did not make too many people or too little stuff. Ghandi once said, "There is enough for everyone's need but not enough for everyone's greed."[14] So why do a few have more than others, and so many feel that they do not have enough? Well, simply because we have not trusted in "this day our daily bread."[15] Instead, we stockpile money in banks, like the guy Christ spoke about who stores all his stuff in barns, when God is leading us to give it away.[16] Stashing away our resources is not how we are supposed to live.

John and I don't have much of a problem with having too much since we can usually put every penny we get to work and milk a buck for all its worth, but there is often the temptation to save more for hard times in the future or for projects on the horizon rather than live in the simple purity of the lilies and the sparrows. Sometimes it's tempting to hold a little back . . . like what to do with the royalties when this book hits a million copies sold!

There's a great story, though a scandalous one, about a shrewd manager. This guy uses his position to forgive debts, even subversively (unbeknownst to his boss), and makes friends for himself . . . as he sliced certain debts down over and over. He spun the system of debt on its head and made a mockery of the power of mammon.[17] Just goes to prove that the best way to take away money's power is to give it away. Keep doing that, and eventually it won't be worth much. Meaning will be left to relationships and friendships and the sense of community. Now those *can* sustain us even when systems collapse, when Wall Street flounders and when Ponzi schemes are uncovered. No wonder the scandalous story of the shrewd manager ends with the words: "The Pharisees, *who loved money*, heard all this and were sneering at Jesus . . ."

John: It takes courage to lead. But what is courage? Courage is not the absence of fear; rather, it is the ability to follow one's convictions in the face of fear. It takes courage to do what is expected of you in life, to not back off, to not cave in . . . to not even dance around it.

SHANE: I once heard it said, "Courage is fear holding on for one minute longer." Actually, I think it was a general who said that. I don't quote generals every day, but that's a good word.

John: One of the most popular preachers I've heard in a long time was an astronaut named Scott Carpenter. In February 1962, Carpenter became the second American to orbit Earth. Upon reentry, the pitch horizon scanner malfunctioned, and he had to manually take control of his Mercury-Atlas 7 rocket. It was one of the most successful of the early NASA missions. Carpenter is a humble guy, but to hear him tell the story is to hear a powerful message on courage. He says, all he did on that flight was everything that he had been taught to do. And though he maneuvered the spacecraft with precision, he felt it (and his own life) might be lost. Finally, he brought Mercury-Atlas 7 in for a splash landing—several hundred miles off course, but safe. Now we call him a courageous hero.

Moses came from a family of courage. Despite considerable fear, he was able to exercise a decision to go before Pharaoh. Moses' fight was a fight between the God of heaven and Pharaoh's god. That's what the plagues were about. And the invisible God of Abraham won! The God of heaven and of earth won—the same God who comes down and energizes people through His Holy Spirit to do courageous things today.

SHANE: Sometimes it's not that good leaders are fearless . . . it's just that they don't have anything left to lose. They are willing to put everything, even their life, on the line for what they believe. It's what the martyrs did, and it's what people have done in movements for freedom and justice throughout history.

I went to Iraq during the recent war to be part of a Christian witness for peace and reconciliation and to stand against the bombing and fighting. Folks often ask me, "How did you have the courage?"

The truth is, I counted the cost of going, and I counted the cost of not going—and when I thought it through, I felt so compelled; it was as if I could not *not* go.

When I was in Iraq, community was key. Just as happened with the Israelites, and with blacks in the civil rights struggle, the people carried the weight of the struggle together.

But fear is powerful. At some point, especially as Christians, we say with Paul, "To live is Christ, to die is gain"[18] . . . if we die, so what? We believe in resurrection. We'll dance on injustice till they kill us . . . then we'll dance on streets of gold. Many Christians live in such fear that it is as if they don't really, I mean really, believe in resurrection.

John: The late Peter Drucker and I talked about leadership. One time we discussed where great leaders come from—leaders who impact history and liberate people. We struggled with whether or not these leaders were just born great or whether they were trained to be great. You know what I say? Great leaders emerge. They appear out of, or enter into, the agony and pain and struggle of their day. They meet God somewhere, maybe on the backside of a mountain as Moses did, and they get a vision from God. You've got to have vision to lead. They get a glimpse of the promise of God. You must be conscious of the fact that God is calling you to carry on the promise. There has to come a time in your pilgrimage when you become conscious that God put you in a specific place, for a specific time and He's leading you. It's fearful. It's painful. It's too big for you. Moses experienced all of these things. But, like him, you must feel that quiet sense of serenity that God has called you for this moment. It is humbling.

I don't talk about this much, but I knew my time had come when almost a hundred men would come at night and protect my house. It was Mississippi in the mid-1960s, and the civil rights movement was already going. Those men would say, "You go to bed. We'll protect these kids. You are here to do what we can't do, and it's our task to protect you." That's when I knew that God had called me. These men were so noble. They loved me so dearly. They were old men, and they said they had been dreaming and longing for someone to come and lead them. I respected them so much that I was afraid of them.

Bruce Stillman said, "You don't lead to be loved, you lead to be truthful." You lead toward the goal that God has called you to. That's part of the promise. But unless the people you lead love you, they're not going to follow you with their whole hearts. That's why Paul tells the Ephesian believers to preach the truth in love.[19] He instructs them on how to behave. Peter says, "Don't rebuke an old person." Suck it in! Because sucking it in is going to work something in you. It's going to create humility inside. And Peter also says that God "resists the proud, but gives grace to the humble."[20] When you are called, the proper inner response is humility. Moses was the most humble guy who ever walked on earth.

GOD SHOWS US IN MOSES A
PICTURE OF HOW IMPORTANT HUMILITY
IS TO BECOMING A LEADER.

God shows us in Moses a picture of how important humility is to becoming a great leader. In the situation where Moses struck the rock, and thus didn't get to enter the land, we see how angry God becomes when our egos get in the way of His glory. The reason Moses didn't go into the Promised Land was that when he struck the rock he didn't give God the credit. It is almost blasphemy against the Holy Spirit for us to take credit for what He has done in our lives. God had told him before: "Moses, speak to the rock." And Moses spoke to the rock, and water came gushing out. And God told Moses a second time: "Speak to the rock. I'm the one that's going to release the water from the rock." Moses got so angry in the situation, he went up and he slammed the rock instead of speaking to it. From the people's perspective, it looked like *he* was cracking the rock and causing the water to run out. Moses didn't go into the land because he'd messed up his picture of himself. He lost the big picture, which was submission and humility.

SHANE: That seems like something that happens over and over. Leaders start to trust in their own strength and gifts and get impressed by their credentials. It's why God chooses the least likely candidates to bring the Kingdom—like a barren woman (Sarah) to be the mother of a nation; like a stuttering prophet (Moses) to be God's voice; like a little shepherd boy (David) to be king; like a reborn terrorist (Saul) to be a trumpet for grace. But Moses, like so many others, started to second-guess God. David did the same thing. We remember him as a man after God's own heart,[21] but in reality he royally screwed up—he lusted, coveted, committed adultery, lied about it, committed murder to cover it up—he pretty much broke every command in about two chapters of the Bible.[22] And David is not alone.

We can all name great leaders who began to lose it near the end of their lives; even folks we remember as heroes. Just like Moses and Dr. King, their stories don't always end perfectly, and we get to see their lives were not perfect—not even close. We are all tempted with the counterfeit power our hands can wield and the sense that we are invincible because God is on our side. That's precisely when God starts to switch sides. It is at the moment when we think the power for change is in our own hands that God sometimes leaves us to let us give that a shot, until we crawl back praying for help.

John: The Bible lays out seven things that God hates: haughty or prideful eyes, a lying tongue, hands that shed innocent blood, a heart that devises wicked plans, feet that make haste to run to evil, a false witness who breathes out lies and one who sows discord among brothers.[23]

Right now we're talking about the first one. With pride, you are taking the credit. Although leaders play a role (we are the hands and feet), the credit always goes to God. We are always the sheep. He's the ultimate Shepherd. That's what makes David such a powerful leader. In the middle of all David's sinning and all of his "stuff," he says, "The Lord is my shepherd. I shall not want. He leads me beside still waters . . . He prepares a table before me . . . He leads me in the path of righteousness for His name's sake" (Ps. 23:2). And David ends with, "Goodness and mercy will follow me all the days of my life because I'm going to dwell in the house with this One who led me, my Great Shepherd" (v. 6). We're here because of the grace of God and must always remember that He is the potter; we are the clay.[24]

Moses himself is a model of a shepherd leader. That's why God took so long to raise him up. It took 80 years to prepare Moses to become the kind of exemplary leader that we can look to—one who molded a people so damaged by enslavement into what became a model nation.

SHANE: I'm picking up a trend here. Abraham was 80. Moses was 80. John you must be just getting started. What does that mean for me?

John: Don't forget, Jesus only made it to 33.

SHANE: Good word.

John: Back to Moses and our passage in Hebrews. Finally, it says in verse 29, "And they passed through the Red Sea." Moses didn't lead them to a place of his choosing; rather, he led them where God told him to lead them—out of Egypt. Joshua would eventually lead the Jewish people into the Promised Land, but Moses led them as far as God wanted him to lead them.

In the year 2000, Tommy Tarrants and I traveled together to Amman, Jordan, to speak at an international meeting on peace. So there we were: Tommy, a former Ku Klux Klansman, and myself, a black from Mississippi, standing next to a lineup of Nobel Prize winners for peace and reconciliation. The king of Jordan was there with his delegates too. He said, "When a black man from Mississippi and a white Ku Klux Klansman can become friends, there is hope for the Jews and Arabs." That was wonderful. But that hope has to be in Jesus Christ! The reconciliation came because that Ku Klux Klansman met Jesus Christ, and because that black boy from Mississippi met Jesus Christ. It was His death on the cross that pulled this white supremacist and me together. Only because Jesus reconciled us could we stand side by side on a platform next to the king of Jordan as a symbol of hope for peace in the Middle East.

SHANE: It is an exciting time to be alive. In some ways the issues that demand leadership and courage are not the same today as they were 30 years ago. The KKK, while it's not dead, is at least wilting. Many of the old beasts have not produced a new generation of charismatic leaders, but there are other beasts . . . new giants to be slain. There is a new exodus journey too. And there is a generation that is stepping up to the challenge.

I was just over in Sweden, where I had the privilege of witnessing a historic moment for the Church in Sweden. A growing number of people over there have become convinced that they need to unite across denominational lines as a Church, and that Jesus longs for us to be one as God is one. So they have worked and led the way and have now signed a declaration with the Bishops of the major denominations to merge as one Body—*and the initiative was led by the young people.* In Ireland, there are groups of young Christians, both Protestant and Catholic, who are ashamed of the bloodstained pages of history there—of Catholics and Protestants killing each other. So what are they doing? Some are starting up intentional communities where Protestants and Catholics can live together. It's stunning. God is moving. Yes, the challenges are all around us—slavery did not end; it only changed . . . and evolved, and mutated. There are slaves in sweatshops, and there is human trafficking all over the world. But there is also a generation that is convinced that these things matter to God.

John: Our hope today for reconciliation is in Jesus Christ. We do have a Leader we can follow.

SHANE: Every age has its own exodus.

John: And every generation needs a new Moses.

Notes

1. See James 1:2-3.
2. See John 2:1-11.
3. See Luke 8:26-33.
4. See Luke 8:41-47.
5. Throughout this book I will say "our" when referring to life in Philadelphia. I am a part of The Simple Way community and a part of the neighborhood on Potter Street. It is always "us."

6. See Deuteronomy 11:20.
7. See Esther 14:13-17.
8. For the entire story, see John Perkins, *Let Justice Roll Down* (Ventura, CA: Regal, 2006).
9. This is my paraphrase. See Mark 16:15.
10. For more information, see Spencer Perkins and Chris Rice, *More Than Equals: Racial Healing for the Sake of the Gospel* (Downers Grove, IL: InterVarsity Press, 2000); and Millard Fuller and Diane Scott Fuller, *No More Shacks: The Daring Vision for Habitat for Humanity* (Waco, TX: Word Books, 1986).
11. George Bernard Shaw, *Back to Methuselah*, 1921.
12. See Mark 6:8-10.
13. Society of Brethren, Eberhard Arnold, ed., *The Early Christians: In Their Own Words* (New York: Plough Publishing House, 1998).
14. Rajendra Pachauri, quoting Ghandi in his Nobel Prize acceptance speech in 2007. This is a popular quote from Ghandi and appears in various translations. I like this one the best.
15. As prayed in the Lord's Prayer. See Luke 11:3.
16. See Luke 12:16-21.
17. See Luke 16.
18. See Philippians 1:21.
19. See Ephesians 4:15.
20. See 1 Peter 5:5.
21. See Acts 13:22.
22. See 2 Samuel 11–12.
23. See Proverbs 6:16-19.
24. See Isaiah 64:8.

The abbot or abbess, once established in office, must often think about the demands made on them by the burden they have undertaken and consider also to whom they will have to give an account of their stewardship. They must understand that the call of their office is not to exercise power over those who are their subjects but to serve and help them in their needs.

—St. Benedict of Nursia (480–547)

THE ACHE

(Beginning Where It Hurts)

John: As I look at the leaders I would follow, I think of men and women who actually enter into the real pain, suffering and agony of the people. It is one thing to say racism is bad and wrong; it is altogether another thing to have held a sick child in your arms, waiting until all of the white patients have been seen at a medical clinic before the doctor will see you—a medical clinic where you had to enter by a side door and sit in a "blacks only" waiting room, not knowing how sick your child was or how long you would have to wait. (Yes, this happened to me in Mendenhall, Mississippi, in the 1960s.)

Most effective leaders are the ones who recognize real pain, lead from within that pain and lead the people out of their own pain. Of course, joy is a wonderful emotion and experience. God created joy, but it is not the starting place. Joy is a result or outcome. Pain is the beginning. We are born in pain and we live in pain—sometimes a lot of pain. The leader who can tap into our pain and walk through it with us—bearing our burdens like Jesus bears them—is going to be a real leader.

Pain. We want to avoid it, but we shouldn't. We really need to get the pain part right. In the Bible, we see where God appears to have put people in some really hard situations where they had to actually bear the pain of others—sometimes many others. Look at Moses, Ezekiel and Jeremiah. Jeremiah, in his own expression of life, understood and responded to the misery of the people. He wept. In fact, he wept so much that he became a spectacle and is still known as the weeping prophet. He identified with the pain of the people. Not only did he weep because of their wounds, but he also wept because he saw greater pain coming.

Hosea wept too. God was trying to show him the adultery of the nation, how the Jewish people had turned away from God, and how they were following after many other gods. So God gave Hosea a wife who turned away from him and was going after many men. He had to live with the shame and the pain of her transgression. Today we don't quite get why what Gomer (Hosea's wife) did was so bad and why it cut so deep, because our culture has almost made having sex outside of marriage okay, or at least not unusual. For Hosea, Gomer's infidelity clearly was shameful and an embarrassment to him personally.

And Jesus wept.[1]

SHANE: The Scriptures are all about a God who feels the pain of the people, who hears the cries of the slaves in Egypt and rescues them, who is continually responding to the pain. The coming of Jesus is about God entering the pain. Pain is where Jesus began. He did not arrive as the celebrity messiah everyone was expecting. He came unassumingly as the suffering servant, the baby refugee, the homeless rabbi . . . the God who suffers.

Too often well-intentioned leaders are quick to stand up to be a voice *for* the voiceless rather than being a voice *with* the voiceless. We assume that because people's voices are not being heard, they're not speaking. And the truth often is that people on the margins are weeping, wailing and crying out from the depths of their souls, but the rest of the world has hands over their ears. Leaders are folks who can help remove the earplugs and the blinders so that we all can hear and see and feel the pain of others; so that the ache touches us and we cannot help but begin to carry the burdens and wipe the tears away.

Most great social movements in history have similar beginnings: they start with pain, and then emerge from the streets, slums and abandoned corners of the earth . . . places like Nazareth, of which folks said nothing good could come. People most affected by the pain and closest to the injustices make the best leaders. They feel and understand the problems better than anyone else. I think that's why Jesus did not simply come to help the poor; He came *as* the poor. Mother Teresa used to say that we cannot understand the poor until we stand under the poor and live among them. I love that verse in Romans that speaks about how the world aches. It says that all of creation is groaning for its liberation, like a mother giving birth . . . and then Paul says something so powerful: "And we have begun to *ache* with it."[2] Every leader who is not indigenous to struggle needs to take that pilgrimage into the pain.

John: Today, Christians tend to put leaders on a pedestal. We have megachurch pastors, televangelists and Christian celebrities. It is hard for the leader to enter into the pain of the people when he only sees it from the other side of the camera or sitting at the boardroom table. We do leaders a disservice sometimes. We think we are protecting them, prioritizing their time and doing wonderful things for them, when in actuality, by shielding them or filtering what information they get, we distance them from real people and real needs. By always having a catchy slogan, a positive spin, a trendy campaign or a big reward, we end up not dealing with real issues or the heart of the matter. I am not saying we cannot have slogans, campaigns or rewards. And I am not saying that megachurch pastors cannot be justice leaders. But some leaders are talking out of that place of pain and others are just talking. We need to stop and ask ourselves what is show business and what is God's business.

SHANE: Compassion does not mean only "to care about." It means "to ache from the bowels"—to literally become nauseated with injustice and to get sick to our stomachs with suffering.

At one point, Jesus says blessed are those who hunger for justice—some of us have heard that so many times it has lost its punch, but to hunger for justice is a powerful image. Justice is not just something we want to happen. It's not just something we hope for, like a new car. It's something that starves us. I think that's why fasting (going without food) can be such an important Christian practice—because we begin to feel, our bodies ache a little, along with the 2 billion starving bellies of our world. It affects us physically, then emotionally and spiritually. Not many of us hunger for justice like that. Lots of us want justice. But it's something else to hunger for it, to be kept awake at night because we are starving for the Kingdom to come on earth. Consider folks like Oscar Schindler in Nazi Germany, who rescued thousands of Jews, or Paul Rusesabagina in Rwanda, who rescued folks in the genocide . . . they became tremendous leaders because the pain touched them so deeply. It haunted them. They could not *not* lead. They certainly could have fled the chaos and saved themselves and their families, but instead they risked their lives because the pain of others chose them—they were drafted into leadership by the suffering around them.

The pain of others has to become our pain. I like the saying, "The gospel comforts the disturbed and disturbs the comfortable." As we move closer to the suffering, the problems and struggles become our own. We have come to share the struggles of our neighbors on Potter Street. My friends Nate and Jenny Bacon have lost more than one friend to gang violence in San Francisco. My new friends at FreeSet in Calcutta, India, have spent many nights helping women escape the snare of forced prostitution. Hebrews says, "Continue to remember those in prison as if you were together with them" (Heb. 13:3). We begin to carry some of the pain of the world. That's what Jesus is all about, and that's the path of the cross He invites us to follow. Where there is pain, there is also a cry for freedom.

Not only are we to be in touch with the pain and brokenness of others, but we also have to face our own brokenness. It is through the cracks that the light comes in.[3] It is knowing our wounds that helps prepare us to lead. That's why God prefers the weak over the strong and uses the foolish to confound the weak. For this reason, He can make something beautiful out of a mess. The best leaders have battle scars. Jesus Himself was a wounded healer. And it is our wounds that empower us to be healers of others. The best domestic abuse counselors often are women who have been in domestic abuse. The best teachers in recovery are addicts themselves. And the most powerful voices for grace are those who have experienced tremendous violence and still been able to forgive.

Henri Nouwen coined the term "wounded healer." He put it like this:

Compassion grows with the inner recognition that your neighbor shares your humanity with you. This partnership cuts through all walls which might have kept you separate. Across all barriers of land and language, wealth and poverty, knowledge and ignorance, we are one, created from the same dust, subject to the same laws, and destined for the same end. With this compassion you can say, "In the face of the oppressed I recognize my own face and in the hands of the oppressor I recognize my own hand. Their flesh is my flesh, their blood is my blood, their pain is my pain, their smile is my smile. Their ability to torture is in me, too; their capacity to forgive I find also in myself. There is nothing in me that does not belong to them too; nothing in them that does not belong to me. In my heart, I know their yearning for love, and down to my entrails I can feel their cruelty. In another's eyes I see my plea for forgiveness, and in a hardened frown I see my refusal. When someone murders, I know that I too could have done that, and when someone gives birth, I know that I am capable of that as well. In the depths of my being, I meet my fellow humans with whom I share love and have life and death."[4]

John: Leaders need to be in touch with the deepest longings of the people they expect to follow them. We have said that this often comes out of pain, shared experience and common hope. But leaders need to speak to the people of God. They need to listen to their deepest longings—to not assume but pay attention to their words.

Not long ago, I stood outside the Family Health Care Clinic in Mendenhall, Mississippi—about 35 miles southeast of Jackson. We had purchased the building and integrated it more than 30 years ago, and Dennis Adams—a brilliant, kind brother in Christ from New York—has been the resident doctor there for the past 30 years. In the 1960s and early 1970s, there was a longing in the hearts of the people to have good health care. As leaders, we listened and found a way to answer that longing—together. That longing is still being answered today with the clinic.

That's the good news! Good news is the answer to people's longing. What are your longings? What are your greatest pains? What do your followers long for? Beautiful are the feet of those who bring good news.[5] How can our longings become good news? And remember, all of our longings can only be met in Jesus and His Church—His people in the Body of Christ.

SHANE: Here is where you get to make a list. What are some of the things that make you ache with those who suffer? Things that make you starved for justice? What are some of the things that you think break God's heart and should keep you (and all of us) up at night? (See, I do know what a list is . . . and there are probably more than three things, so keep going if you want to!)

1. _____

2. _____

3. _____

Notes
1. Check out John 11:35. The vulgate says "*et lacrimatus est Iesus*." Jesus literally cried upon hearing the news of the death of His friend Lazarus.
2. See Romans 8:22-23.
3. Variations of this phrase have been attributed to St. Augustine and to St. John of the Cross.
4. Henri Nouwen, *With Open Hands* (Notre Dame, IN: Ave Maria Press, 1995).
5. See Isaiah 52:7.

THE VISION

(Carrying a Cause)

John: Jesus said, "Follow me" (Matt. 16:24). He knew where He was going and why people should follow Him. If we are going to be audacious enough to ask people—even expect people—to follow us, it is not enough to know there is a problem; we also have to ask ourselves, *Where do we want people to go?*

Leaders need vision. Mine is for reconciliation. Shane's is for the poor. To live out our vision, we must start by truly identifying closely with folks, with their pain. And we need to carry a vision for moving away from or beyond that pain toward reconciliation and healing. We need to know where we are going.

People follow vision. Most Christians follow Christ for His provision—emotional, physical and spiritual. If we are really honest about it, most of us would say one of the primary reasons we follow Him is because we want to go to heaven—we want to live forever, and we want it to be good.

Jesus spoke with such great certainty that His followers would get to heaven that I don't think about it very much. I am a follower of His, so He has that covered. He also gave us an example of caring for the least of these while here on earth, and that is my day-to-day motivation.

SHANE: I remember when I was in college. (It wasn't *that* long ago!) One day my prof, Tony Campolo, talked about how many of us come to Jesus with such mixed motivations. He asked: "If there were no heaven and there were no hell, would you follow Jesus anyway?" Like John (and Tony), I do believe in heaven and hell. I am excited about the afterlife . . . but at the end of the day, I did not choose Jesus because I wanted crowns in heaven or because I was scared to death of hell. I chose Him because He is good. He is love. He is peace. He is all that my heart longs for. And He is taking us on an adventure that begins right now, not eventually, when we die.

I am convinced that Jesus did not just come to prepare us to die; He came to teach us to live. The vision that Jesus invites us to follow is not just a vision for heaven . . . seriously now, how hard can it be to love our enemies in heaven?! Jesus is teaching us a vision for how to live on earth, to care for others. Here and now is where and when we need to figure out how to love those who are against us. The Kingdom of God that Jesus spoke of wasn't just something we hope for when we die, but something we are to bring on earth as it is in heaven. It's not just about us going up, but about bringing God's kingdom down.

John: When Jesus called His disciples, He was very careful with the words He spoke: "Follow Me." To "follow me" is to be with me and to watch me. To "follow me" is to see the vision and embrace it as your own. To "follow me" is to hear my words and speak them as your own.

So leadership starts with identifying with the pain of the people you will lead. A leader must have vision and be able to articulate hope. And he or she must pray. But that is not enough. We must live out our vision with character and values; we must live honestly before people and before God.

SHANE: A good leader's life gives credibility to his or her words. A good leader's life becomes her or his gospel. John's life is his best sermon. Mother Teresa's life is her best book. Her life embodied her words, theology and politics. Think about it. She didn't become a champion for life and for unborn children because she went around wearing a T-shirt emblazoned with the words "Abortion is murder!" She became a champion because she came alongside women in tough situations and offered to help raise their kids with them. That approach to the pain of abortion carries an integrity that no one can argue with. Even President Bill Clinton invited her to speak at his prayer breakfast. Here is a hilarious aside amidst my rather serious point: A friend of mine who was at the breakfast tells about how the organizers had saved a VIP seat for Mother Teresa, right up front next to the President. As the meal was being served, the seat was empty and she could not be found. She was in the back with the kitchen staff and servers, eating her meal.

Too many people try to lead just with writing books or preaching sermons, but they don't realize that's the easy part. Anybody can write a book. But words on paper (even partially recycled paper like this book) only come to life when they get lived out—when the word becomes flesh. We lead out of who we are. At our best we can say, "If you want to know what I think, then watch how I live."

WORDS ON PAPER ONLY COME
TO LIFE WHEN THEY GET LIVED OUT—
WHEN THE WORD BECOMES FLESH.

I've submitted my writing and speaking schedule to my community, elders and close friends at The Simple Way. I have a little committee that sorts through all the speaking requests with me, and they protect my time so that I have time in the neighborhood. They will not let me travel out of town more than 12 days each month. They make sure I am not just talking about the gospel but that I am living the gospel. That's why John and I have such wild lives. We don't compartmentalize things into safe little categories or have a time clock as if the gospel were a 9-to-5 job. We are on the streets, in our neighborhoods and out where people live. Some people might try to put some kind of urban, community or grassroots label on what we do. As I look at Jesus, it's just what makes sense. So let's put aside the labels and just live the gospel.

Being present in people's lives keeps us in touch, but it also keeps us honest. Even when I travel, I try to take someone along everywhere I go. Jesus sent the disciples out in pairs, and there's a lot of wisdom in that. It's also how you make disciples; they see all the parts—good and ugly, joyful and tedious—of our life work. And they also keep us honest. When someone from your community is present and listening, it affects how you tell a story. There is no room to be "evangelastic" and exaggerate something. The person with you will say, "No, actually that's not how it happened. We didn't really raise four people from the dead that day. It was only two." It's much easier to be a soloist (with no accountability). But that doesn't have the same dazzle of a full symphony or a Gospel choir. Seems as though too many leaders have been soloists, and I guess that's why so many of them are lonely people.

John: One of my greatest pains occurs when I go into my neighborhood—the poorer urban area of Jackson, Mississippi. I see the amount of money that flows in from government and nonprofit aid, and from illegal activities such as drugs. I watch the way money is spent and wasted. Everyone thinks they need personal stuff that has no meaning—Nikes, iPods and plasma screen TVs. There are plenty of resources that could do the important things, such as education, better housing and medical care—but so many of the people are not properly utilizing what they do have.

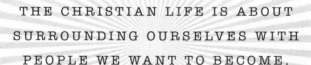

THE CHRISTIAN LIFE IS ABOUT
SURROUNDING OURSELVES WITH
PEOPLE WE WANT TO BECOME.

Seeing all of the waste stirs up pain for me. The same thing happened 70 years ago when I was growing up in New Hebron, Mississippi—a little more than an hour south of Jackson, in the country. We were sharecroppers, but to make money on the side, we were also deep into bootlegging and gambling. There was money, but it was just money. It didn't amount to anything and it did very little to improve the conditions of our people. So I grew up with this kind of a economic model: It was easy to make money and even easier to immediately spend it all on meaningless things that only provided a moment of self-satisfaction or looking away from reality. It is much more difficult to be thoughtful and utilize our money to achieve something good. There is nothing wrong with getting a milk shake at Dairy Queen, but do we really need one every day? We all need shoes, but do we really need the $100 pair? We don't need the drugs, the drinking and other addictions that drain wallets and lives. The pain comes in looking at the community after the waves of destruction and then you have to live with that pain.

In response, we need a holistic teaching—we need to be concerned about the body, the soul, the experience, the quality of life of people within the community. The leader is symbolic of the problem that God has called that leader to address. We are also called to challenge the folks around us. Shane's commitment to his dress and the way he lives challenges us to rethink how we use our resources. Now, when a leader challenges people in a big way, he needs to be careful. He can end up being entertainment or written off as an extremist. Shane is able to speak above and beyond his dress and lifestyle. So he is able to connect, and people take him seriously. But finding the balance is a challenge for leaders.

SHANE: Of course, there are always folks who push us to have more and more integrity. I remember showing up to speak at a conference where a friend of mine was also speaking. When I saw him, I ran up to give him a hug. I noticed that he looked terrible—all red in the face, sweaty, disheveled. I wondered if he had the flu or something, so I asked, "You're looking rough, bro. Is everything okay?" He smiled with an ear-to-ear grin and said, "Yeah, man, I'm just worn out because I biked about 700 miles to get here. I'm doing a workshop on 'Creation Care' and decided I needed to practice what I preach." Ha-ha. It made me blush, as I had just strolled off my plane complaining about how long the security line had been in Philadelphia.

I want to surround myself with people like the one who biked to the conference—people who push me to risk more, to love more, to laugh harder. The Christian life is about surrounding ourselves with people who look like someone we want to become, people who may be a few steps ahead of us on the journey.

After that encounter with my cycling buddy, I sat down and rethought how I travel. I saw that there are tons of Christian writers and speakers who are talking about how we need to live simply and responsibly (thank goodness), but I also saw a need to do more work to put flesh on our words. Many of us catch planes and use lots of fuel every few days so we can travel to far-flung cities to talk at conferences about how we need to be good stewards of the earth. I realized that I had to do something, so my cycling buddy, a few other friends and I created a contract that I now use when going to any speaking event. Others reduce their fuel usage to offset the carbon impact of my travel. Another group of speakers and writers that I am a part of is trying to be "certified green," meaning that we are careful to erase the environmental footprint of our travels. I give folks all sorts of ideas for how they can do that—riding a bike, car-pooling, fasting from fuel, planting trees . . . I even had a group of Mennonites pick me up by horse and carriage, then drive me 30 miles to an event. So there is always more, and there are always folks who are taking the gospel to new dimensions. We need to surround ourselves with these people, no matter how many years, sermons or books we have under our belts. We will keep moving each other a little closer to who Jesus wants us to be, even though that doesn't mean we will all end up doing the exact same thing . . . after all, I'd still be hard-pressed to bike 100 miles, let alone 700.

John: Amen to that. Reconciliation assumes equality; that all people are equal. For people who look different and live different lives to become friends, we first have to be reconciled. For me to be reconciled to you, I have to feel and see dignity in you, not just accept you because the Bible tells me to or because it is comfortable. I have to ask myself, *Do I really see you as equal?* Sometimes this can happen simply by seeing something of value in the other person's life that we wish we had in our own. Rather than becoming jealous, we value certain abilities or characteristics we see in our friend. So that friend enriches us.

Leaders and followers are equal too. Leaders must look at their followers with dignity. And followers must see their leaders as human beings, with the same aspirations that they have. There also has to be a love between leaders and followers. When leaders and followers value each other's strengths and cover each other's weaknesses in love, then we enrich each other. Effective leading and following is never a one-way street when it comes to respect. A certain quality of life rises up when there is equality. When people see that quality in a leader, they want to follow.

Remember when Colin Powell declared his support of Barack Obama for president? Powell was a Republican. He had served as Secretary of State under George W. Bush. Why would he endorse a Democrat? I think he saw a quality in Obama that he wanted to follow. Obama exuded hope for change. Powell saw excellence in the way Obama carries himself. He heard it in his words. Agree or disagree with Obama's policies, this is what a lot of people see in him and why they followed. Now, Obama isn't John the Baptist, but I think we see the same dynamic at work in Scriptures. People followed John the Baptist because of the power of his message and the content of his character. What is said about John is said about no other person— that he was "filled with the Holy Spirit, even from his mother's womb" (Luke 1:15). That was the spirit of truth, sacrifice, selflessness, courage, honesty and all of the other healing virtues.

SHANE: The Scriptures have a lot to say about a tree being known by its fruit, and about how there are certain fruits of the Spirit—things like love, joy, peace, patience, kindness, goodness, gentleness, faithfulness and self-control. It seems that looking for these fruits is always a healthy litmus test as we try to identify the good folks we want to follow or align ourselves with.

Is there fruit? Does the fruit look like the character of God? We can call anything Christian, but the real question is, Does it look like Jesus? When I was in Iraq back in 2003, it was painful to see and hear about all sorts of acts being perpetrated in the name of God that must have made Jesus nauseated. I remember some Iraqi people calling leaders of the U.S. "Christian extremists" in the same way we hear Islamic leaders called "Muslim extremists." One Iraqi mother spoke about how she had given up on God and renounced both Islam and Christianity. She said, "Your government is doing terrible things in the name of God, and asking God's blessing on its war. That is the same thing my government is doing. My question is, what kind of God wants to bless this? What has happened to the God of love, to the Prince of Peace?" What becomes at stake in situations like Iraq is not just the reputation of America, but also the reputation of Christianity. And it has everything to do with leadership . . .

When we have leaders who closely identify with Christ but then publicly behave in ways that do not look like Christ, it becomes very confusing for people. I'm not picking on George Bush and the Iraqi War. Bill Clinton committed adultery. I am not saying that leaders who err should be ostracized or that we should say, "They aren't real Christians," or something like that. But what we can say is, "Even though you are Christian, what you did does not look like Jesus." We then invite confession and repentance, and offer restorative justice by surrounding the struggling leader with grace. But we do not take it lightly when those in positions of leadership publicly embarrass God, and misrepresent our faith.

> WE INVITE CONFESSION AND REPENTANCE, AND OFFER RESTORATIVE JUSTICE, BY SURROUNDING THE STRUGGLING LEADER WITH GRACE.

The Scriptures have much to say about taking seriously a public platform, and make it clear that leaders will be judged very strictly if they abuse their position of power. Certainly, in the end, mercy always triumphs over judgment. That's the good news. Meanwhile, we cannot cheapen grace and excuse mistakes like adultery and the invasion of Iraq . . . the list goes on and on. We always need to test the spirit of what we see . . . lift it up to Jesus and see how it holds up. A tree is known by its fruit. I say the names of the fruit of the Spirit—saying them one by one, several times a day, praying that they would live in me and come out of me in every interaction. I even have them written on my chapel wall, and I have hung them on four-foot wooden planks from the window of our community house.

I think the early Christians had it right. They said, "If someone's a healer, don't let them go around saying it, let them show it."[1] If someone's a prophet, you'll know it not by what they say but by the fruit of their prophecy. Does it edify? Does it happen? Who is doing the speaking? My Pentecostal friends joke that in some churches the same three men have been saying the same three prophecies at exactly the same point in the service for years! I suppose anyone can claim to be a prophet and someone might be edified, but what really is important is the fruit!

Anybody can say he or she is a leader. Anyone can say, "Hey, I have this great idea to build fresh water wells in Cambodia." And others can raise tons of money for wells in Cambodia. Still others will make great websites for wells in Cambodia. But it will just stay a good idea until someone actually risks something and goes to the people of Cambodia. Like John says, it can even be a good idea. But a real leader has more than an idea . . . she or he has followers who are eager to carry out a vision with all sorts of skills and passions. And a real leader will be the first to recognize someone who is going to lead one part of the project better than he or she can, and will be the first to step aside and follow.

John: Leaders need to have vision. But not just any vision. It needs to be inspired foresight—a big dream. Scripture didn't just spring up out of the minds of some smart men. (Men aren't that smart.) It was prophetic, given by God. So our vision must also come from God and His Word. Leadership books about vision can help. But they can also mislead. If we take a personality test, make a list of goals and get motivated, but it is all out of our own willpower, then ultimately, if it succeeds, it will only result in self-gratification, not in real change. If our leadership is designed to satisfy only ourselves, ultimately we will not have many followers. George Barna, in *The Power of Vision*, wrote, "While He [God] allows us ample latitude and creativity to articulate, disseminate and implement the vision, make no mistake about it: Visionary leaders receive their vision for ministry from God."[2]

When we receive a vision from God—and we are sure that it is from God—it just makes sense to throw our whole life into that vision. But how do we know whether it is actually from God? We should start by asking ourselves, *Does this vision correspond with God's Word?* The most important thing we can do is to align our particular vision with the Word of God . . . as God's plan for our lives will come out of that juxtaposition.

No matter how exciting the vision (and it will be exciting when it comes from God), we always need to remember who created that vision. Sometimes we make the projects and structure more important than the vision itself or the One who provided it to us. Take family, for example. We've got to understand that God's vision for the family is for it to be the vehicle of reproduction and nurture in the world. To accomplish that end, we need houses, discipline and structure, but we can't let these pursuits get ahead of the original, bigger vision. God wants us to provide for the family, but that provision should never overshadow the family itself.

Now look at the bigger picture of the family of God. The vision of the family of God relies on evangelism and nurturing. We lose that focus and vision when we fuss too much over buildings, budgets and institutions. Why are we building bigger churches when we have trouble nurturing the people already coming through the doors? Too often, our vision has turned into creating institutions rather than developing people. We have to keep our focus on the people of God—reconciling them to God and to each other.

Tom Skinner once talked about how people warp an initial vision by using the example of the creators of the railroad system. These individuals launched their success with a vision to create a system that would transport goods from coast to coast in America. When they started, they were "transportation people" and dreamed up new ways to get people and stuff from one place to another. However, as the system grew and became more effective, they changed from transportation people to "railroad people," and in the process they lost their original vision. Instead of talking about the transport of people and goods, they began to define themselves in terms of their tracks—their network.

Later on, President Eisenhower came along and built a network of highways across America. Now people could get their products at their door! The railroad system was no longer needed for the basic transport of goods and people now that there was a better way. Although today railroads still have a place in our economy, they are nowhere near the system they once were. The railroad people were myopic and lacked foresight, and as a result they lost their original vision of transportation.

SHANE: Vision is not enough. Think about the Tower of Babel. It may have seemed like a good idea at the time, and good visionaries and leaders no doubt headed up the project. The Babylonians probably even had an amazing development director. But they also had a big problem: they thought they could make a name for themselves. They thought it was their duty to bridge the heavens and the earth . . . which may have impressed the paparazzi, but didn't impress God. He toppled the tower and scattered them.[3] They couldn't even communicate with each other anymore (this is where we get the word "babbler").

The only hope for reconciliation was in God—that's the only thing that could bridge the heavens and the earth (and it still is the only thing). The only hope for understanding each other again would be a mighty move of the Spirit. This is exactly what happened on the Day of Pentecost, when people who spoke different languages understood each other again.[4]

God seems to have an aversion to power . . . not because people are a threat to Him, but because they are a threat to themselves. In the case of Babylon, it was not a lack of leadership or vision that destroyed the people. They were destroyed because the vision had become an idol and needed to be toppled.

I often remind myself that it is God's work, not mine. What we do in North Philly is God's work, not ours. In *Jesus for President,* Chris Haw and I wrote:

> We have a God who enters the world through smallness—a baby refugee, a homeless rabbi, the lilies and the sparrows. We have a God who values the little offering of a couple of coins from a widow over the megacharity of millionaires. We have a God who speaks through little people—a stuttering spokesman named Moses; the stubborn donkey of Balaam; a lying brothel owner named Rahab; an adulterous king named David; a ragtag bunch of disciples who betrayed, doubted, and denied; and a converted terrorist named Paul.[5]

John: Leaders need to ask themselves about the future. They should think about it, pray about it, talk to others about it and envision it. True leaders need to envision a better future. That is prophetic. And good leaders will be able to communicate the hope, the dream, to followers. Martin Luther King did that. Mother Teresa did that. Billy Graham did that. Shane Claiborne does that.

Proverbs 29:18 says, "Where there is no vision, the people perish" (*KJV*). We need a hope for the future. The leader is the one who receives and carries this vision, articulates it and helps people embrace it as their own. Most followers only see pieces of what lies ahead, but a leader has what I call full knowledge or a complete picture. Everyone can see the individual trees in a forest; the leader has to see the entire forest. Not only does the leader have to see every tree, hill, valley, crevice and stream, but he also has to be able to lead people onto a path, point them in the right direction and walk through the forest with them. A leader needs to anticipate what lies ahead. Not just the now—not just leading and living in the moment. When the sun is shining bright, we may all want to go jump in the lake for a swim. We don't worry about a place to camp for the night, but a good leader thinks ahead, knows the sun will go down, and prepares.

Notes
1. Society of Brethren, Eberhard Arnold, ed., *The Early Christians: In Their Own Words* (New York: Plough Publishing House, 1998).
2. George Barna, *The Power of Vision: Discover and Apply God's Plan for Your Life and Ministry* (Ventura, CA: Regal Books, 2009), p. 28.
3. See Genesis 11 for the whole story.
4. See Acts 2.
5. Shane Claiborne and Chris Haw, *Jesus for President: Politics for Ordinary Radicals* (Grand Rapids, MI: Zondervan, 2008).

TO FOLLOW

(Choosing Who to Follow)

SHANE: We all begin as followers. But who should we follow? It's a good question.

John: It is so important to *choose* wisely when you decide whom to follow and not simply follow by default. Followers may be asked to get a donkey or work in the wake of one of the most devastating hurricanes in recorded history.

SHANE: Who have I followed? I've tried to follow people who remind me of Jesus. I looked to men and women of whom I admire the integrity of their lives. And there's so many. John's one of them.

I can remember when I first came to be on the board of CCDA, about 10 years ago, and I told John, because I knew that I was vulnerable and coming from a different background, "If you ever hear me say anything that you need to correct me on, you do it. And if you ever think I should speak less, you tell me I should speak less." You know, if he told me to stop writing so much, I would stop writing so much. I wanted to be submitted to an elder, and as a white man, I wanted to be mentored by an African-American elder.

This kind of submission to men and women who are wiser than me has shaped me. It has changed me and made me stronger. I remember that at one point after my first book, when there was quite a bit of fresh hype, John pulled me aside and asked me how my soul was. And he reminded me to make sure that I was not leading people to myself or to my vision of revolution, but that I was leading people to Jesus and to His revolution. It was a good word, which I will never forget.

Tony Campolo is another man of faith and integrity I follow. He is one of the first folks who taught me that loving God and loving my neighbor have to go together. Tony was my prof at Eastern University where I studied sociology. He's still a close friend and mentor. I have so many Campolo stories that I don't know where to start. I had some classes with him where he custom-designed our papers—one of my assignments was to write a paper analyzing the problem of homelessness in Philadelphia . . . but I had to write the paper as if I were Friedrich Nietzsche. I remember having Tony for six hours straight. He'd get to preaching (and spitting) and say things like, "You are as young as your dreams and as old as your cynicism . . . and I am younger than any of you." That's a good word, eh, John? Tony would really push us. He didn't settle for easy answers. I remember him debating students so aggressively that they cried (they also had an audience). That makes some strong minds . . . like a good football coach. You don't want a teacher that let's you get away with sloppy arguments, just like you don't want your dad to let you win at chess.

I remember one time when Tony was talking about Cooley's idea of the "looking glass self," which says that we end up wearing different masks and façades as we present ourselves to others. He talked about authenticity and transparency in leadership, and said no one is *really* completely honest about who they are. This one young woman raised her hand, bless her heart, and said, "Not my pastor . . ." (not a good way to start her argument). She went on to talk about how he was totally honest and transparent. Tony shot back (with an audience of 100-plus), "Does your pastor masturbate?" It was silent (except for a few snickers). He went on, "I'm sure he does, but he's not going to talk about it on Sunday morning or in the trustee meeting." That's Tony for you.

Tony doesn't really go easy on those of us he admires, either. In my second year at Eastern, there was a crisis in Philadelphia where homeless families were being evicted from an abandoned cathedral where they had been living, and it sparked a massive student movement on our campus where about 100 of us basically moved in with them and faced the possibility of arrest. (John mentions this in the introduction.)

Tony threw his support to us and told me I could miss class as long as I wrote papers about the sociology I was learning. And then one day he invited my friend and me to speak to his class. We were honored and showed up all excited to give a passionate plea for support and to tell a few stirring stories. But Tony ripped into us. "Have you talked to the Catholic Archdiocese that owns the cathedral? I'm sure they aren't malicious people. What is their side of the story? Is there liability? What if it catches on fire? What if a kid gets abused? How are the families governing themselves? What is your end goal?" By the end of it we were practically in tears, but years later I grew to appreciate exactly the kind of character and wisdom Tony was instilling in us. And besides, a few years later we got to return the favor.

WE HAD SOME SERIOUS DEBATES
AROUND THE LAST ELECTION ABOUT
HOW TO ENGAGE. WE DISAGREED.
AND IT WAS BEAUTIFUL.

We had some major disagreements with Tony about some things he had said, and sat down. I remember challenging Tony on how long it had been since he had hung out with a homeless person or helped a kid with homework. I was a bit pretentious, but Tony listened and responded. He even had us bring a couple of friends who had been homeless to meet with him and help him craft a new sermon. That's good leadership—neither timid, nor haughty . . . ready to challenge and ready to be challenged. To this day I get frequent emails from Tony, kind of like a father, telling me how much he loves me and how proud of me he is. But if there is any time he disagrees with me or wants to call me out, he doesn't hesitate. In fact, we had some serious debates around the last election about how to engage. We disagreed. And it was beautiful.

I am also a follower of Mother Teresa. After college, I was asking myself, "Where can I learn from God at work? Whom is He working through?" Mother Teresa was one of those people who fascinated the world with God's love. Talk about a leader, and even a reluctant leader. I wrote her a letter and ended up talking with her on the phone and then heading over to India. There are more stories than I can do justice to here, but I tell the whole story in my book *Irresistible Revolution* (another thing I've learned from John is to give a pitch for my books here and there. John says, "If it ain't worth pitchin', it wasn't worth writing").

One of the stories I have not told very often has to do with this idea that leaders are able to pull out the best in others. When I was in Calcutta, another one of the volunteers told me that she was wrestling with her sexuality. She was a lesbian and had all sorts of questions about why she was attracted to women and how to live a holy life. So she told me she was going to talk to Mother Teresa about it. *Hey, why not?*

The next day, I asked her how it went. What did Mother Teresa say to her? She said, "Mother just listened and held me . . . and then she asked me if I would read the Scripture in Mass tomorrow." It was a great honor to be asked by Mother Teresa to read the Scripture in Mass. It was as if she was inviting God to continue to move and stir and work in the woman as she read Scripture. And Mother Teresa seemed to have the firm confidence that the Spirit could be trusted to guide and convict and sort through those things. As Billy Graham said (actually when asked about this very issue of homosexuality), "It is God's job to judge, the Spirit's job to convict, and my job to love." Perhaps that was what made Mother Teresa such a great leader: she knew that she was not God. And that it was her job to encourage people to keep moving closer to Jesus. So often, Christian leaders have been the very obstacles standing in the way of people taking a step toward Jesus.

So it was a gift to work with Mother Teresa. I will say that as I watched her and walked with her, I discovered that she's a person who led out of her emptiness, goodness and faithfulness. Since her death, we have all heard about her own crisis of faith—her doubts and struggle with God. In *Mother Teresa: Come Be My Light,* she writes about her loneliness and questions.[1] I think she came so close to Christ and to the poor, that she felt the pain and suffering so deeply, that it was almost as if she had been utterly abandoned, like Christ on the cross.

But she never doubted God's love and faithfulness. She often spoke about how puzzling it was that God had put her in a place of influence, and what a huge responsibility that was. One of her classic quotes is when she said, "I know God won't give me more than I can handle . . . I just wish he didn't trust me so much." On another occasion, I remember some journalist asking her if she was married (incidentally, a very weird question for a nun), and her response was brilliant: "Yes I am. And my Spouse can be so demanding." But there was never a moment when she thought that her work was hers—she even lamented that people followed her. That's a pretty good sign that her motives were pure, and probably why she was a safe person for God to trust. The best leaders will always struggle with this sort of internal resistance. Mother Teresa would constantly write in her journals, "More of You, less of me. Because the more glory I get, the less Jesus gets." One time a reporter asked her, "Is your work going to live after you?" She quietly and respectfully dismissed the question, saying, "That is of no concern to me." It was like she was saying, "That's God's business."

That is a lesson for all of us. This is God's work, not ours. The moment we lose a sense of that, we start to lose our bearings. It is a danger sign.

After Mother Teresa died, a reporter asked me, "Is the spirit of Mother Teresa going to live on?" I said, "The spirit of Mother Teresa died a long time ago. What people love about Mother Teresa is the Spirit of Jesus in her, and that's going to live forever." I would say the same thing about John Perkins. There are all kinds of ripples of his life or witness, but ultimately it's the work of God.

We've picked up some cues from Mother Teresa's leadership. In our bylaws for Simple Way, we wrote, "This is the work of God, and so it's God's responsibility to prosper it or to end it. And either way we rejoice, because we know this is about God's work."

Today we have so many people to follow. It is said that we stand on the shoulders of great men and women of God. It's true, and sometimes we do not appreciate it. We get too caught up in the latest scandal or wrongheaded legalistic act from some pastor or church member, and we forget that the church is bigger than that. Sure it is a mess. People are a mess. But we are all better than the worst things we do. And just as we can see the evil that humans are capable of in the worst sinners, we can also see the goodness we are capable of in the saints.

Not all of my teachers and leaders and heroes and sheroes have names you would recognize. My mom is one of my best friends and most faithful supporters. My neighbors are some of the hardest-working people I've ever met and are defying the greatest odds. And of course there is Sister Margaret. She's an 80-year-old Catholic nun that I've stirred up a lot of holy mischief with. We've gone to jail together for protesting bad laws like Philadelphia's anti-homeless laws and for putting our bodies in the way of death penalty executions. I figure if you are going to go to jail, you should have a nun next to you. She's just got so much of the Spirit of Jesus in her. I've seen her stare into the eyes of mean people and whisper to them that they are better than the mean things they are doing. She can find the image of God in folks that others would have written off.

John: Who do I follow? What are the ingredients I look for in a leader? I have followed my friends over the course of my life, and I'm so thankful I did.

Friendship is one of the greatest of God's graces that can come to a person. A friend, many times, sees in you what you don't even see in yourself. They see the possibility, and sometimes the hope, of their lives being enriched by this relationship. Having friends is a compliment. They see something in you. I am the receiver of what they bring—that makes friendship a grace. They saw what was in you, they saw what they had to give and they directed that toward you. You don't become a friend until you see that in each other. Sometimes it's the other person who takes the initiative and breaks through your barriers. My friends have broken through my barriers, and I respond through that. Love and friendship are similar. When that barrier is broken, it's powerful—a gift from God.

Relationships start when you see someone you're attracted to, and as you get to know each other, you fall in love. It's very similar in friendship. You see how much you enrich each other's lives.

There's an interesting element in leadership and followership, and it really comes out in friendship. There is an authority established in friendship. Your friends have authority over your life. They will confront you in your ignorance and you can't ignore them because of your respect for them. If you have weak authority in your life, you will be a weak person. Without it you might not amount to anything. These are all people who have at one point had authority in my life.

My friends have been people who have loved me. I saw the virtue of love in them. Friendship is a longing for love. You see other people in the shadow of your longing. I turn it into a negative when I meet people who don't have a capacity for love. I put love and well-being together. That's what makes me want a health center. That's why I want to help kids. I want to take what they already have and try to get them to expand it and reach out with it. That's how I love people.

My friends are also people who have had my best interests in mind. These are people who think about what I'm doing, not what they can get out of the relationship or how I can help their cause. I grew up without a mother. So deep down, I have a need for acceptance. Perhaps that has something to do with the kind of person I choose to follow. People who get me on board quicker, and the people who I have followed in life, are the ones who approve of me right away. They don't necessarily approve of what I am doing or what I say, but they approve of me as a person. They accept me. They validate me.

THERE IS AUTHORITY ESTABLISHED

IN FRIENDSHIP. YOUR FRIENDS

HAVE AUTHORITY OVER YOUR LIFE.

Mary Nelson is one of those people I follow. She is on the CCDA board of directors and was the founding director and CEO of Bethel New Life in Chicago. Bethel New Life is a very effective family and community development organization. Mary accepts me, but she doesn't hesitate to correct me or make suggestions. Usually when she says I need to change, I already know she is right. It works that way with people who have our best interests in mind. She isn't trying to get me to fall in line with her agenda. No, she wants me to thrive in the agenda God has given me.

The late Bill Grieg, Jr., and Gary Vander Ark are like brothers you would have wished for in your life. These are friends of mine that compliment me—they don't compete with me. I think my friends are superior to me, and they feel the same way about me. I became the brother that Bill and Gary never had. I filled a hole in their lives, just like they did for me. We weren't afraid of each other because there was equality. We actually saw each other as more than equals. Being friends enriched all of our lives deeply—it went past the material things of this world. Authentic friendship always eclipses the "goods."

Wayne Gordon is another friend. He has a deep ability to love. It is almost contagious and trapping. I would follow him, because I see his love for his church members. It is unusual for Wayne to say something negative about someone. When we talk about something that's going wrong, we talk about the issue, not the person. I'm impressed by that quality in him. I want to follow people who have that kind of love.

R. A. Buckley, who was a 75-year-old man when I met him, was the most brilliant man I'd ever known. He could take anything you said and turn it into something profound. He told the best jokes (that were really profound in the end). "A white man and a black man were dog trainers. The black man was an expert, but the white man wasn't as good. The white man would never humble himself to ask the black man to teach him, so he would watch the black man and steal his tricks (this is the evil deprivation of racism). One day, after the white man saw the black man work a miracle with one really bad dog, he broke down and said, 'How did you do that?' Without looking up, the black man calmly responded, 'You gotta be smarter than the dog.' "

I have long-time friends like Howard Ahmanson, Roland Hinds, Bill Hoehn and Malcolm Street. There are others too numerous to name, but these friendships represent the quality of friendships I've had over the course of my life. The effectiveness of my work and my so-called success are tied to the quality of friends God has given me. Your friends see value in you and you meet that with value. The pursuit of that value is the friendship. If that stops because something got in your way—time, goals, or something else—it becomes a grace, because you benefit from something you did very little for.

Friendship is a win-win! That's what Job's friends were to him. They were tough and they grieved with him. The only problem with them was that they didn't know what God was doing. They didn't know that nothing could separate them from the love of God. But they were his good friends. I see genuine love in all of them. I recognized something in all my deep friends that I didn't quite have. They continue to enrich my life to this day. Most of my friends fall into this category, and I'm so thankful for all of them.

That's been my model. It was what I saw in the Presbyterian elder who discipled me long ago, Mr. Wayne Leitch. He would listen and then instill hope. He almost dreamed his dreams through me. He thought I could achieve things that he couldn't. He always said, "If I was you . . . this is what I would do." These would be creative ideas—powerful ideas. One time he told me to get a barn and not have any membership, just have a choir, like a pick-up game of basketball. I still wish that I could have pulled something off like that. I have almost lived out what he told me I could do.

I admired Tom Skinner's ability to communicate the truth despite his big and intimidating stature. He was a tiger in the pulpit, but through our friendship I could really tell he loved me. Barbara Skinner, his wife, and chairwoman of the board of CCDA, has her own captivating, dynamic presence—just like Tom did before he passed away. I followed Tom because of his strength in the Word of God, his desire for truth and his perspective on living out the kingdom of God.

In Monrovia, California, Mama Wilson helped and loved me so much. I was out of town when her son was killed in a car accident. When I got back, she put me in the place in her life where her son had been. She gave up her son and took me on. She treated me as her own. I had never had a mother's love. And she became the mother that I never had.

Mama Wilson was such a wonderful lady, a solid Christian. And she talked real talk. She would say, "Most preachers, all they want to do is get in the bed with women." That was an eye-opener, and there was truth in it, at least in our town. She was the most honest person I have ever known. When I left Monrovia to come back to Mississippi, she had a party for me. This initial party turned into a weekly prayer meeting for my ministry in Mississippi. These faithful friends became the foundation of my support. And it lasted for a long time. For those 19 or 20 years, their home became our home in California. Vera Mae and I had the pleasure of burying both Mama and Papa Wilson. Even after they died there were still prayer meetings for our ministry. That's when leadership and followership become a powerful friendship.

SHANE: It is true: I have not always agreed with the people I have followed. In fact, when the Scriptures speak of iron sharpening iron . . . that's the kind of thing that happens when you rub and collide with people and their ideas.

John doesn't just make you feel good all the time. He isn't an endless flow of flattery, despite what he said about me in the opening of this book. He is too honest for that and cares too much about me, and he respects me enough to keep his criticism private.

We can learn from our enemies too. Some of my best teachers are my critics. We learn more from people who challenge the things we say than from people who just parrot "Amen" to everything we say. We all see through a glass dimly. And I think that's where, for me, John has been really important. Our experience forms us, and so when you've had really different lived experience, you arrive at some different conclusions. But that's the gift of being part of a Body . . . our vision is made more complete when we are able to see through each other's eyes.

John: Who are some people you follow? (I hope you list at least two people we have never heard of!)

1. _____

2. _____

3. _____

4. _____

5. _____

6. _____

7. _____

Notes

1. See Mother Teresa, Come Be My Light: The Private Writings of the Saint of Calcutta (New York: Doubleday Religion, 2007).

TO LEAD

(Becoming a Leader)

John: Where *do* leaders come from? Young King David's brothers chided him when he told them he wanted to fight Goliath. He responded, "Is there not a cause?" (1 Sam. 17:29). What an astute and powerful comeback. David was just a teen, but he knew the answer. True leadership comes from a cause or a purpose.

Leadership emerges from within the leader. It's akin to a longing for something better; a hunger for dignity. We cry out because we're created in the image of God. Whether leadership ends up for good or for bad, it is the inherited desire for dignity that will motivate people to follow. The American forefathers understood this innate need. When they declared their independence from the tyranny of British rule and taxation without representation, they proclaimed that every human being has "certain unalienable rights."[1] This declaration includes the pursuit of dignity.

In *Dynamics of Leadership: Open the Door to Your Leadership Potential*, author Harold W. Reed discusses a handful of powerful modern leaders—even people we might not hold in the highest light, such as former communist Chinese leader Mao Zedong. Reed looks at leaders from a wide range of disciplines, showing their skills, intelligence and motivations. He concludes that leadership comes out of a major crisis: "All great leaders have the willingness to confront unequivocally the major anxiety of the people in their time."[2] That's my motivation—my people's pain. When I focus on helping to redeem and transform that pain into true life—here on earth and in eternity—my motives remain pure and the opportunity for leadership is always there. Because of our fallen world, we're constantly surrounded by pain, aren't we?

Every day I wake up to see nothing but opportunity. As a leader you need to have a sense of beauty in your heart. When a leader looks at the world he sees that beauty marred and says, "This doesn't have to be this way." We see a canvas; Michaelangelo sees a masterpiece yearning to be created. When I look around my community, and ghettos across the country, I see God's creation. People only see the trash-littered streets and broken-down cars and lives, but I see a piece of art waiting to be created—redeemed by God's love. You have to see the opportunities all around you!

There's a story about a shoe salesman who goes to Africa to sell shoes. He looks around, and seeing that no one wears shoes, he goes back home. Another man goes to Africa, and seeing all of the people without shoes, says, "Let's put shoes on everyone!" Of course the second man had the vision and the motivation that was bigger than just making money for himself. He saw that it was a great opportunity to provide a service and do it creatively.

WHEN I LOOK AROUND MY COMMUNITY, AND GHETTOS ACROSS THE COUNTRY, I SEE GOD'S CREATION.

Look at Warren Buffett. The last I heard, Buffett lives in the same house he's been living in for a long time. He walks to Dairy Queen to get his breakfast. He's a multibillionaire, in the same orbit as Bill Gates in terms of wealth, but he takes a salary from his company that is only a fraction of what he could take home. Along with this humility he has provided thousands of jobs across the country and around the world. Buffett has had a cause and he has been a great leader in the business community. Over the life of his career, he's been motivated by something bigger than himself—unlike an investment banker I recently saw testify at a congressional hearing who's motivations in life were completely backwards.

Someone asked the investment banker how he felt taking $500 million in compensation while the company was in a tailspin. He said,

"Well, it was a lot, but it wasn't $500 million. It was closer to $400 million." This guy was a crook if I've ever seen one. His main motivation was money, and his life reached a dead end. Your motives have to stay pure. You have to be very careful to not let money or fame become your main motivators, and you have to be very careful that neither one becomes an idol.

Recognition is different from fame. In some cultures (and in some families), if a person does not perform to a certain expected level, they are ridiculed, mocked or cast out. Then shame sets in. The person who has "failed" sees it as a flaw in himself as a person. This denigrating form of shame is not healthy and should be avoided. But I think the flip side of shame does have some value. One outward form of shame is being embarrassed. Shame is saying, "I'm not doing my share." Wanting to do your best to avoid shame and embarrassment isn't necessarily a bad thing.

SHANE: Sometimes the people who are quickest to lead aren't necessarily the best leaders either. And some of the folks that would make stellar leaders never get a chance to give it a shot. That's why some folks, especially white folks and male folks, sometimes need to pause before jumping into the driver's seat. I've had folks on my block who have been asking me to be block captain (which is the most localized form of leadership in the intercity, sort of like a village elder, though they are officially recognized by the city)—and yet I insist that I will only be an assistant block captain, to make sure there is room for others, and especially folks indigenous to the neighborhood.

Many folks do not believe in themselves—just like Peter when he looked at Jesus walking on water. He could have just sat in the boat and admired Jesus' skills. He could have just felt like crap thinking he could never do something like that. But Jesus told Peter to get off his butt and walk. And even when he stumbled, Jesus didn't just let him sink, nor did He give him a piggyback ride to the boat . . . He simply put out a hand and lifted him up and kept Peter going.

Some folks have just never had a chance to get out of the boat and take the risk of leading. We've got a recovery community in Philly made up of folks who are recovering from substance addiction, mostly crack and heroine. And it is led by people that are recovering addicts themselves. One of the realities we have learned there is that everybody is a teacher and everybody is a learner. We are all recovering from something. Everybody can lead out of his or her experience and woundedness. It is brilliant engineering for God to use the weak and the foolish rather than the strong and learned—as it puts us all in a place where we can be used by God. All it takes is the humility to recognize that all have something to teach, and we all have something to learn—especially when it comes to recovery.

I can remember years ago when we had folks using heroin living in our house; it was a disaster. Needles were left in the house, someone overdosed in the bathroom . . . Eventually we said, "What a mess! Why are things so bad?" The answer was pretty clear—because we didn't know much about heroin, the beast of addiction. So that's where we have to become learners and have others lead us in how to set up a community that moves people toward goodness and healing.

I think a lot of white guys get to be leaders because they're white guys, not because they're leaders. A lot of books sell, not because they are good but because they are marketed well and have money behind them. That's not the way Jesus did things. Instead, Jesus said that we should expect the world to hate us. There should be a collision with the culture. So if people speak well of you, woe to you; that's how they treated the false prophets. We cannot just listen to the hype and to the loudest voices. Some of God's most precious saints are quiet people, gentle prophets, secret saints that live in the shadows.

As a white man, it means I've got to be creative and take risks to create space for those other leaders. A few years back, I was a speaker for a large leadership conference for pastors, and I noticed there weren't any women in the lineup. I didn't like that, so I talked to the leadership about it and said I'd give up my place so that a woman speaker could speak. I even told them I could give them a list of dynamic women communicators. But they didn't take me up on the offer. So then I consulted some of my female friends and came up with a little idea. I still gave my plenary talk and just wore a sign that read: "God loves women preachers." I got in a little trouble for that one.

We—especially we men and we white folks from backgrounds of "so-called privilege" (note: I say "so-called privilege" because I do not consider it a true privilege to come from an ancestry and history built upon genocide, displacement, bloodshed and slavery)—need to take creative risks to make room for other leaders and voices. It's certainly not that women or people of color are not good leaders or dynamic communicators when we see a conference brochure with all white guys talking. It's that we haven't been careful enough, and humble enough, and creative enough to make sure every voice is at the table.

John: Sometimes they are not invited, and other times it's just that folks are not motivated. People sometimes ask, "What initiates leadership? Where does the motivation or inspiration come from?" People can lose their ambition to lead. You know, it seems to me like the best motivation should be our daily bread—the very fact that we need energy to live and we want others to live. And that should be our basic motivation. Some people believe that is a basic motivation of man, which he needs to eat to live. That gives you motivation to get up. And if you put food before that person without him understanding the need to contribute to that, things get messy. I think what motivates you, what inspires you, is a big question . . . because it has to be more than money.

SHANE: There are all sorts of things that can motivate people to lead—prestige, money, the ladies. Or guilt. Guilt can motivate (haven't you heard the pleas for volunteers in the nursery?!). Guilt can be a major reason why people lead, but it doesn't last, you know. Guilt can be a good thing at first, like when you realize the truth about poverty, slavery or the amount of stuff we consume in America. Guilt can be a good indicator, but it is a terrible motivator. You cannot lead out of guilt. Once you have paid your dues or appeased your conscience, then you need some other motivation or you'll just move on. Or else you'll just get paralyzed in the guilt.

Like John mentioned, folks in the ghetto can have a low self-esteem that cripples motivation. There are plenty of kids in the suburbs that react with guilt and shame because of the affluence of their parents—they turn into young hipsters with no real initiative to lead anything, or they become sort of cynical, timid, self-deprecating adults because they are reacting to the so-called privilege that can also cripple. They don't want the responsibility that comes with leadership, so they flat-out reject any offer of it.

That's where the freedom stuff comes. Good leaders are able not only to identify what's wrong in the world but also to point toward what's right. Moses saw the slavery and pain of his people, but he also had a vision of the Promised Land. Dr. King saw racism and slavery and humanity at it's worst, but he also had a dream of the beloved community. At The Simple Way, we talk about the importance of not just protesting, but "protestifying." It's also where you need visionary leaders.

> GOOD LEADERS NOT ONLY IDENTIFY
> WHAT'S WRONG IN THE WORLD, BUT
> ALSO POINT TOWARD WHAT'S RIGHT.

One of the shortcomings of the Reformation was that the Reformers knew what was wrong (after all, half of the word "Protestant" is "protest"). But once they were in charge, they didn't know what to do. And I think most people want to do what's right. They just don't know the alternatives. For instance, people don't want to buy clothes that are built on the backs of sweatshop labor. But a lot of times they don't know where else to buy or how to sew. And part of the marketing job is to insulate people from the faces of injustice, from the invisible people behind the way of life that we have. So you see the celebrity, but you don't see any of the 14-year-old girls making that celebrity's brand of shoes. So the job with all the advertising and commercials is to keep us away from the pain. I think the job of leaders is truth-telling . . . unveiling. Like revelation, which means to "reveal" or disclose or unveil, it is our job to disclose what lies underneath the surface. Then we are compelled, not just to sweep something under the rug but to get our hands dirty and do something about the problem.

There are a lot of people that can identify with problems. A lot of people say "Amen!" when John preaches about the systemic injustices like those in the prison industry—folks respond when John says that 70 percent of folks in prison are people of color, or 97 percent of them don't have fathers. But then he says, "So what are we going to do about it?" And there is silence . . . just crickets. But if the only message is what's wrong with the "system," then it doesn't lead you anywhere. You are just a victim or something to be pitied, or powerless under "the Man." As leaders, we have to have the ability to say, "So here's what's wrong and now here's what's right." We have to have some good news.

E. V. Hill, the late, great preacher, used to talk about a woman who would sit on the front row of his church in Los Angeles. He would be talking about all the things that were wrong and she would say, "Get to the good news. Get to the good news, pastor. Get to the good news." A lot of people never get to the good news. Certainly we have to start with the bad news, with the problems, the pain . . . but we also have to get to the good news. That's what Jesus brought. There had been plenty of prophets and zealots that knew everything that was wrong—just read the Old Testament and weep. People need good news. And the good news is that we have a God who so loved the world that He sent His Son, not to condemn it, or to leave it floundering in sin and injustice, but to save it.

We are neither invincible nor indispensable. That would be a good saying to put on a plaque and hang on the wall.

John: That thought, "We are neither invincible nor indispensable," brings me to the place of "rest" in the life of a leader. I've been looking through the book of Matthew where Jesus said, "Come to Me, all you who labor and are heavy laden, and I will give you rest. Take My yoke upon you and learn from Me, for I am gentle and lowly in heart, and you will find rest for your souls. For My yoke is easy and My burden is light" (Matt. 11:28-30). All of the great words in the Old Testament are captured in that one passage. Particularly in the word "rest." Rest is symbolic of God finishing creation and then resting. Therefore, if we are to be more like God, there is rest for the people of God, too. For six days God created—we know the story in Genesis. Then He stopped. As leaders we need to see that there is a time for God's work and a time to cease, to rest, to have a respite.

But there is a paradox in this passage. God makes us His workmen, but we are to rest in Him—always rest in Him, not just on the seventh day. When we learn to rest in Him while we work, the work is no longer ours. It becomes His work because He is bearing the burden. He is bearing the load. If you are a leader of any type, you have a vision. When you start to lead others in that vision, you will have burdens, not only to complete the vision or task itself, but to see the vision come alive and be completed in others. You will never see this happen if you try to carry your vision and force it into reality. You will only see it completed in others when you learn to let God carry your vision.

SHANE: I did some study on that same verse in Matthew about Jesus telling us to come to Him and take up His yoke. Scholars say the particular word Jesus uses to describe His burden is better translated as "good," "kind" or "full of grace" rather than that it is "easy" (a word that appears many other places in Scripture). That makes more sense to me; after all, Jesus is inviting us to carry a cross . . . a little bit of a daunting invitation. Throughout Scriptures the images of "yoke," such as the "yoke of slavery," seem anything but light. But part of the good news of the gospel is that we are not alone. Others will help bear the burdens with us. Even Jesus had help carrying His cross. The burden Jesus invites us to bear is not easy, but it is good and full of grace. And compared to the yoke of the empire, compared to Pharaoh's yoke of slavery, it is light, even liberating.

Leaders need to be able to rest. In our community, we give each other permission to take space—to rest, to pray, to take time away. Above our door there is a sign that says, "Today, small things with great love . . . or don't answer the door." Leaders need to learn how to rest and learn that they are not indispensable. We take a Sabbath day each week—where everything rests—all of our programs, all of our activities. We don't even answer the phone or a knock at the door. Jubilee and Sabbath are a couple of the distinctive marks of God's peculiar people. Not only do they know how to work, but they also know how to party (Jubilee) . . . and they know how to rest (Sabbath).

Resting and playing help us keep a perspective of things so that we can sustain things for the long haul. I remember hearing the story of some young missionaries that came down to Central America during one of the civil wars. With youthful passion and a deep sense of urgency they began rescuing people's possessions from homes that had been destroyed, holding kids that had been traumatized, cooking, cleaning, doing just about anything they could to help. At one point though, they became a bit frustrated by a group of women who were sitting on their porch sipping tea when there was so much work to be done. The kids went over to the women and said, "How can you be sipping tea in the middle of a revolution?" The women looked delicately at the kids, and with a large, gentle smile that comes with age and wisdom, one of the women said, "How can we not drink tea during a revolution? There will always be work to do. There is always a crisis at the door. We've seen young missionaries come and go, and we are thankful for you. But when you leave we will still be here. And if we do not sip tea, we cannot make it until tomorrow."

That's the sort of wisdom and pace that can sustain us for the long haul. True movements and true leaders are not measured in years, but in decades. That kind of longevity takes not only working our tails off, but also sipping tea together.

John: Let's look at Psalm 1:1-2: "Blessed is the man who walks not in the counsel of the ungodly, nor stands in the path of sinners, nor sits in the seat of the scornful; but his delight is in the law of the LORD. And in this law he meditates day and night." The law that was revealed through the justice leader Moses was completed in Jesus.[3] So those of us who are in Jesus (the fulfillment of the law) are to meditate on Him day and night.

I think there is something in the Incarnation (the Son of God coming to Earth as a human being) that God wanted for us to have as a model. He was meek and in many ways lonely. Leaders are often lonely because their concern is about others. Others cannot always physically be present with you.

To be lonely for me is to be thinking about my wife, Vera Mae, when she's not by my side. When we were younger and I traveled a lot, I would think about Vera Mae and the children, and all things happening at home, like homework and sporting events. Now that we are older and have had a good life together, I think of her health and comfort. Sometimes I think of what it will be like when one of us is no longer here. I can lose myself in thoughts about her. Sometimes I return home late after being out of town and she is already asleep. I see all sorts of pots and pans on the table, and I know she has been cooking. She likes to prepare meals for her family. Even if I am not hungry, I will peek into the refrigerator. Often, right on the top shelf, there will be something that I like. In that moment, I know that when I am away, she grows lonely too.

To a certain degree, we become so absorbed with Jesus and God's will that we die to ourselves, to our selfish desires. His ambition becomes our ambition. His ambition drives us and becomes our purpose. Jesus promised, "If you *abide* in Me, and My words *abide* in you, you will ask what you desire, and it shall be done for you" (John 15:7, emphasis added). Too often we look at the end of that verse, which is about getting our desires. But the first part sets the condition of abiding in Christ. Abide means to reside, to continuously meditate, to dwell. When we abide in Christ, who is the vine, we die to ourselves. We surrender our desires and replace them with His desires, which are better desires anyway.

As leaders, our ambition is not for a certain achievement, award or word of praise. As much as we want to change the world, our goal cannot even be a particular change. Our ambition is the will of God. We need to meditate upon God as revealed in the person of Jesus Christ and in His Word. As we meditate day and night, He then gives us the wisdom and understanding to do what He has called us to do.

SHANE: Early in my youth, way back in the 1900s (wink), I spent a lot of time thinking, *What is God's will for my life?* You know how it goes— as if the whole universe kind of revolved around me. One day, I caught this idea from a priest: "Good things come to those who wait, but great things come to those who get off their butts and *go find God at work*." That's a very different way of thinking of things. And it's very liberating to know that I don't have to wait for God to write a magical formula on the wall for me, but I can look around for where God is at work and join in. Instead of staring at my sandals, I walk out my front door and look into the eyes of my neighbors.

Community is a way to discern our calling. A lot of the time we act like we can just discern God's will in a vacuum, but I think there is something to Jesus' words when He says, "For where two or three of you are gathered together in My name, I am there in the midst of them" (Matt. 18:20). One of the ways we hear God's voice is by listen-

ing together. I've learned a lot about that from the Quakers. They often have "clearness meetings" when folks gather a group of elders
around them in order to discern major decisions or callings. In our
community, we did that when two of my community mates were trying to decide how best to raise their kids, whether to keep them in
public schools or home school. I had discernment meetings when I first
felt the nudge to write a book, and I have had all sorts of discernment
meetings trying to decide whether to be single or get married (and I
may need a few more). But community helps us discern our callings.

As we seek God's will, it seems to me that one way to discern our
calling is to ask: How do my gifts intersect with the needs of the world?
We really come to life when our gifts meet with the needs of the world
around us. That's where the Kingdom happens. We are made to live for
something bigger than ourselves. A leader who really begins to bear
fruit is somebody who's felt the needs in the world and then said,
"So how do the unique gifts that I have intertwine with that?" I see
examples of this all over the place.

I recently met a young man who is a robotics engineer (which I
thought was really cool). He told me about how he originally pursued
the career because it made a lot of money and folks were impressed by
his skills (after all, he makes robots). But then he said he began to
rethink his career and his gifts in terms of the kingdom of God . . .
and the needs of the world. Now he has pulled together a group of
robotics engineers that are designing robots that can dismantle
landmines so they can send them over to Afghanistan—the robots can
do the job that little kids are getting their hands blown off doing, and
can disarm fields so that children can play again. He's been able to see
his gifts come to life for God.

There are also a group of nurses around the corner from us in Philly
who became deeply disturbed by the crisis in health care in our neighborhood (around 47 million U.S. citizens do not have adequate health
care). Rather than whining or waiting for politicians to solve everything, they just opened up a free clinic. Now there are doctors, chiro-
practors and even nurses, dentists and massage therapists that are a
part of the clinic. Some of them have their own private practices on the
side, but if you ask them, the highlight of their week is always working
at the free clinic.

John: Gifted people do not necessarily rise to the top, but sooner or later they will be identified. The whole idea behind spiritual gifts in the New Testament is that God gives different gifts to different people. We just have to find out what those gifts are and why God has given them to us . . . and it is not just for ourselves.

In the mainstream world, we would say bring the most gifted people possible alongside of you. President Nixon had a strategic mind. He identified and brought gifted men and women into his administration. As dynamic as Nixon was, he knew that he could not lead this nation alone. This has nothing to do with political leanings. It has to do with how you go about leading and finding the right team.

I'm great friends with Chuck Colson. I've served on the board of Prison Fellowship and can tell you he's a great guy. Chuck's strength is his loyalty. If you are his friend, you've got a *friend*. But his loyalty was his downfall. He served on Nixon's Committee to Reelect the President and was so committed to Nixon and his reelection that he lost his moral grounding. Since then he's been a powerful force for restorative justice and righteousness in America and around the world.

SHANE: In the best cases, leaders are not appointed; they're recognized. So many people talk about electing elders or appointing elders, but I've got a pastor friend that told me in their congregation they just "recognize" the elders. Folks already know who the leaders are; they've already risen to the task by the time they are recognized. It's the same kind of thing as if you're a prophet: don't say it; show it. You know if you're an elder, so we don't need to cast lots or put names in a fishbowl.

We started our community with a whole bunch of us. And then as it doubled in size, everybody was like, "Well, who's leading this thing?" I mean, it was a mess. We had people that were there for two months and people that had been there for three years that were trying to lead the thing together. So we just stepped back and said let's talk about it. Who are the people that it's hard to imagine this community without them? Who are the people we recognize as leading us? And then we kind of submitted to each other in what we voiced. So I think that's a real difference. It's the sign of a strong community as well.

John: Shane said it. I say the same thing. Leaders emerge. Leaders sort of appear. Some people wait for the right time for leadership. It comes out of their faithfulness. And many times, failed leaders are people who are anxious to take over. But leaders generally are the ones who start doing the work and then others discover them. An education, a briefcase and a corner office don't make a person a leader.

SHANE: That's a good point.

John: We also have to grapple with knowing what kind of leader we are. In South Africa, Bishop Tutu was called upon to be a political leader, but he was reluctant. He was a church leader. So for a time he played both roles. It is important to know what kind of leader you are and to know your arena. If you try to lead a bunch of wild mustangs on a ranch in Wyoming but don't know the first thing about saddles and stirrups and all, it is not going to matter much if you are Donald Trump. You need to know about Mustangs, not Wall Street, to be that kind of leader.

SHANE: Sometimes it's harder to be part of a community than it is to just be a lone ranger or vigilante. It can seem easier to be a soloist than part of a choir—but ultimately this is a story about community. I've got a quote on my wall that says, "I know you're strong enough to do it alone, but are you strong enough to do it together?"

John: I like that one.

SHANE: Here's another one: an old African proverb says *if you want to go fast, go alone, but if you want to go far, go together.* In a sense, leadership is a choice to go far together rather than just run as fast as you can on your own. Being someone who is always going fast, I am tempted to do things alone, but I have chosen to do life together. I have intentionally joined with others. Ultimately, we can do more together than I can on my own.

Jesus taught the disciples a little something about empowerment and community. Look at the story of the miraculous feedings. The disciples start pointing out to Jesus that there are hungry people all around them (as if Jesus hadn't noticed). Jesus' response is brilliant. He says to the disciples, "Well, feed them." And the disciples are stunned—they start complaining about how much money it would take and how far away the nearest fast-food joint is. Jesus stops them in their tracks, saying, "What do you have?" All they can round up is a little kid's lunch of fish and chips. But Jesus tells them to start sharing what they have, and they do it . . . only to find out that there are baskets of leftovers.[4]

Jesus took what the people had and added a little God stuff to it. He teaches the disciples to offer what little they have and promises that when we do that, there will be enough. It is not the same miracle as when God rained down bread from heaven, though it is reminiscent of that. This time the miracle is that God can take frail, meager offerings from our hands and do the work of the Kingdom. What a crazy idea—the God that can feed the masses on His own resists the temptation to turn stones into bread or rain down manna from heaven and chooses to use us, to need us, to want us! Jesus chose to do the miraculous work with a group of followers, albeit a ragtag bunch that over and over were arguing, flailing, denying, betraying and embarrassing Him. But that seems to be the nature of the kingdom of God. It is the story of community. We have a God that doesn't want to change the world without us.

John has an incredible motto: *When a leader's task is done, the people say, "We did it ourselves."* John says, "A good leader motivates followers to do what he wants them to do, and they think it was their idea." This is where good leadership is an art form. Leaders who may be perceived to be strong know that ultimately they are trying to work themselves out of a job, and they are not indispensable. When the leader has earnestly listened to the people and built on their gifts, and stepped out of the way every chance he or she gets to make room for others, then naturally the people begin to own the work. When the leader makes himself smaller and smaller, the people no longer see the leader, only the vision. And when the followers own the vision of the leader as their own, the leader has succeeded. The word "succeed" literally means "to pass on," "to come after," "to follow after." Success has nothing to do with money or notoriety, and everything to do with whether or not people will carry on the vision when we are dust.

Notes

1. The second sentence of the Declaration of Independence reads, "We hold these truths to be self-evident, that all men are created equal, that they are endowed by their Creator with certain unalienable Rights, that among these are Life, Liberty and the pursuit of Happiness"(July 4, 1776).
2. Harold W. Reed, *Dynamics of Leadership: Open the Door to Your Leadership Potential* (Vero Media, Inc., 1982).
3. See Matthew 5:17-18; Luke 24:44.
4. See Luke 9:10-17.

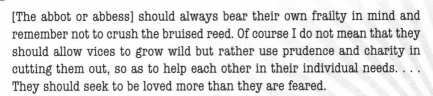

[The abbot or abbess] should always bear their own frailty in mind and remember not to crush the bruised reed. Of course I do not mean that they should allow vices to grow wild but rather use prudence and charity in cutting them out, so as to help each other in their individual needs. . . . They should seek to be loved more than they are feared.

—St. Benedict of Nursia (480–547)

FOLLOWERS

(Finding Others to Join the Cause)

If anyone desires to come after Me, let him deny himself,
and take up his cross, and follow Me.
MATTHEW 16:24, *NKJV*

John: We are all followers. We start and end as followers of God. We follow our hearts, our vision and our instincts. A good leader will be a good follower, and good leaders are always following someone else.

SHANE: I remember John saying to me a long time ago: "A good leader is somebody who teaches what he knows and admits what he doesn't know." Some leadership gurus suggest that you talk big. Hype it up. If you sound like you know your stuff, then everyone will think you do. If you talk like an expert, you will be one. I've never seen that really work. Even if it did, the leader would be establishing his authority on false pretenses. The real test of a good leader is whether he can say, "I don't know." And that leads to the willingness to find someone who does know. Too often so many of us think that we have to have all the answers. When we don't, we just make something up. Eventually, that approach comes back to bite us.

That's what is so fun about being a part of a Body with lots of different parts. For example, Bob Lupton is a close friend of John and me. Bob started a great work in Atlanta and has been a great advocate for meeting gentrification head-on. There are some things that we see very differently from each other when it comes to politics and economics. In fact, I tell folks he is my favorite "responsible capitalist."

Bob was one of the first folks to jump on board when we started The Simple Way. He probably thought that we were a little naïve and nuts. But I also am confident that he saw a fire in us that he admired, and maybe even a youthful idealism that he thought CCDA needed. And you had better believe when we started facing issues of gentrification in our neighborhood, we called Bob. When a fire burned down our block and we needed to figure out how to rebuild our neighborhood, we called Bob. Granted, I may not ask him who to vote for in the next election, but neither he nor I believe one election is ultimately going to change the world anyway.

> TO KNOW WHAT A FOLLOWER
> LOOKS LIKE, ALL WE HAVE TO DO
> IS LOOK IN THE MIRROR.

A few years ago, we were a bit paralyzed by a pattern we saw here at The Simple Way. Many of our visitors and new members, and long-term leadership were made up of young white folks, and yet we wanted to be about the work of reconciliation, and we sought to reflect the diversity of God's family. Some of my African-American and Latino brothers and sisters began to critique the "whiteness." It was hard. I ended up calling up some of these friends and asking, with tears in my eyes, for them to help us figure this out. Eventually we made some significant shifts, and we continue to make them—but it started with us becoming good listeners, not being defensive. We had to be willing to bring some of our critics to the table and even create spaces for them to lead us, for we were heading into some uncharted waters. We had to be able to say . . . there are some things we do well, but this is not one of them. Hopefully, it is becoming one of the things we do well, because our "we" is much bigger now.

John: To know what a follower looks like, all we have to do is look in the mirror, or sit on a park bench and watch people as they go by. Sometimes it's the people who look like us who are going to listen and join; others times one who will follow will be a complete surprise. We should avoid putting followers in boxes, just as we don't want to be stereotyped.

When I started the co-ops in Mississippi, in the 1960s, it was the blacks who listened and followed. They were the ones who needed some kind of economic breakthrough, not the whites. We wanted and needed the support of whites, but that would take longer to come.

We need to teach what we know. What we have experienced is what is going to communicate to people. When folks share our demons, our struggles and our pain, they also will want to share our hope.

SHANE: We talk a lot around my community about how we are called to harmonize but not homogenize. To us, this means that we are singing the same tune and dancing to the same drum, but that doesn't mean we are all identical. Just because we follow the same Rabbi doesn't mean we end up in uniformity. In fact, it seems to be just the opposite. Uniformity and sameness (homogeneity) are a part of the empire and the systems of this world. People are taught conformity and are socialized into ways of acting, dressing, eating, speaking.

It's funny that John encouraged leaders to avoid putting followers in boxes. It's a good word . . . and isn't that exactly what we do in our culture all the time? There's an old song that starts out, "Little boxes on the hillside; little boxes made of ticky tacky." (I cannot quote it all here, but you can find the lyrics to "Little Boxes" on the Internet. Just Google it.) In the song, Malvina Reynolds describes the empire to a tee. In a poem and with a jingle, she shows how we are put in boxes as children, students, lawyers, business executives—the list is long.

It's the system, the empire, the Matrix. That's Caesar's world. Caesar makes coins that are all identical. But our God is a God of diversity. Our God is an artist. The kingdom of God is a place where every person is unique, just like our fingerprints. So when folks follow us we cannot pretend that they will make the exact, same choices or responses. There are certain things that we can say are clear gospel mandates—like caring for the poor and sharing the salvific love of Jesus with others. But Jesus doesn't tell everyone the same thing when He invites them to follow. To one person He says, "Be born again." To another He tells him to sell all that he has and give it to the poor. There is an unmistakable call in Scripture to "not be conformed to this world" (Rom. 12:2). But just because we are called to be radical nonconformists doesn't mean that we all end up doing the same thing.

Nonconformity doesn't mean uniformity. We are all called to carry a cross, but that doesn't mean all the crosses look alike. Consider the two tax collectors who followed Jesus—Matthew and Zacchaeus. Even though they both had the same profession, their responses to Jesus were not identical. Matthew leaves everything and follows Jesus, barefoot on the streets. Zacchaeus doesn't. He sells half of everything and gives it to the poor, and then he begins paying people back four times what was owed them. He is a different kind of tax collector, doing Jubilee economics and spinning debt on its head. Neither Matthew nor Zacchaeus conformed any longer to the patterns of their world and the oppressive systems of taxation they found themselves in. But they responded in different ways.

One little non-conforming adventure we have been on—one that needs good leaders and prophets these days—is fair-trade clothing . . . we are trying to bring an end to sweatshops, child labor and modern-day slavery. So many of us see that something needs to be done, but we will not all combat these injustices in the same way. I see so much creativity. One of my friends started a T-shirt company in the Philadelphia area. They are committed to creating desperately needed jobs in the neighborhood with eco-friendly inks and fairly-traded shirts. Then folks like Tony Campolo and me, and maybe John next (wink, wink), ask that all of the events we are speaking at support the local business. Specifically, we seek to ensure that the T-shirts at Christian conferences are not made with the blood and the sweat of the poor. And this strategy is working . . . not only is it fruitful for the gospel (we are being good stewards), but it also provides money for jobs and work in the neighborhood. How cool is that? So, if you are ever printing T-shirts, call my buddy Adam at Dotted Line.[1]

We always need to keep our eyes open for what could be next and not just assume that we have arrived. Recently, I met some folks who had left their corporate jobs to start a fair-trade T-shirt and bag company, giving jobs to women in Calcutta whom they had helped escape from sex trafficking in the red-light district. It's called Freeset, and it looks like they may be our largest T-shirt supplier.[2] We even want to distribute their goods to other T-shirt printers around the country who care about this stuff. Freeset cofounder Kerry Hilton says, "The business we're in is actually freedom, and to obtain that, we manufacture and export quality jute bags."

It is awesome to see how everyone finds his or her own gifts and passions come to life and how different people take the pilot seat on their little piece. No one has to do everything, but everybody has to do something. Like pieces of a puzzle . . . we are a Body, God's Body, getting in the way of injustice and inequality. I've heard John say that we have to take on poverty and injustice on all sides. Give a person a fish and they'll eat for a day; teach them to fish and they can feed themselves. But we also have to ask, "Who owns the pond?" Others will ask, "Who polluted the pond?" Others will say, "Why does a fishing license cost so stinking much?" We need to keep asking the questions, and eventually we will get at the root of the injustices that keep some people from being able to eat while others live it up.

As we "seek first the Kingdom of God," some of us may lose our jobs. Some of us may redefine them. Others may turn the systems on their head as we pursue the upside-down kingdom of Jesus. What we can say is that we can be assured that an encounter with Jesus will mess us up and transform not only what we believe, but also who we are—our economics, our politics, our families, even our very lives. So don't follow us. Follow Jesus, and follow us in as much as our footsteps lead closer to Him.

John: We tend to follow leaders who reflect our perception of what we think or hope life is all about—or at least our basic viewpoints. A leader, operating within his vision, gives people a deeper perception of existence. Good leadership brings to life a more qualitative type of day-to-day experience for followers and for the community. This "good life" is not based on materialism. It's grounded within the human spirit.

How we view material possessions affects our perception of life and how we lead and how we follow, whether we are in an extreme prosperity gospel camp, within the Amish in Pennsylvania or in the inner city. In my community, some poor people have a mindset that if they can't have stuff (a nice car, nice clothes, diamonds, and so on), they can give those things to their leader. And some leaders go along with it. I call this a Solomon mentality. Solomon, of course, was one of the wealthiest men of the Old Testament.[3] Solomon had 12,000 horsemen; today, religious leaders just drive cars with a lot of horsepower.

Here is the principle: people collectively tend to give their leader what they individually want for themselves but realize they can't have. Some leaders play on that kind of mentality and soon enough they are leading not for the good of the people but for their own success. Some of the best-known television preachers use just the right words to justify consuming on a large scale: boats, houses, airplanes and the like.

Jesus says it's more blessed to give than to receive—it's a spiritual gift. It's the one gift that everyone can have. The real issue I have with the prosperity leaders is that they manipulate people's good-natured giving—the gift of God.

> WE TEND TO FOLLOW LEADERS WHO
> REFLECT OUR PERCEPTION OF WHAT
> WE THINK OR HOPE LIFE IS ALL ABOUT.

"In their prayers for you, their heart will go out to you for the surpassed grace that he has given you. Thanks be unto God for this unspeakable gift" (2 Cor. 9:14-15, *NIV*). This unspeakable gift is the gift of giving. That's the idea behind John 3:16. God gave His only begotten son to us. I'm angry that we take the most divine gift, this gift of giving, and we corrupt it, using it for our own selfish ends. That is why it should not be manipulated.

This affects black and white preachers alike—it's a human trait. Many of the black prosperity preachers got their training from their white counterparts. I'm not against fundraising as a cause as long as it's not for the benefit of one person but rather for the release of the poor and the general good of the society . . . "general good" being hospitals, art and all of the cultural developments that enhance humanity.

Shane rode in a veggie-powered bus on his *Jesus for President* book tour. Now that is making a statement, but I hope we aren't climbing into a bus for this book. I'm not sure I'm ready to filter that stuff.

SHANE: Don't worry; the veggie bus thing has already been done. For this book, we are going to have to try something else—maybe a book tour on horseback, like John Wesley and the revivalists! Actually, the veggie bus was an incredible adventure. We hit up over 20 cities across North America, and traveled 11,000 miles in that old thing, smelling like French fries, pulling up to restaurants and asking if we could have their waste veggie oil. But it all goes back to integrity. As we planned the tour we decided that if we were going to be traveling the country talking about the peculiar politics of God's kingdom, then we needed to practice what we preached. So we ended up asking some friends who had converted their diesel bus to run off of waste veggie oil if we could use it. It became a part of our message, part of our politics. We even had CNN come on the bus. It was part of our witness—that God cares about how we travel, how we live, how we use resources. Not to mention it was a cheap ride. The whole *Jesus for President* book and tour was a project to provoke the imagination—to get people to think, not just about how we vote on November 4, but about how we live on November 3 and November 5 and every day.

We have to scratch where folks are itching. That's what the whole *Jesus for President* project was about. Folks were talking about important issues and things that really matter—like health care, immigration, abortion, poverty, the environment, militarism . . . and we wanted to contribute to that conversation without allowing the media and hot-button issues, the old camps and the stale debates to provide the framework for discussion. We had to think outside the box. That's one of the things Jesus always did so magnificently. He colored outside the lines. He didn't just answer the questions; He questioned the questions.

Leaders identify the things that people care about (for better or worse). People want to be safe, and are scared to death of death, so they follow leaders that make them feel secure (of course, Jesus challenged and continues to challenge the things we hope and trust in—and offers a security plan that would never win an election—"Lose your life to find it" . . . it's a wonder He even had 12 followers with a plan like that). People want to go to heaven, so we see books and movies about that. I am not so sure about all of the theology in the *Left Behind* series, but Tim LaHaye and Jerry Jenkins sure do sell a lot of books.

As leaders, we have a duty to pay attention to the things people care about and gravitate to. It says something about their deep longings. We can't just write people off because we disagree with them. We need to start thinking, *What* is *behind that?*—even when we disagree them or don't particularly like their style. Even the Religious Right has leaders, albeit leaders some folks may disagree with. But if we aren't careful we will write off all of their followers if we don't engage their message and the reasons that folks followed and are still following them. Jesus was always inviting dialogue with His critics. He was able to draw together a pretty eclectic dinner conversation. Look at His followers. He was able to bring to the same table a zealot revolutionary and a Roman tax collector. Zealots killed tax collectors for fun on weekends. What a mix . . . and all of them were being transformed into a new creation in Christ.

Good leaders do not fear those who see things differently. In fact, I think it is a sign of weakness, not strength, when we try to silence the voices of dissent. I had one speaking engagement cancel because I was too "liberal." A few months later, I had another engagement cancel because I was too "conservative." Maybe that's a sign we are doing something right. But it is also a sign that people are fearful, as if the Spirit is not capable of guiding us into truth, and needs us to be truth's gatekeepers.

John: When I first met Al Whitaker at a rushed airport meeting, I never thought he would become one of my greatest friends. We disagreed on just about everything. He was a conservative investment banker guy. But along with his business savvy he understood the value of a good relationship. Because of our initial meeting, he came to Mississippi and spent a week with me. We traveled all around and got to know each other's hearts. Because of that week he got involved with the Christian Community Development vision.

He's the guy who made the initial movement toward the development of CCDA. He created the first Christian MBA program at Eastern University. He started Opportunity International that is a small international bank that makes loans to banks in developing nations that in turn make micro-loans to bakers and tailors and all sorts of other people in poor communities. I'm so thankful that we took a chance on each other. Despite our initial differences, our lives were so enriched by our friendship—and together we made a difference in the world.

§ⅢⒶⓃⒺ: Some of us follow people not because they hold any truth, but because they make us feel loved. That can be a dangerous reason to follow. It's often why folks join gangs and extremist groups. One of our deepest longings is to be assured that we are beautiful, that we have dignity, that we have meaning; and we can find that in all sorts of ugly places. The needs are real, but we can end up settling for something that does not really meet the need. It's sort of a counterfeit community or a counterfeit gospel. That's also why prosperity preachers have such a following. They tell people what they want to hear— promises of health, blessing and prosperity. They say "peace" even when there isn't any. This sounds too similar to the false prophets in Scripture . . . and false prophets can have followers. They can even have an alluring message and a charismatic personality.

The real test is the fruit, and the litmus test of Jesus. If the gospel we hear is not good news to the poor and freedom for the oppressed, then it is not the gospel of Jesus, no matter how many followers there are. There is another gospel out there. It is a self-centered, blessing-obsessed gospel of prosperity. *Become a better you. Find your best life.* If we are not careful, in all of our infatuation with ourselves we lose the secret of Jesus: "If you want to find your life, you've got to give it away." Lose yourself. We're designed to live for something bigger than ourselves. When we spend so much time looking in the mirror, we are no longer looking at Jesus.

That's exactly what discipleship is all about, surrounding ourselves with folks who remind us of Jesus, and hoping they rub off on us a little. As one of my friends says, "Discipleship means finding a Rabbi we follow so closely that we get covered in the dust behind him." Intentional community is just choosing a group of folks to do life with because they will move us closer to the person God wants us to be.

That is one of the key ways we discern God's will, by asking, "Does this—this community, this spouse, this leader—move me closer to Jesus?" Can I smell the fragrance of Christ on them?

I have a friend in Philly who is always giving stuff away. In fact, nearly every time I see him he's given his coat or shoes or blanket away, so I always ask if there is anything he needs. I found out that it was his general policy to give things away any time someone compliments what he has or is wearing, lest he become too haughty and lest the person need the item more than he does.

Once he had a bike one of the kids said he liked, and before I could turn around the bike was gone.

One of my buddy's general rules is that there are senseless amounts of food getting thrown away, so he committed to eating discarded food whenever possible. One time, I was speaking at a prestigious Ivy League school, and I took my friend along. After the speaking event, there was a nice full-spread VIP buffet dinner arranged for us with the deans and heads of the university. As we all waited in line, I noticed that my friend had slipped away and was in the dishes line, scraping some of the leftovers folks were throwing away, which were not the same selections as the foods on the buffet. When he came back to the table, he actually had a full plate of rather delicious looking food and got a few inquisitive stares from the administration folks. One of them said politely to him, "That looks really good." And with a nice smile and a wink my way, he pushed the plate forward to offer a bite. That's the kind of person I want to be around. They keep us from getting complacent.

As a leader, there needs to be a sense of moving people closer, not to ourselves but to who God is. And as leaders, we have to say, with Paul, "In as much as I'm like Jesus, follow me" (and inasmuch as I am not like Christ, don't!).

In my generation, there's such a suspicion of leadership, partly because there are so many terrible leaders. People have seen televangelists take people's money, priests abuse kids, and pastors indulge in extramarital affairs. I guess that's nothing really new, but what is new is that every time there is a "scandal," the world knows about it—with the media, the Internet, Twitter and blogs, the poop hits the fan pretty fast these days, and it at least *seems* like every leader is up to his elbows in trouble. The nice thing is that, as Scripture says, it's hard to hide . . . what's done in private will be proclaimed from the mountains.[4] But it's a little lopsided, because the scandal stories make much hotter news stories than stories of grace or reconciliation. Bad leadership gets more airtime than good leadership. Yet while the scandals do make us a little suspicious and hesitant to trust the next charismatic leader, we should never forget there have been many good leaders, even in the last 50 years.

John: Good leadership produces good followership. This section is on finding good followers. So what should we look for when gathering together people who can help carry our vision?

1. Of course, consider their commitment to Christ. How strong is it? Do they have a good heart or do they come on as too religious or pious? How dedicated are they to a cause? Look for people who have ideas. Look for learners and listeners. Followers need to be firm in their faith but also malleable in how they go about living out that faith.

2. I like thoughtful people. These are the people that will question motives and direction while continually moving forward. You have to be going down the road while noticing the potholes along the way.

3. Honesty and integrity are hugely important.

4. I look for someone who can write well and communicate the vision in a variety of mediums. Good note takers. Habakkuk 2:2 says, "Write the vision and make it plain on tablets, that he may run who reads it."

5. I love people who are passionate about people, not about buildings.

6. I love high-energy people! Vision can create energy within people, but for the most part, people are either high- or low-energy. High-energy people give me more energy to do what I do! These are the visionaries a lot of the time.

7. I look for people with discipline. When they have discipline, you can help them discover God's purpose in their life. You have to have some personal resolve and grounding. That works itself out in a lot of ways.

8. I look for people with a large worldview. When you set out on a journey, the spark of initial motivation may be a single act, but you need to arrive at a more holistic end.

9. I look for thrifty people. There is a difference between thrift and stinginess when it comes to money. Stinginess is hoarding it. Thrift is placing it where it will go the furthest.

10. I look for people with joy in their hearts—people who can laugh and joke. If someone is buttoned-up too tight, they might not be open enough. I love lighthearted people— they make life so much more enjoyable.

SHANE: Certainly God loves us as we are, not for who we could be— not in spite of our shortcomings, but with them. And yet being a Church of and for the broken doesn't mean we stay in our brokenness. We need to be healers, communities where people can heal. As Dorothy Day says, we have to create an environment where it is easier to be good. That means discipline. The word "disciple" shares the same root as "discipline." And that's not a word we like very much.

For many of us, the judgmental, arrogant, legalistic Christianity we might have known growing up has created a suspicion of discipline and order that can lead to a pretty sloppy spirituality. By reacting to the institutional sickness, we can easily find ourselves with little in place to help us heal from our wounds, create new disciplines and carve out a space where goodness triumphs.

I just read an article that spoke about one of the parenting gurus who died a few years back. He was one of those psychiatrists who pioneered the movement that taught parents not to discipline their kids but to allow autonomy as kids make mistakes and decisions on their own (let them touch a candle so they learn what "hot" is . . .). Just let the children make mistakes—that's the best way to learn! On his deathbed, this doctor confessed that the social scientists were wrong, saying, "We've raised a generation of brats."

Much of the seeker-sensitive, postmodern church is in danger of making the same mistake. We can raise a generation of spiritual brats that do whatever they want and no one can tell them otherwise. People come to the altar singing "Just as I am" and leave just as they were—a church that teaches what to believe but not how to live. A church that is scared of spiritual disciplines like simplicity, fasting, solitude and chastity will not produce very good disciples.

Community is pretty hip these days. The longing for community is in all of us, to love and to be loved. But if community doesn't exist for something beyond ourselves, it will die, atrophy, suffocate. Without discipline we become little more than hippie communes or frat houses; we fall short of God's dream to form a new humanity with distinct practices that act as contrast culture to the rest of society.

Like any culture, we who follow the Way of Jesus have distinct ways of eating and partying that are different from the culture of consumption, homogeneity and hedonism of the world around us. Discipline and discipleship don't just happen; they have to be cultivated.

John: What 5 or 6 qualities do you look for when choosing disciples? Okay, I had 10, so you can have 10, too . . . but don't just duplicate my list.

1. _____

2. _____

3. _____

4. _____

5. _____

6. _____

7. _____

8. _____

9. _____

10. _____

Notes

1. See www.dottedlineshirts.com.
2. See www.freesetglobal.com.
3. See 1 Chronicles 22:14; 1 Kings 9:14; 10:14,26-29.
4. See Mark 4:22.

SOMETHING BIGGER

(Seeing That It's Not Just About Us)

John : Rick Warren had it right in the opening line of his book *The Purpose Driven Life*. It's not just about us.

If someone shares in prayer meeting that they need a wheelchair ramp, well don't just pray for it. Do pray for it, but also get some carpenters together. I could help build a wheelchair ramp (or find someone to do it) and so can many of you. If someone has chest pains, you don't just pray. Pray, but also see if there is a doctor in the house and call an ambulance. If a single mom has been laid off from work, pray, but also invite her over for dinner. Maybe help her with her résumé. Ask around to see if anyone is hiring. A good leader will be the first to pray *and* the first to bring everyone together to help be the answer to that prayer. We cannot always be the answer to every prayer, but good leaders bring folks together and do life.

SHANE: Good leadership will not only be inspirational and motivational, but there will also be some action to it. We don't just draw up blueprints for the wheelchair ramp, but we actually get it built.

In our community, we have a little litmus test to check our motives. We ask ourselves, *Would I do what I'm doing regardless of whether or not I get paid?* For 10 years, the answer has been, "Absolutely." The Simple Way didn't have any paid staff because we said we wanted people doing what they love to do and what they're gifted at doing without any strings attached. When people started getting married and having children, and developing bad knees, new questions arose and we evolved. That's a good thing—change means something is alive. Some folks get paid now. But we still ask the same question:

Would I do this even if I didn't get paid—because it is worth doing, because I believe in it? What we do needs to ignite such a fire inside of us that we can't just watch someone suffer. The point is not whether we get paid; rather, it's the fire. Is it burning? Do I love what I am doing? This is a question for leaders and for followers. Out of people doing what they love doing comes fruit. I remember one time hearing a reporter tell Mother Teresa, "I wouldn't do what you do for a million dollars." And she shot back, "I wouldn't either . . . but I'd do it because it matters to God."

John: Tradition says that when the disciple John was an old man, his friends would take him to church and stand him up in front of everyone. He would say, "Children, love one another. Children, love one another." And the people said, "Why do you always say that, old man?" John never flinched. Every time he would say, "That's what Jesus taught us." Indeed, Jesus taught us to love one another. That's the acid test. Do we really love one another? If we do, getting a thousand dollars or even a million dollars will not make much difference in how we go about things. Okay . . . a million dollars would buy a lot of malaria vaccines for Africa or houses for single mothers in Jackson, but it should not affect our hearts or increase how much we love. That should always be the same.

SHANE: When John the Baptist was in prison, he heard reports about a great prophet rising up. So he sent two of his disciples to investigate. They found Jesus easily enough. He had been in a city called Nain, teaching and healing people. The two disciples asked Jesus straight up, "Are You the one who was to come?" (Luke 7:20). The *International Standard Version* records it this way: "Are you the Coming One?" With His usual creative flair, Jesus' response was just brilliant. He didn't say, "Yeah, I am the Messiah . . . and what's your name?" Rather, He said, "Go back and report to John what you have seen and heard" (Luke 7:22).[1]

What did the disciples see? The blind could see. The lame walked. The lepers were cleansed. And let's not forget that the dead were raised *and* the poor heard the gospel—the good news. I love this story. Basically, John the Baptist's emissaries asked, "Are You the one we've been waiting for?" I am sure they didn't expect His answer. In effect, He said, "Come and see. Then you tell Me." It was an invitation to read the trail of crumbs behind Him. This answer was so consistent with Jesus' character. These were not just words. He didn't go around flaunting that He's the Son of God. In fact, half the time, when folks discovered He was the Messiah, He would tell them not to tell anyone, to keep it on the down low. He didn't command people to worship Him, but He did invite everybody to follow—and as they followed, they discovered who He was (and still is today). They worshiped then, not because they had to but because they wanted to.

I'm hard-pressed to find anywhere in Scripture where Jesus commanded people to worship Him. His life was simply an invitation of grace. I heard one theologian say that one thing we can learn from Jesus is that the gospel spreads best not through force but through fascination. That's Jesus. He doesn't force; He fascinates us with love. Good leaders live in ways that woo people into their vision. Force, coercion, manipulation, aggression . . . these are weapons of the weak. These are the devices of empires. These were the tools of Caesar.

We can learn from Jesus. As evangelicals, we want people to know the love of Jesus. But that doesn't just happen by saying a magic prayer. It only happens by saying, "Come and see. Come and follow. Come and feel. Come and experience the goodness of God."

John: CCDA started as a longing in the hearts of just a few people. Most of us were already working in urban areas and were the only ministry in town, or at least it felt that way. Through the years, taking the good news to the poor, oppressed and needy had been a rather lonely mission. What faith-based efforts existed tended to look inward, because there were so few. One common longing we had was to take Christian community development public, so to speak—to make it more visible. When a leader or group of leaders has a longing, they have to ask themselves the hard questions. We had to ask ourselves, "Is there a people out there who are thinking like we think? And who are those people?"

We took a risk, sent out about 100 letters to people we knew who might be interested. We invited those folks to come to the airport in Chicago and spend a day together. Representatives from 37 groups showed up. It was quite a diverse gathering. I was surprised and excited. We exchanged stories and ideas. Quickly, we saw that our longings and dreams were similar. A few months later, we got together again and pretty soon we had something going.

Forming a group from scratch is an interesting process, especially when the members of that group are already leaders with followers. Nonetheless, CCDA needed a leader. I was set to be the chairman of the board, and Lemuel Tucker was going to be the president. We penciled in a date for our next meeting and were eager to see how this group would take shape.

A GOOD LEADER WILL ASK HIMSELF,

WHAT IS IN THE BEST INTEREST

OF MY TEAM MEMBERS?

There are always surprises along the way, and leaders have to adjust. For us, the surprise was a sad one. Lem got sick and he died. Now who was going to lead CCDA? I said, "I'm not going to be the leader. I want to be the organizer." (There is a difference between a leader and an organizer, and we will look at that later.) When we learned that Lemuel Tucker had died, the air went out the room. Wayne Gordon had stepped out of the meeting, and while he was gone I said, "Wayne's going to be the president." And that's how it was. Wayne Gordon became president of CCDA. And he was a good choice. Usually it is obvious who the leaders should be because people are already following him or her. That's how it was (and is) with Wayne.

Wayne Gordon is the most effective indigenous leadership developer that I know of in the world. He's simply the best. He founded Lawndale Community Church on the west side of Chicago and has developed an indigenous team of leaders there. It's not an accident that he is nicknamed "Coach." He takes the coaching style into his leadership and believes deeply in each person. A coach wants his team members to excel. A good leader will ask himself, *What is in the best interests of my team members?* When a person sees a leader with that attitude, he or she will want to follow.

The key is the phrase "best interests." Sometimes a person doesn't know what is best for him. A child rarely sees the best interests that her mother has for her. A son will balk all day long when a father doesn't want to hand over the keys to the family car on a Saturday night. A good leader must have clear vision that enables him to see past the emotion of the moment and through to the best interests. We all know stories of teenagers who hated their parents' "rules" or "decisions," but later in life thanked their parents because those rules and decisions had resulted in the person's best long-term interests.

SHANE: A leader should never be leading people to herself or himself. A good leader leads people to something bigger and beyond themselves. Moses and Dr. Martin Luther King, Jr. were leading people to a Promised Land, to that Beloved Community. Really, with CCDA and his whole life, that is what John Perkins has done. He has envisioned something beautiful and is leading people to it. It is a vision of a Church as diverse as the Kingdom.

I heard a pastor who put it well. He said that too often we become like the donkey that carried Jesus into Jerusalem. We have this cool little journey with God. We are chugging along doing the work. Then one day it happens. We start to hear folks singing praises and shouting acclamations. What began as God's work becomes our work. We come to think that our narrow little vision is about ourselves. Maybe like that donkey carrying Jesus into Passover, we start to think we are something spectacular. Hearing all the chants and seeing all of the people laying down palm branches, the donkey gets excited and starts strutting his stuff. Halfway down the street, the donkey realizes, *Hmm, it's not my name they are calling*, but he says thank-you nonetheless. The donkey takes the credit! How often is that us? But you know, we're just the asses who get to carry Jesus in. We must always remember that we are carrying something big, and it's not just ourselves. We're carrying something beautiful, bold and precious. Something eternal.

We have to temper ourselves when we realize we carry something that can literally and radically change the world. The temptation will come to be the greatest, most talked about, most honored. We will want all the buzz that comes with being the greatest this or that. We will want to be first in line, first on the bestsellers list, first as the fastest-growing, most effective nonprofit around. What did Jesus say about those who are first?[2] I like to think that His answer was "Grab a plunger and follow me to the toilets."

It's not a call to lead like the Gentiles and lord over people, but a call to be the least.

So that's the call—a call to be the least. And following the call means together we can all move closer to the suffering, no matter where we start and no matter how great the divide.

John: What if Jesus is taking us to the dump, but people do not want to go there? We need to ask ourselves that question. And I think that some teaching has to be done. We need to understand the virtue of suffering. Suffering, in the real sense, is the removing of instant gratification and replacing it with a promise for the future. Discipline is not giving people what they want right now—that will destroy them. Discipline is to delay that self-gratification in relationship to the future of life. As there is virtue in delaying, so there's virtue in suffering. This is a lost art in our society.

SHANE: It is important to distinguish between types of suffering. After all, there is redemptive suffering and then there is "stupid" suffering. When a woman is getting beat up by an abusive husband, that is stupid suffering. When kids are dying of malaria because they don't have $3 mosquito nets, that's stupid suffering. It is stupid not because the victim is dumb, but because it has no value. It is hurtful. Redemptive suffering is when we suffer with someone, when we *choose* to enter into the pain and suffering of others, when we bear their burdens with them.

Isaiah talks about the fasting we've chosen—a fasting for the release of the captives. He says that as we spend ourselves on behalf of others, *our* healing comes, and *our* light begins to shine.[3] We talked a little about that earlier, but it is important to remember when we consider suffering. We will not always suffer for ourselves. We will suffer for others, and some people will even give their lives for others. This is the greatest love of all.

We begin to heal as we pour ourselves out for others. It's what we are made for. Don't just take my word for it. Try it.

Sometimes folks say, "What about the poor in spirit? Rich folks need Jesus too." That's true, but too often we pretend that we can heal in the very environment that made us sick. Much of suburban life has been around cultural values that have very little to do with the gospel—folks have conformed to a cultural pattern of moving away from difficult neighborhoods, away from folks who don't look like them, away from areas of economic plight and high crime . . . and these patterns are the antithesis of the Incarnation, which is precisely about a God who moves into the neighborhood, a Savior who moves closer to suffering and comes from an area where people said nothing good could come. One of the remedies of the poverty of spirit, and the loneliness and isolation of suburbia, is to "go into the world," to bust through the walls and fences like in the story of the rich man and Lazarus, to get rid of the stuff and live closer to the poor. It is what Christ was inviting folks to do 2,000 years ago. And the invitation is the same today.

ONE OF THE REMEDIES OF THE
POVERTY OF SPIRIT, AND THE
LONELINESS OF SUBURBIA,
IS TO "GO INTO THE WORLD."

Now, that doesn't mean that everyone has to move into a row house with a half-a-dozen other people and one bathroom. In fact, we don't even live exactly like we did 10 years ago when we started The Simple Way. And John and I live very different lives. But there is a pattern in the gospel, and the pattern is that when we live in proximity to those who are suffering and spend our lives caring for the "least of these," not only does it give life to others, but it also gives life to those who choose this crazy gospel way of living.

I've become friends with a kid who has a fantastic story. He got on the game show "The Price Is Right" and ended up winning a car. Then he hit it huge on the big wheel and got into the "Showcase Showdown." Now you're not going to believe this, but in a rare stroke of brilliance, he bid perfectly and ended up winning absolutely everything in the "Showcase Showdown." So he ended up with two cars and all sorts of prizes totaling around $60,000. But then he read his Bible, and he prayed (sometimes a dangerous thing to do). He felt the Spirit move him to do something different, something crazy, something that would make God smile. So he cashed in all the winnings and flew to Uganda, and spent time in orphanages all over Uganda, secretly giving all the money away. And here's the incredible thing . . . when you talk to the kid, he is ALIVE. Like never before. It isn't even as if he did something heroic or noble. He just did something that made sense in light of the gospel. And, not only did it bring life to some kids dying of poverty in Uganda, but it also brought life to this kid who gave it all away. I mean, really, what would you rather have, two cars and a bunch of stuff from a game show that will eventually break or rust or get sold on eBay; or the precious memory of those faces and smiles, and the deep sense that you've done something of lasting significance for another human being? That's life.

John: I have a little story. There was a guy named Ralph Opgenorth who had just retired from one of the big computer companies. He lived in Colorado Springs. He had suffered a heart attack and was still recovering, but after Hurricane Katrina hit, he came down South. After Katrina, we helped in a lot of places. I sent this man to Biloxi to help coordinate aid. He was good at communicating with people, but he was an old man. In Biloxi, he burned himself out and returned to Colorado.

Long after we had finished the main push of our post-Katrina work, I called him on the telephone just to see how he was getting along. He told me how he had returned home and talked with the people at his church. They then organized a whole system at that church so that whenever a disaster strikes, he can go out and take a team with him. Now, he and his church are a beautiful example of what it means to be the hands and feet of Jesus. His story caused me to pause. Out of the tumult during Katrina, and the suffering of the people during the rush to help after the hurricane (it really was a mess) and his personal aching, something beautiful and very helpful had risen. He found a better way to respond than we had found. Sometimes people are following us even when we do not know it.

SHANE: That's an incredible story. And there are hundreds like it. I've got friends who are teaching kids to do sound design so that they can edit their own hip-hop. We've got friends that used to develop fancy condos and are now making affordable housing out of recycled cargo containers like the ones on freight trains—crazy, creative ideas. Some other friends of mine started a fair-trade T-shirt company where they rescue women out of the sex trafficking in Calcutta to make the shirts. Many of the folks in these examples used to run their own businesses just to make profits for themselves, but every single one of them says they have never looked back. They are more alive and full of joy than ever before. Deep down, all of us know the joy of giving, and that we were made to care for others. Even the drug dealers in my neighborhood, while they are still making some terrible choices, often surprise me by bringing one of the elderly women a rose on her birthday or buying all the kids ice cream. Those are the places where Jesus seems to point out the glaring contradictions, like when He said to the religious elite who were looking down on others: "The tax collectors and the prostitutes are entering the Kingdom ahead of you" (Matt. 21:32, *NIV*). We are made to love and to be loved.

I think of the landscaping architects that heard about the big fire we had a couple of years back and are volunteering to rebuild and green our neighborhood (and these are folks that do some serious corporate landscaping projects) . . . pouring all their energy into our block right here in Kensington (I'm sure it's their first project in Kensington, ha-ha). And they are so alive. It's contagious—they'll call friends who are fencers and tree people and fancy concrete folks. All they needed was to be asked.

Sometimes it is really true, we don't have because we never asked. Bob Lupton talks about how Jesus tells one of His disciples, "Go to this man's house. He's going to have a donkey. Tell him you need the donkey." The disciple goes down there and says, "The Lord's in need of this animal." So the stranger gives him his donkey. Bob said, "That's what I get to do now. I get to tell these business people, the Lord's in need of your gifts." The cool thing is that once people have that invitation, they begin to see all sorts of possibilities. I even have a friend who just brought his business into the neighborhood to create jobs here, even though he could be anywhere else. One congregation we are connected to in the Philly suburbs now has a Vocation and Imagination evening each month where folks share creative ways they are using their gifts and redefining their careers in light of God's kingdom and the needs around us.

John: When you get right down to it, something bigger might actually start with something smaller, and it might be right before your eyes.

Notes

1. See Luke 7 for the entire story.
2. See Matthew 19:30; 20:16.
3. See Isaiah 58:6-8.

JUSTICE

(Considering the Will of God)

John: As we seek to lead people to something bigger than ourselves, even larger than our communities, we often talk about justice. It has become quite popular to speak of justice as it relates to almost everything these days, which is good and not so good. It is good because we have the opportunity for an entire generation to understand and carry forth the message of justice, which is interwoven with the message of reconciliation. It is not so good because justice becomes a trend, and trends do not tend to remain at the forefront of the Church's focus.

Just as people in the culture at large dart from the hot button of the day to another hot button the next day, so we do the same. Those of us who have a heart for justice issues need to take advantage of the opportunity to grasp this trend. We could resort to shocking people with facts about poverty, racism and all sorts of ills, and we would get lots of checks in the mail. But I think God wants, even demands, more from us. If there is even a prayer of justice becoming central in the church's consciousness and heart, then we must have a full understanding of the justice will of God.

The justice will of God is indeed the heart of the gospel, and it is revealed throughout the Scriptures. It's clear that God's own holiness, righteousness and justice were the motivation for man's redemption. God created you and me for His own glory and honor, so that we could bring Him joy, happiness and fulfillment. He wanted a family. But in the Garden of Eden we sinned through Adam. Now God had a major problem: How could a holy God have this fellowship with you and me? How could He stay just and yet justify you and me? This quest is what brought God down from heaven to redeem us! So God had to work out a just plan of redemption.

And so justice was always on the heart of God. His righteous justice is revealed through His coming Himself to endure the death we ought to have died. *He that knew no sin was made sin for us that we might be made the righteousness of God in Him so that He could bring us back to Himself.* The Bible says that God was in Christ, *reconciling the world unto Himself.* And so justice is at the heart of God's concern for us.

In Romans 1:13-17 we see the apostle Paul's heart to serve God, and to bring this same concern that Christ had for justice to a perishing world. These passages also speak forth my own heart for all who would endeavor to join us in the work of saving our communities:

> Now I do not want you to be unaware, brethren, that I often planned to come to you (but was hindered until now), that I might have some fruit among you also, just as among the other Gentiles. I am a debtor both to Greeks and to barbarians, both to wise and to unwise. So, as much as is in me, I am ready to preach the gospel to you who are at Rome also. For I am not ashamed of the gospel of Christ, for it is the power of God to salvation for everyone who believes, for the Jew first and also for the Greek. For in it the righteousness of God is revealed from faith to faith; as it is written, "The just shall live by faith."

It is not news that many of the societal problems we experience in our urban communities—the gangs, the violence and the drugs—are now moving to our suburbs. The jails are too full and the killings too numerous to ignore. There must be a challenge put forth for us all to do some things we haven't done before to reach people, particularly our young people. None of us knows how to address this perfectly, but I believe Paul shows us an example of the heart condition that must precede any great work for God. While God's motivation is His justice, Paul's motivation is gratitude for the grace God gave to him on the Damascus Road.

Paul says simply, in verse 14, "I'm in debt." He is not talking about paying back a debt to God for saving him. You can't do that. You're not saved by your own works. "For by grace you have been saved through faith, and that not of yourselves; it is the gift of God, not of works, lest anyone should boast" (Eph. 2:8-9). So he's not talking about paying a debt for his salvation. He is talking about a debt of gratitude. The apostle Paul's motivation for carrying the gospel to the world is his gratitude to God for coming into his life, forgiving him for his sin and then calling him, sending him and making him an apostle to the world. Let's take a look at Saul, this young madman, before Jesus met him on the road to Damascus and renamed him Paul.

> THERE MUST BE A CHALLENGE
> PUT FORTH FOR US ALL TO DO
> SOME THINGS WE HAVEN'T DONE
> BEFORE TO REACH PEOPLE.

Saul was really the original Osama Bin Laden, or as we might say in the urban community, an O.G.—Original Gangster. His goal was to erase all Gentile influence, to basically snuff out Christianity. He wanted to lock them all in jail, and kill them all, too, if possible. That's why he stoned Stephen, a Gentile who had been a proselytized Jew. Saul heard Stephen preach, and he preached so well that it inflamed this former bigot to his core. When he caught hold of Stephen, he ordered him stoned to death. What you have here is Saul, who is not only a murderer one time, but he is a murderer many times. He says, "I persecuted this Way to the death, binding and delivering into prisons both men and women" (Acts 22:4). The *Contemporary English Version* states it this way: "I made trouble for everyone who followed the Lord's Way, and I even had some of them killed. I had others arrested and put in jail. I didn't care if they were men or women."

"And when the blood of Your martyr Stephen was shed, I also was standing by consenting to his death, and guarding the clothes of those who were killing him" (Acts 22:20). He's showing the absolute awfulness of himself . . . but that God's grace has no limits.

So here we have this madman, this multi-murderer (who called himself the greatest of sinners) on his way to Damascus in search of all those Christians who had fled and started a fellowship there. He's going there, and he's not afraid to bust right into the synagogues. If he finds any Christians inside, he's going to tie them up, bring them back to Jerusalem and stone them, making them an "example," as he thought he had done with Stephen. His ultimate goal was to remove all influence of the Gentiles within Judaism, because after all, he was *a Pharisee of Pharisees*.

So this madman got almost to Damascus; in fact, he could see the city in the distance, and I know he was anxious to get there to kill some more. But God came down from heaven and struck him to the ground. Lying there in the dirt, Saul heard a voice. I believe this voice could have sounded something like this: "Saul, Saul, I love you. I love you." Now you know, that's the gospel message. Love is what the gospel is all about. *For God so loved the world . . .* The cross is an illustration of the extreme that God went to in that great love. God had one begotten Son, and He gave the life of that one Son for you and me. *Greater love has no one than this, the one that laid down His life for His friends.* "Saul, Saul, I love you. Why don't you love Me?" "Who are You, Lord?" "I'm Jesus. I'm Jesus, whom you are persecuting." (Later, Paul tries to explain this experience to the Galatians.)[1]

Of that road to Damascus, Paul says, "God apprehended me. He reached down from heaven with His long arms and He put His arms around me and He squeezed me in His arms. He loved me. He laid hold of me. And the rest of my life I want to lay hold of Him, and squeeze Him back the way He squeezed me on that Damascus road. Christ has shown me that what I once thought was valuable was actually worthless. Nothing is as wonderful as knowing Christ Jesus, my Lord" (Phil. 3:12-14).

Note this: The first thing he cried out in response was, "Lord, what would You have me to do?" And God outlined to him, as he lay on that road, where He wanted him to go. He sent him directly to the people he was killing—those same folks that he was trying to eradicate! And then He gave him a vision for what that world looked like out there—and it wasn't so nice. Paul describes the Gentiles (that's you and me, too, so change "they" and "their" to "we" and "our" as you read) by saying that when they knew God, they glorified Him not as God. He goes on to say that neither were they thankful, but they became vain in their imagination, their foolish heart was darkened. They professed to be wise. They became fools and they changed the glory of the incorruptible God into corruptible beings.

Romans 1:26-27 describes the rest of the corruption Paul would encounter on his assignment, seeing how they *lost their sexual drive for women and went men for men and women for women* and, basically, this world was (is) all messed up. God said, "Yes, I'm sending you to that world. I'm sending you to turn them from darkness to light, and from the power of Satan to the power of God." What a job! Would you take it?

What is more, Paul said, "I also count all things loss for the excellence of the knowledge of Christ Jesus my Lord, for whom I have suffered the loss of all things, and count them as rubbish, that I may gain Christ and be found in Him, not having my own righteousness, which is from the law, but that which is through faith in Christ, the righteousness which is from God by faith; that I may know Him and the power of His resurrection, and the fellowship of His sufferings, being conformed to His death, if, by any means, I may attain to the resurrection from the dead" (Phil. 3:8-11).

JESUS EMBRACES US IN THE PRESENT AND WILL GUIDE US IN THE FUTURE— THROUGH OUR OBEDIENCE.

When the apostle Paul recognized God's love and how extreme that love really was, that God would not only go to His own death on the cross but would also reach down and pick up somebody like him and save him, he realized his debt. I like to say that salvation means that you are "sho nuff" saved. You've been saved from your past, forgiven from murder, or whatever you've done. Paul was forgiven for all that. Jesus embraces us in the present and will guide us in the future— through our obedience. The will to obey is also a grace act. The redemptive grace of God is released in our obedience. He gives us the will to obey. There is a supernaturalness in serving God. There is a miracle-working power in God's redemptive act. The forgiveness of sin is the miracle of miracles.

Paul talks about his gratitude. We just don't have that now. We don't have a Christianity today that is equal to Paul's faith. It is easy to get our convenience ahead of obedience. We put our little needs, our little provisions in first place. It's not a sacrifice; it's a *perceived* sacrifice. We perceive that when we are going to make a sacrifice, it is too much of a "give up." It's actually at that point of the give up that you actually receive more than what you gave up. My provision comes out of my obedience. God hears our cries and knows our need. If our plans don't have obedience to God's will at the core of them, they will always be empty.

That's why fasting is so important. It's an exercise of delaying gratification. One of our most self-gratifying actions is to eat food, and that's why we give that up. There is no doubt that Paul is asking the Church to imitate him. That's why he says all of what he does in Philippians. "I'm not perfect. Christ apprehended me. I keep struggling. But I keep running toward the prize." Paul calls us to lay hold of Christ as Christ has laid hold of us.

SHANE: I like to say, "If we believe that terrorists are beyond redemption, then we should rip out half of the New Testament . . . as it is written by one."

John: That's good. So then salvation means that we have a future. Jesus said, "I go to prepare a place for you. And if I go and prepare a place for you, I will come again and receive you to Myself" (John 14:2-3). You are not working for this, you are not setting up timbers, trying to build your own place—you can't get timbers up there anyway! He doesn't need them. He has provided that for us as a part of redemption, and we are going there. We *are* going there.

One of my main concerns is that we as Christians today don't understand what God has done for us the way the apostle Paul did. We don't understand the salvation plan He's worked out. We don't understand the extremity of God's love for us. Paul tries to explain that by asking the question, "Who can separate us from the love of Christ? Life or death, angels or principalities, things present or yet to come, height or depth?"[2] No! Nothing! God has worked out for us a salvation, and He's going to take us to heaven. I challenge us to question whether or not we have really accepted our salvation. Really. We need to examine whether or not we have truly given our lives to God. Because I feel that if we understood that, we would feel a sense of debt. And that sense of debt would propel us into sharing that love and move us to bring about that same justice for our neighbor.

I began to see and understand the oppression and effects of slavery, the same tension and pain that Moses and his people suffered. I saw how it was not only taking an emotional toll, but it was also a physical toll on my people—particularly poor Southern blacks. We now have diabetes, high blood pressure and heart disease; and unless we could get freedom—in knowing Jesus Christ and His healing power—and get access to health care—both physical and psychological—we would not be truly free. When I became a Christian, I began to understand that we become new beings but we need freedom and we need healing—we need an ongoing redemption.

For much of my early life, I was a part of the civil rights movement in the 1960s and 1970s. As I pondered the problems of oppression, discrimination and poverty, I began to see that justice is really a stewardship issue. It has to do with how we manage the earth God gave to Adam—and to us—to subdue. It is also an educational issue. We need to acquire the skills, the wherewithal, to use those gifts God has given us to manage the earth in a way that enhances lives and brings about justice. Ultimately, justice is an economic issue, because that is how we implement what we have learned in order to be good stewards of this planet, which includes every human being.

Since we are assigned to care for and be blessed by earth, injustice is to deprive any other person from open access to this creation; to disallow them from reaching their full potential in life; to subjugate, deprive or exploit them. That's injustice.

Why would anyone want slaves? Why would anyone want to work people for less than minimum wage? People who approach business that way want to increase their individual profit at someone else's expense. That is not God's way. That is anti-God. And so justice is fundamentally a stewardship issue. How do I use my gifts and skills to make sure that someone else has a better chance? That's justice. And so we work toward it.

I discovered this truth early on and ended up helping to start the Cooperative Movement in Mississippi. That was an economic development movement with poor people, and I will tell you more about that later. As a part of the economic movement, I traveled to Israel and studied the thriving economic systems there, specifically their Cooperative Movement and the kibbutz system. I took notes on how they ran it all. My goal was to come back to the South and, with the help of others, stimulate economic development projects. We started a development bank, based in Louisiana, and I stayed on that board for a long while. I remember that we began with $200,000 in our little bank. That was a lot of money! When I left the bank 10 years later, we had around $30 million in deposits.

> GOD CREATED US SO THAT WE
> MIGHT BE HIS WORKMANSHIP. WE ARE
> HERE TO SERVE HIM, NOT TO
> USE HIM TO SERVE US.

When my family and I were ready to move to California in 1982, it was hard for me to give up being on the board of that bank. The idea was to loan the farmers money, and they would pay back an additional 5 percent to earn a stake in the bank. Those investors—the farmers that owned the shares—would be the owners of the bank. That was a true cooperative. That's investing in people. That's stewardship. If we are to ever find any measure of freedom today, then our leaders must be faithful stewards of the blessing being passed along for our care.

Right now, too many of the people I meet are getting God to be the therapist for their addiction. They are getting God to help them take care of a headache. I don't use God to take care of my headache. I use Tylenol—that's a good medicine! I want God to do those things in my life that I can't do. We're so busy serving God for what we can get. But why? Don't we know our redemption is complete? God has paid it all, all to Him I owe! We serve God in gratitude for what He has done for us. We should feel a sense of debt, a deep sense of gratitude. We should be able to say: "It was good when they said, 'Let us go into the house of the Lord.'" Let us go worship Him. Let's go pay our vows to Him. It ought to be our joy to serve God.

I don't understand begging Christians to do God's work. I don't understand it at all. It's a contradiction. He created us and saved us so that we might be His workmanship. We are here to serve Him, not to use Him to serve us.

Do you feel a sense of debt as a Christian? Do you feel a sense of gratitude? Let me share a little of my life regarding these two points. I am here out of a sense of gratitude. I'm an old—79-year-old—man, but 50 years ago, my life of faith in Christ began.

It was in Monrovia, California, that my little son got involved in Good News Clubs. There the women would gather up the children in the community and tell them Bible stories. He went there and fell in love with Jesus. Then he came home and began to tell *us* about Jesus. As I said, I didn't care much about Jesus. And I particularly didn't care much about the church. I had been in Mississippi, and I saw those big white churches. They would have signs up saying, "Revival tonight! Everybody welcome!" Well, if I, a black man, had gone in there, a riot would have broken out. "Everybody" didn't mean everybody. I saw that as hypocrisy. Then I would go to the black church and see them fall all out on the floor and use up all of their energy, but they weren't doing anything in the community. And so I didn't care much about religion until I found myself confronted by the Word of God.

My son began to come home with these little books to read. You know, he was too little to read. But they knew what they were doing. They were giving him books for *me* to read. And I began to do that, and I started to see that it was pretty good stuff. The stories we were reading together painted a different picture of Jesus and Christianity than I had seen before. At the same time my son was bringing all these stories about Jesus home, I started going to a Sunday School class in Pasadena.

I went out and bought a Bible—the first time in my life. I remember I found one at the old McMahan's furniture store (anyone who grew up in California in that day will remember McMahan's! Sadly, after 89 years, they closed their last retail operations in 2008). When I went there, they had a sale on Bibles. I bought one, and I began to read it. What impressed me most was the life of this apostle named

Paul. He was going everywhere, telling everyone about Jesus. He's being stoned (not high on pot, but literally having rocks thrown at him!). He's suffering for his faith. I thought religion was something you suffer *with*, not *for*, but here's the guy suffering *for* religion.

I noticed that this Paul was so energetic. I kept reading to try to find out what made him tick. I visited the church for about six months and asked these religious people my questions. (Everybody in that church probably thought that surely by then I was a Christian, because in America we have an easy Christianity, you know.) And though I was sitting in the pew on Sunday mornings, I didn't understand how God, Jesus, the Holy Spirit and His Word all fit together, let alone what I was supposed to do about it. I'm just enjoying this history, enjoying this apostle Paul. And I'm trying to find out what makes this guy do all he's doing. And then we came to Galatians 2:20. This is Paul explaining exactly why he is behaving the way he's behaving. The verse goes something like this: "I have been crucified with Christ; it is no longer I who live, but Christ lives in me; and the life which I now live in the flesh I live by faith in the Son of God, who loved me."

Now, I grew up without a mother. She died when I was seven months old. My father dropped us off at his mother's house, so I also grew up without a father. I had none of the institutional family love that we are now learning is so instrumental to a healthy life, and the lack of it is much of the cause of the great crisis we have in America today . . . the broken family. The kids don't have that institution of love. *Love.* This is the reason God wants us to get together with one wife and stay with her until death do us part. Not because God doesn't like for us to have sex. But God wants us to have sex responsibly, with one woman, and to take care of those children so we can raise them in love. The problem we have now is that we don't have the fathers in the home to love those children they father.

But even fatherless, I saw that *He* loved me. And I began to reckon with that concept. If there is a God in heaven who loved me enough to send His only Son into the world to die for me, and to bring a salvation that frees me from my past sin; if He was willing to provide His blood so I could wash away my sin daily, and then offer me an eternal home in heaven, I wanted to love this God! I want to love this God *in gratitude for what He has done for me.* And so I gave my life to this Christ

the best way I knew how. It wasn't the most informed decision because I definitely didn't have it all figured out. I just wanted to love
Him. Romans 10:11-13 tells us this: "For the Scripture says, 'Whoever
believes on Him will not be put to shame.' For there is no distinction
between Jew and Greek, for the same Lord over all is rich to all who call
upon Him. For 'whoever calls on the name of the LORD shall be saved.'"
I remember that I was so excited about it. I began to share this with
others. But I heard people say, "You're on fire, but you're going to cool
off." I didn't want to cool off! Cooling off to me would mean I would
stop loving God. I didn't want that.

A LOT OF PEOPLE HAVE ASKED JESUS
INTO THEIR HEARTS, BUT THEY ARE
NOT LIVING WITH ANY GRATITUDE.

Fifty-eight years ago, I fell in love with a woman, and I'm still in
love with her. I still got her. I don't want to fall out of love with her.
I want to stay in love with her! And so I wanted to stay in love with Him
too. But they always kept telling me, "You're gonna cool off . . . you're
not gonna always behave like that." But you see, I was behaving "like
that" out of gratitude.

And so I went to my old man, a Presbyterian elder, and he discipled me. I told him my struggles. One of the problems we have in the
church today is that we have over-evangelized the world too lightly.
We've gotten a lot of people to have supposedly asked Jesus into their
hearts, but they are not living with any gratitude. They've got Jesus
working for them instead of them doing His work in the world. We've
got to start discipling people. Jesus has no hands but my hands and
your hands. Jesus has no eyes but our eyes. We are His workmanship:
"As He was, so are we in the world." We're His body. We're all that
God has to reach out to the homeless and the poor in our society.

I like the 12-step program of Alcoholics Anonymous. But I'm seeing the American church becoming an AA center where people are
never healed from their problems. They are always taking care of their

own addiction or ailment but don't make time for other people. As a result, they haven't been healed. They need their sins forgiven. They need to get rid of their addiction and come off of that mentality that they can never be healed! It's a good place to start, but you cannot stay there. Jesus came to make us whole. He came to mobilize us so that we could rescue the perishing and care for the dying.

And so I wanted to love God back. And I said to my old discipler, "How can I love God back?" I remember it like it was yesterday—he told me to open my Bible to Matthew 25:31-46, and I read it. "For I was hungry and you gave Me food; I was thirsty and you gave Me drink; I was a stranger and you took Me in; I was naked and you clothed Me; I was sick and you visited Me; I was in prison and you came to Me . . . inasmuch as you did it to one of the least of these My brethren, you did to Me" (vv. 35-36,40).

How do you love God back? Through gratitude. Like Paul said, "I too am in debt. I have a debt of love. I have a debt of gratitude." That attitude was what provided his motivation to serve. That's why he said: "I'm in debt, both to the Jew and to the Gentile. Both to the wise and to the unwise, as much as lies in me, I'm ready to pay."

Are we ready to pay? One thing with me, I've found it easy to let people be in my debt, but the hardest thing is to get them to pay their debt! Paul said, "I'm ready." Then he added, "For I'm not ashamed of the gospel."[3] I don't think we understand the power of the gospel. The gospel is God's love. And love is the greatest power on earth. That's why we've got to live it out. Jesus says, "By this all men will know that you are My disciples, if you have love for one another" (John 13:35). Love must be displayed. I'm not ashamed of it, for it is the power of God.

The gospel, when we live in obedience to God, releases all of those virtues that God works in us. It's in the gospel that we see the righteousness, the justice of God. Jesus Christ died on that cross and paid for our sins. God was in Christ, reconciling the world unto Himself. He that knew no sin was made "to be sin for us, that we might become the righteousness of God in Him" (2 Cor. 5:21). And so the righteous justice of God is revealed, and we, then, as God's people, live out that justice in society. Let justice roll down like water and righteousness as a mighty stream. Justice and righteousness are one and the same! And righteousness is you and me out there in society.

Righteousness is the Good Samaritan. Righteousness is seeing people wounded and in a ditch, helpless, almost dead. Justice and righteousness is you and me going out there, embracing them like we were embraced. I can see that Good Samaritan. He reached down in order to give some water to this guy. He had to embrace him, pull him up, show him love, and then put him on *his own* donkey and take care of him. He didn't wait until he could organize a 501c3—he used his own resources! And then he carried him into town and invested in the life of this man. There was a commitment to him being well—a commitment to his future. He was ready to go in debt for this guy's future. He did not just put him in therapy. He wanted him well. And so he said: "Until he gets well, here is some more money. And if you need any more, just put it on my account. I'll take care of him." This man was paying his debt of gratitude and love.[4]

I, as a member of the urban community and a member of the Christian Community Development Association, beg you, suburbanites and *all* Christians, to join with me as we tackle some of the severe problems of the urban community. (We don't want to be too confrontational, but we want to inspire all people—especially Christians who aren't involved—to have the fire of gratitude lit under them.)

The things we associated with the poor are now coming to the suburbs. The suburbs have become the "urburbs." We must address it. But we cannot do what I've outlined in our own strength. We also cannot wait for tomorrow. Now is the day you hear His voice; harden not your hearts. Resolve today that you are going to embrace the justice will of God; *become* someone He can use to transform your street, your neighborhood, your place of work, your school and, yes, your church.

Notes
1. See Galatians 1:11-24.
2. See Romans 12:35-39.
3. See Romans 1:15-16.
4. See Luke 10:25-37.

SIN, WOUNDS AND FORGIVENESS

(Breaking Through the Real Problem to the Real Answer)

SHANE: As John was talking about justice, I kept thinking about how we've lost touch with people and their pain. Jesus never did that— He never lost touch with people and always had His feet on the ground. God so loved the world that He didn't set up a committee or an organization; He sent His Son. And that personal experience is what is so consistent all through the Incarnation. Jesus hung out in a town where they said nothing good could come.[1] You know, He died on a cross. He went into the world with no place to lay His head. He suffered with people. That is the model I think we've got so much to learn from.

I'm sure there was much temptation to organize on a movement, an institution, like "Throw Herod Out." There are so many ways God could have done His ministry. There's a great example for us in the first chapter of Mark that people were coming to Jesus for miracles. Jesus was off by Himself, praying. And Peter goes to Him and says, "Oh, there's all these people, and they're waiting at the house." And Jesus says, "Well, then it's time to move on." Basically, He says, "We've got to go out of this place." He resisted the idea of just setting up a distribution center. His plan was to spread a much broader movement among people, but He was always getting interrupted.

Another idea that comes to mind is that there's something deep in the ideas "judge not lest you be judged" and "inasmuch as you forgive, you will be forgiven." When we talk about judgment, sometimes our minds immediately jump to the final Judgment; but I think Jesus is offering us some really helpful advice for our lives as Christians and as leaders. We can really see that both finger-pointing and forgiveness are equally contagious. When we forgive others, they are more likely to forgive us. And the same is true with judgment. Think about it. If I go around telling everybody it's wrong to smoke and then I'm seen smoking, folks are not going to go easy on me.

I'm thinking of some of the religious leaders that have made mistakes. Often, what is so tragic and surprising is not that they made a mistake but that they have been quick to point out others' sins and appear beyond sin themselves. I think of Ted Haggard, the former head of the National Association of Evangelicals, when it was revealed that he had been with a male prostitute. What was so troubling and confusing to folks was that he had been very vocal against gay and lesbian rights and spoken so sharply about homosexuality as a sin. It's no wonder folks were hard on him.

JESUS DID NOT COME TO SAVE THE
RIGHTEOUS, BUT THE BROKEN; HE DID
NOT COME FOR THE HEALTHY,
BUT FOR THE SICK.

But there were also beautiful voices of grace in the midst of that crisis, just as there were with Bill Clinton. My friend Tony Campolo was a constant whisper of grace to both of them. Now, that is good leadership—not jumping ship when someone in power falters or falls, but walking with him or her through the darkness (even as others pounce on that person like wounded prey). Tony said in a television interview during the Haggard incident, "When one part suffers, all of us suffer." I remember hearing Tony, who had many differences with Haggard, speaking with such gentleness and grace about his hopes that this would be an opportunity for evangelicals to step down from the high horse of moral superiority and identify with the brokenness of others, even the gay community. And he said that in this scandal, neither the gay community nor the evangelical community was being seen very well. And maybe it was a chance for us to hear God whisper, "All of us are better than the worst things we do."

Jesus did not come to save the righteous, but the broken; He did not come for the healthy, but for the sick. That is the sort of grace that Christian leaders should be known for, not the judgmentalism that has come to characterize Christians in the minds of many onlookers.

John: Sin is the fulfillment of our own selfish desires, separating us from God and from our brothers and sisters. It's difficult to communicate truth when we're separated from God. The only way to deal with sin is to feel the conviction of the depths of your sin against God and your fellow man.

In the movie *Amazing Grace*, the powerful, true story of William Wilberforce's lifelong struggle to abolish slavery, we see John Newton living in service to God through the motivation of the grace given to him despite his wretchedness. He had a humble understanding that he was the devil's workman during his slave-trading days, and now he was motivated to be God's workman through gratitude for God's grace: "Amazing grace! How sweet the sound, that saved a wretch like me! I once was lost, but now am found, was blind, but now I see." He lived out the rest of his life humbly in the midst God's grace. We are to walk in that same humility.

When I came to know God, and was drawn to Him, I felt my sin becoming more sinful. Since the time I became a Christian, I have sinned against someone without repenting—and that haunts me. If I don't repent and become clean, my sin stays with me. Sin is a cover-up. That's why God wants us to confess our sin as soon as we're aware of it. That's hard to do today, because people never talk about anything openly. The biblical principle to follow if our brother sins against us is to tell somebody and go to that brother collectively. But we have erased the consciousness of sin. We don't really believe that God sees us or that we are in His constant presence. Because of that unbelief, we cover up our sin, and that blinds us to further sin.

When sin is forgiven, all of God's redemptive grace is unleashed. We get to be a part of that. Jesus came to earth to die once for all. There is an eternal fountain of cleansing in His shed blood on the cross, and we are to come to that fountain. This is the essence of the gospel.

To miss God's forgiving grace as it relates to sin is to miss the redemptive purpose of the Incarnation. Every other grace is a contributing
grace to the act of Jesus dying on the cross. To miss that is to miss the
Christian faith. The preacher that minimizes or ignores sin doesn't understand the big truth of the gospel that we can have our sins forgiven—daily and eternally.

The burden of the leader is to live with a consciousness of his or her
sinfulness. When a leader stumbles, he needs to confess it to God and
to someone in his fellowship. The consciousness of the grace of God is
key. The Father loved us so much that He sent His only Son to die for
our sin. If not for the Holy Spirit and my studying the Word of God,
I would be like everyone else—broken and fallen. My sin is tragic in re-
lation to the redemptive work of God. If we aren't conscious of our
sin, we spit on the work of God. But 1 John 1:9 says, "If we confess our
sins, He is faithful and just to forgive us our sins and to cleanse us from
all unrighteousness." Many Christians today haven't grasped the power
of that thought.

When sin becomes a bigger factor in our own conscience, it's not
necessarily a bad thing. The dangerous pitfall is when you become
desensitized to your own sin. If you can't recognize it, you can't confess it.

Confessing to your brother is almost as important as confessing to
God, because it relates to your life here on earth. Without that confession, your life becomes shallow and you begin to live it too lightly.
Instead of becoming Christians—Christ-followers—we become play-
actors—hypocrites. A part of conversion is discovering your true self.
Like it or not, sin is a part of our lives, and we have to recognize that,
but also recognize that God has a purpose for our lives and wants to
redeem us.

The holiness movement ties it together. Whenever there is a renewal or revival, the people and the evangelist agree that our lives
should be lived in honesty and confession; and when we sin, we have
an advocate with the Father in Christ Jesus. Foot washing is symbolic
of the Christian life. You go out into the world and you get dirty with
sin, and you need to get cleansed. Peter said to Jesus, "I won't let you
wash my feet." Jesus told Peter that He had to wash his feet, and so
Peter asks Him to wash his whole body. Jesus says that He only needs

to wash Peter's feet. Our bodies are clean, but because we walk in this world, we must constantly confess—get our feet washed. This is good for us! Why have we made this Christian walk so horrible—thinking that if we obey God we will be so miserable? Confessing our sins is so necessary for an effective life.

CONFESSING TO YOUR BROTHER IS ALMOST AS IMPORTANT AS CONFESSING TO GOD, BECAUSE IT RELATES TO YOUR LIFE HERE ON EARTH.

Pastors sometimes hide out in their office—much like the monks hid in the monastery. A leader has to carry with him an exemplary life. When Paul says it's not only necessary that we follow Christ, but that we suffer—suffering is a given. Even if it's nothing but the suffering to *avoid* temptation. Being tempted to sin can be just as heavy as yielding to sin. Billy Graham never got in an elevator alone with a woman, and he always had a third party in his office when a woman was with him—he didn't even want the appearance of sin, let alone the temptation of sin and, in that case, sexual sin.

We put sexual sin in a big light—and it is big. Because it has the potential for life, it is dangerous to be reckless with sexual sin. God is concerned about the holiness of life. If we recognized that, then maybe we would be more responsible. We put our own desires over that. That's why prostitution will never go away—it's one of the biggest instant-gratification temptations in life. And again, that is why we sin when we give in to our own selfish desires.

SHANE: Leaders know how to nudge folks without pushing them. We have to learn how to encourage others to take baby steps, and any step we take toward Jesus is something we should celebrate. For some folks, the first step toward faithful discipleship is bringing a homeless person to their house for dinner with the family. For another person, the first step is just pausing to talk with a homeless person for the first time. What's radical for one is old news for another, but I think Jesus loves every step we take, perhaps even gets the most excited when someone way off takes his or her first step—sort of like when He talks about leaving all the sheep to find the lost one. So leaders know how to walk alongside folks as they take those steps toward Jesus and toward loving others. Maybe walking alongside means encouraging someone to smoke a few less cigarettes. Maybe it means not Googling their name as many times or wasting as much time on the Internet. Maybe it means writing some letters to folks in prison or spending more time with their kids. Baby steps.

I remember seeing a sign that read: "Dear God, please protect me from myself." Leadership is about protecting folks from themselves before they destroy themselves. That is what sin does . . . it destroys us. God hates sin, not just because we are disobedient to the law, but because sin destroys us, and God can't stand to watch us destroy ourselves.

Much of the discipline in Scripture seems to be God smacking our hand to keep us from burning it on the stove. It is not the sort of vengeance of a malicious Master; it is the liberating hand of a loving Father.

Note
1. See John 1:46.

CIVIL DISOBEDIENCE

(Taking a Stand)

*You will be handed over to the local councils and flogged in the
synagogues. On account of me you will stand before governors and
kings as witnesses to them. And the gospel must first be preached to
all nations. Whenever you are arrested and brought to trial, do not
worry beforehand about what to say. Just say whatever is given you
at the time, for it is not you speaking, but the Holy Spirit.*
MARK 13:9-11, *NIV*

SHANE: Let's talk about this whole idea of civil disobedience (or as we
like to say, "holy mischief"). Others might call it "upholding the law of
God over the law of man." Some would argue that a leader who gets
his followers arrested is not a good leader. John and I would beg to
differ. Ha-ha. In fact, John and I have gone to jail together . . . more
on that later.

I reckon we could start with Jesus, many of whose followers landed
themselves in jail. John the Baptist, Jeremiah and lots of the prophets
were arrested or even killed. Shadrach, Meshach and Abednego were
thrown into that fiery furnace for refusing a royal order that violated
their commitment to God. Daniel ignored the king's law prohibiting
prayer, and Darius flung him into the den of lions . . . and on and on.
Moses' very birth was an act of civil disobedience when his mother
floated him down a river to escape Pharaoh's slaughter of the innocents.
Jesus, too, was born on the move in the middle of Herod's genocide,
and the magi directly defied Herod's orders in order to protect Jesus.

The book of Acts and the accounts of the Early Church are rid-
dled with jail time, beatings and even state-sanctioned executions of
folks such as John the Baptist. Paul and Silas have a great story of the
Spirit busting them out of that old jail. Paul's letter to Philemon was
written to urge a former slave owner to illegally welcome back a fugi-
tive slave (Onesimus)—a crime punishable by death—not as a slave
but as a brother.

Early Christians tell stories about how they gave witness to the
jailors and officers and soldiers, and many of them came to faith. One
account tells of how James shared God's grace with his executioner
and the man became a Christian and ended up getting killed next to
James. And, of course, the martyrs were known precisely for their faithfulness to God over Caesar. One of the early Christians said that every
time a Christian proclaimed "Jesus is Lord," they were saying "Caesar
is not." The early Christians were known to be rebels and revolutionaries, albeit in a very different kind of revolution—a revolution that was
as much for the freedom of the oppressors as for the freedom of the
oppressed, a nonviolent revolution marked by enemy-love, gentleness
and audacious grace. But it was a revolution nonetheless. "These men
who have caused trouble all over the world have now come here. . . .
They are all defying Caesar's decrees, saying that there is another king,
one called Jesus" (Acts 17:6-7, *NIV*).

Wow, I got to preaching there! Let me slow down. Chris Haw and
I spend a whole lot of time around these themes in our Jesus for Pres-
ident project, but here are a few quotes from folks in the early days of
Christianity . . .

We are charged with being irreligious people and, what is
more, irreligious in respect to the emperors since we refuse to
pay religious homage to their imperial majesties. . . . High treason is a crime of offense against the Roman religion. It is a crime
of open irreligion, a raising of the hand to injure the deity . . . .
Christians are considered to be enemies of the State . . . we do
not celebrate the festivals of the Caesars. Guards and inform-
ers bring up accusations against the Christians . . . blasphe-
mers and traitors . . . we are charged with sacrilege and high
treason . . . we give testimony to the truth. —Tertullian

The Christians form among themselves secret societies that exist outside the system of laws . . . an obscure and mysterious community founded on revolt and the advantage that accrues from it. —Letter to Origen

They form a rabble of profane conspiracy. . . . They despise titles of honor and the purple robe of high government office though hardly able themselves to cover their own nakedness. Just like a rank growth of weeds, the abominable haunts where this impious confederacy meet are multiplying all over the world. Root and branch, it should at all costs be exterminated and accursed. They love one another before being acquainted. They practice a cult of lust, calling one another brother and sister indiscriminately, under the cover of these hallowed names fornication becomes incest. —Minucius Felix

Indeed, as we look at Church history it is hard to miss the collision between the kingdom of God and the kingdom of this world. Jesus promises the disciples that the world will hate them, that they will be dragged before courts and magistrates. It is a promise that if they live real good, they will get beat up real bad. But what is important is that they are to return love for evil. They are to stare into the face of those who persecute them and say, "Father, forgive them, for they do not know what they are doing" (Luke 23:34).

Civil disobedience has had an important place in the black Church in the U.S., and in struggles for freedom throughout the world. Many Christians in the 1960s participated in sit-ins at lunch counters, wade-ins at swimming pools, and refused to honor laws that forbade them to enter certain restaurants or to sit in the front seats of public buses in challenge of laws that promoted segregation.

First-century Christians were branded as lawbreakers for refusing to bow to the Roman emperor or his image. Martin Luther broke ecclesiastical laws of the Catholic church over freedom of religion. American abolitionists broke laws in order to bring about racial equality. Martin Luther King, Jr., broke laws intended to enforce racial division. The American revolutionaries broke laws imposed by King George that oppressed the colonies. During the tyranny of Nazi Germany, Corrie ten

Boom's family disobeyed German law by hiding and protecting Jews. And Dietrich Bonhoeffer and Martin Niemoller stood against German laws instituted by Hitler's Nazi regime. The Anabaptists, Quakers, Mennonites and Brethren communities refused to adhere to laws pertaining to engaging in war. Christians smuggled Bibles into the Soviet Union and other Soviet Bloc nations against laws that prohibited importing Bibles. The list of Christian civil disobedience is endless . . . and keeps getting new additions as time passes.

DISINHERITED PEOPLE ALL OVER THE WORLD ARE BLEEDING TO DEATH FROM DEEP SOCIAL AND ECONOMIC WOUNDS.

John certainly has his stories from the civil rights era, and it seems that there is a general acceptance that the sort of civil disobedience of the bus boycotts and the underground railroad were acts of holy mischief. Many of those leaders are now national heroes (and sheroes), like Sojourner Truth, Harriet Tubman, Rosa Parks, Frederick Douglass . . . and, of course, John Perkins.

Today, some things are different. Some of the bad laws have been changed. But other bad laws have emerged. Dozens of cities in the U.S. have begun to enact anti-homeless legislation that makes it illegal to sleep in public, to be in parks after dark, to lie down on the sidewalk, to ask for money. One city even made all trash government property so that if a homeless person goes into the trash looking for food or clothing, he or she can be arrested. In Philadelphia, a Food Ordinance law was passed that made it illegal to distribute food to the homeless downtown. Many of us were arrested for violating these laws. But we had police officers that testified in court that the laws were wrong. We even had a judge who said, "If it weren't for people who broke the unjust laws, we wouldn't have the freedom that we have . . . that's what this country is built on, from the Boston Tea Party to the civil rights movement." He went on to say that we were not criminals but "freedom fighters," and he dismissed all our charges.

There have been other times here in Philadelphia that we have engaged in civil disobedience that resulted in arrest for remaining in houses, sometimes abandoned houses, when the folks living there were being forcefully evicted without being offered any options for other housing. Sometimes in court the judges have seen our side and even awarded families legal housing rights. In New York, I was arrested for lying down in an area where homeless folks were being forced out, and we won in court. It was a significant legal precedent calling into question whether sleeping in public could be considered "disorderly conduct." Should I stop?

John: No, go on.

SHANE: Okay. One of my favorite lines from Dr. King is this one: "There is nothing wrong with a traffic law which says you have to stop for the red light. But when a fire is raging, the fire truck goes through the red light, and normal traffic had better get out of its way. Or when a man is bleeding to death, the ambulance goes through those red lights at top speed. There is a fire raging . . . for the poor of this society. Disinherited people all over the world are bleeding to death from deep social and economic wounds. They need brigades of ambulance drivers who will have to ignore the red lights of the present system until the emergency is solved."

There are places where injustice is happening that we find we cannot stand by. That is why John and I went to the Capitol a few years ago, disturbed by the federal budget that increased military spending and cut programs for the poor, and we prayed on the steps of the legislature in D.C. . . . and we went to jail with the Lord's Prayer on our lips. I can't remember what ended up happening on that one. I think the judge made us write a paper about why we did it.

John: When we integrated a place in rural Mississippi during the civil rights movement, it was terribly frightful. The worst place that you could integrate was a truck stop. Black folks didn't drive trucks back in those days. You have to remember that. There wasn't anyone there but some white men and the policemen who ate at the truck stop.

The young man who integrated the truck stop was locked in jail, and Vera Mae had to go bail him out. Our rule was that once we had integrated a place, it became our responsibility to keep that place integrated. That's what all our leaders told us. If you didn't achieve integration, you had made one act of being bad—you could have been drunk and gone into a bus stop on a whim. That was not integration. So we had to make sure the place stayed integrated. To accomplish that, we went back every week and reintegrated it. It was best if the first person to integrate the place could be a part of the team that returned. We were very deliberate in what we did, and always peaceful.

And so we thought we would all go to Jackson that day, but we had made up our minds that when we got back from Jackson, we would have to integrate this truck stop again.

So, on our way back, we went by the bus stop, because back in those days the buses were running and there would always be people from Mendenhall coming to Jackson, and we would go by and pick them up and bring them on to the bus station. When we went by there, we saw a veteran. We knew that he was one of our guys from home, but he had been in the service and had missed all of the civil rights movement—all the beatings and stuff. So we picked him up. We had the idea in mind then that we were going to integrate the place, but we didn't want to make it public yet, so we didn't say anything about it on our way home. But that gave us some more coverage. We thought that having a soldier with us would give our actions more publicity—can't you just see the headlines . . . "Soldier Just Back from Vietnam Beaten at Bus Stop." That wouldn't have been good for anyone.

When we went in there, this soldier was scared to death, and I was scared. All of us were scared. I was so fearful . . . and I was the leader. When the waitress went back and talked to the owner, he served us. So the waitress brought the forks and things over to us. You know, forks make a lot of noise when they dingle together. I was so nervous I couldn't hold them without making noise. So I had to sit on my hands. So I'm trying to keep these other guys from thinking that I'm going to crack as the leader.

When I tell this story, people always ask me, "What did you do? What was the outcome?" I tell them, "We integrated the building."

That was the task. Fear had nothing to do with it. "Did you get beat up?" they will ask. "What happened?" That isn't the right question. The question should have been, "Did you integrate the place?" And, yes, we achieved that. You don't focus on the consequences; you focus on the task that is before you.

That's the agony of leadership today. We can't get people emotional enough about the object of leading because so often the object is "me." So when we say we don't have leadership, it means that we are self-addicted. I hate to take Jesus' words and rank them by importance, but in our hierarchy of doing things, Jesus said, "If anyone desires to come after Me, let him deny himself, and take up his cross, and follow Me" (Matt. 16:24). That might be the essence of leadership. That might be the essence of discipleship. It's not the essence of conversion, but it might be the key passage for discipleship and leadership development.

SHANE: That is precisely why I went to Iraq during the bombing in 2003, and I went with a team of Christians, pastors and doctors. We took medication to the hospitals, hung out with families, and worshiped with Iraqi Christians. When we returned, the U.S. State Department declared a lawsuit against the group—with penalty of facing up to 12 years in prison. Both the trip to Iraq and taking medications were technically illegal, violating U.S. sanctions against Iraq. What we argued and continue to believe is that the sanctions and bombing were violating God's law to love our neighbors (or enemies, for that matter) as ourselves. And we were willing to go to jail for that.

Ultimately, not much came of it all. Even the judge said the State had a difficult case to prove. I am convinced that our trip to Iraq was a holy endeavor even though it was illegal. As Gandhi and King said, "All that is needed for evil to triumph is for good people to do nothing." So we have put our bodies in the way of injustices. On Good Friday we often hold a Stations of the Cross service at the corporate headquarters of Lockheed Martin, the biggest arms dealer in the world. We pray there on the property, and when asked to leave, we continue to pray, and are arrested. Another quote Gandhi and King liked was: "Noncooperation with evil is as much a duty as cooperation with good."

This year, we did the same sort of witness at one of the most no-torious gun shops in Philadelphia. There are more than 900 gun deal-ers in Philadelphia, and Colosimo's is one of the most notorious for selling guns that are later used in violent crimes on our streets. In fact, the Brady Center to Prevent Gun Violence rated Colosimo's the fifth worst of the "Ten Worst Bad Apple Gun Dealers in America." This year, a group of clergy and religious leaders approached Mr. Colosimo, asking him to sign a 10-point code of conduct that helps ensure guns don't end up on the streets. When he didn't comply, they simply re-mained in his store and outside his store in a nonviolent, peaceful way until they were arrested (for trespassing when asked to leave). In a highly charged trial later, a judge allowed evidence to be presented that justified their action and their intent to prevent harm to others, and all of the charges were dropped. These are incredible stories.

There are leaders, Christian leaders, of these movements of free-dom that are changing laws and policies out of sync with God's laws and policies. It was St. Augustine who said, "An unjust law is no law at all." As Christians, and as leaders, we commit ourselves to disobey any ungodly, un-Jesus-ly ordinances and laws. We are willing to suffer the consequences with nonviolence and grace, just like Jesus (that second part here is just as important as the first). There is no place for violent rebellion or violent protest. There is no room for killing abortion doc-tors. There is no room in the cross for redemptive violence. We cannot fight fire with fire or violence with violence. The Jesus revolution is dif-ferent. When the soldiers came to take Jesus, Peter picked up his sword and cut off the ear of one of the servants. If ever there was a case for justified violence or just war, Peter had it. But Jesus' response is fasci-nating. He picks up the ear of the wounded persecutor and heals him. Then He scolds Peter, telling him, "If you pick up the sword, you will die by the sword." The early Christians said at that moment when Je-sus disarmed Peter, He disarmed every Christian. Our arms are not big enough to carry a cross and a sword.

Indeed, it seems the Judeo-Christian story is one of collision with empires and kings, one of divine conspiracy and holy troublemaking. The French philosopher Jacque Ellul once said, "Christians were never meant to be normal. We've always been troublemakers, we've always been creators of uncertainty, agents of a dimension that's incompatible with the status quo: we do not accept the world as it is." But we are not just troublemakers for the sake of making trouble—we are people who plot goodness and whose commitment to the upside-down kingdom of God collides with the patterns of the world we live in. And what is very important is the manner in which we engage the powers. We are to practice what some theologians call "revolutionary subordination." We are to respect and submit to the authorities, even as our obedience to God lands us in their jails and courtrooms. We are to realize that our battle is "not against flesh and blood, but against the rulers, against the authorities, against the powers of this dark world and against the spiritual forces" (Eph. 6:12, *NIV*). After all, the same Paul who wrote in Romans 13 that we are to submit to the authorities uses the same word in Ephesians to say we wrestle against the spiritual demonic "authorities." The same Paul who said that the authorities are established by God ends up in jail for subverting them.

At first glance it can seem confusing and contradictory. Though we can't go into too much depth here, there is a whole chapter around this idea of authorities in *Jesus for President* (and we have an appendix in this book based on Romans 13). Simply put, just because the authorities are established by God doesn't always mean God approves of them . . . the same way a librarian can order books on a shelf. After all, it wasn't even God's will for Israel to have a king.[1] But we are always to look to Jesus to know how we are to engage the authorities. We are to engage them with revolutionary subordination.

In Colossians, Paul says that when Jesus rose from the dead and triumphed over that Roman cross, the quintessential symbol of imperial power and punitive justice, Jesus "disarmed the powers and authorities . . . and made a public spectacle of them" (Col. 2:15, *NIV*). It is through submitting ourselves to suffer under the powers that we expose the injustices of the world we live in. That is what happened when we went to jail for breaking bad laws. That's what happened when we exposed the scandal of the sanctions on Iraq. That's what happened when Dr. King and John looked into the eyes of those who were threatening their lives and beating their friends and said, "We still love you."

To our most bitter opponents, we say, in the words of Dr. Martin Luther King, Jr.: "Throw us in jail and we will still love you. Bomb our houses and threaten our children and we will still love you. But be ye assured that we will wear you down by our capacity to suffer. One day we shall so appeal to your heart and conscience that we shall win you in the process, and our victory will be a double victory."

John: I have outlived most of the heroes of the civil rights movement. And I'm honored to share my stories of our civil disobedience.

Civil disobedience assumes nonviolence. Sometimes people ask me if I'm "nonviolent." I say, "Are you a fool? Have I ever killed anyone? Come on now." The civil rights movement from the black perspective was nonviolent—that was powerful. That's where the power in the civil rights movement came from. I don't think there was ever a white man killed by a black man in pursuit of his civil rights from 1955 until today. That's a miracle. The violence came when the non-Christian blacks started rioting in the northern cities. Nonviolent resistance was the way that we followed as we pursued justice in Mississippi.

There was, and still is, a lot of violence within the black community, but I gained a new model when I was converted. "Blessed are the peacemakers for they shall be called sons of God" (Matt. 5:9). I took for granted that Christians ought not to be violent. I read a book about all of the historical martyrs and learned the progressiveness of one's belief in martyrdom. You can kill the martyr but you don't kill what he believes—it only spreads. Martin Luther almost asked for martyrdom. "Here I stand. I can do no other. God help me. Amen." Killing him could do nothing but further the faith of his conviction.

During my lifetime of civil rights work, I have felt a similar conviction. When I was arrested in Mendenhall, I knew I was standing up for not only what I believed but what the people who were following me believed. I was trusted with the voice of my community. That is a lot of pressure, and I felt it in my soul. I knew God put me in that position for a reason.

When we had a break during my trial for contributing to the delinquency of minors, I was really ridiculed by the district attorney. I was sitting by a tree when an old black lady with a flap-down hat came and spoke to me. "Stand up. You're not standing for me; you're standing for all black people." It brought more pressure, but it gave me fortitude to stand. I knew that I was standing for something. I wasn't just standing for myself, and I wasn't just standing alone. "Therefore take up the whole armor of God, that you may be able to withstand in the evil day, and having done all, to stand" (Eph. 6:13).

We created a list of demands from the black community that included, among other things, equal minimum wage practices; equal due process for all arrests, trials and defense; representation in government offices; and all rights and protection granted by the Constitution. "We demand our freedom. We demand the power to determine the destiny of our community. Black people will not be free until we are able to determine our own destiny. Selective buying will continue until employment issue is corrected. Then and only then will the other items be negotiable."[2]

BLACK PEOPLE WILL NOT BE FREE
UNTIL WE ARE ABLE TO
DETERMINE OUR OWN DESTINY.

"We were only demanding those rights that were supposedly ours under the Constitution and the present American system. There was no talk of a 'new order,' it was only a call to live by the ideals that whites themselves claimed as their heritage."[3]

Until our demands for equal percentages of employment were met, we would boycott all businesses in Mendenhall. It was powerful to witness the solidarity of the black community. We held weekly marches that grew in number with the help of the faithful community members and college students from Tougaloo College. (You can read more about this in my 1976 book *Let Justice Roll Down*.) These marches lasted from Christmas 1969 to February 1970—when everything changed.

On Saturday February 7, 1970, after one of our demonstrations in Mendenhall, 19 students were arrested in Brandon, Mississippi, on their way home to the Jackson area. Along with Rev. Curry Brown, I drove up to Brandon to get them out—but was blindsided when more than a dozen white deputy sheriffs and highway patrolmen led by Lloyd "Goon" Jones ambushed us. That night, Curry, Doug Huemmer, a young white volunteer, and I were beaten within an inch of our lives.

They beat us down. They stuck forks up my nose and down my throat. They kicked me in the groin. They dehumanized and tortured us. Here is my recollection:

> When they started torturing us, it was horrifying; I couldn't even imagine that this was happening; one of the officers took a fork that was bent down and he brought that fork up to me and said, have you seen this, and he took that fork and put that fork into my nose; than he took that fork and pushed it down my throat; and then they took me over there and beat me to the ground . . . Mr. Lloyd Jones was sitting down on the front . . . and he got up and stomped me; and by this time, I was almost out.[4]

The Brandon jail experience was destiny—it was an experience that I had to have. As I look back on it, I realize that I had to go through it. I had to be convinced, in a dynamic way, of the evil of racism. It had been theoretical up until that point. I had to see the end of racism. Now I can preach the evil of racism without malice. God allowed me to go through that experience and survive. It was a reinforcement and challenge to my faith. I'm overly competitive, and that time I lost. They beat me—literally. They showed me the evil of racism and hatred. I allowed those 19 children to be arrested, and I thought I would never be forgiven. I thought I would never rise from that again.

I almost lost my faith after that incident. However, every time I would get into a place of doubt and wandering, I would meet someone who envied me. They wanted something that I had. In my time of pain these folks walked with me. Every time I was about to lose my faith, some believer, some friend would come along who had more faith in God than I had and would show me His love. In my times of doubt these people became my strength. My doctor used to come to the hospital and take me out into the country just so I could enjoy some fresh air. Another doctor would come into the hospital at night and sit beside my bed until I fell asleep. These people helped sustain me in my faith.

On May 14, 1970, just 10 days after the Kent State anti-war protest where four students were killed by national guardsmen, Constance Slaughter, my lawyer and the first black female graduate of Ole Miss, took Goon Jones's deposition about the Brandon jail incident. That same night he led a group of highway patrolmen onto the Jackson State University campus to subdue a crowd of students that had gathered in protest, just blocks from where I now live.

Reports vary, but what we do know is that around midnight, the highway patrol and police force under the direction of Goon Jones opened fire on a group of students outside a women's dormitory. They would later count over 400 bullet holes in the outside walls of the building. Two young men were killed and 12 more were injured. They claimed they were fired upon first and that there were snipers on the buildings surrounding them, but no policeman or patrolman was injured in the incident.

It's my belief that Jones was, in a sense, punishing "that little, black bitch" for putting him through that type of misery earlier in the day. This woman asked him all these questions that no one had ever made him answer, and I believe he took it out on those students. I shudder at that thought. But that's how deep the racism was.

Even in 1970, the Mississippi court system was infected with a racism that continued to deny us our human rights. I was unable to get a fair trial, as the majority of the justices neglected the undeniable facts that my civil rights were violated by the police officers. They accepted the police officers' statements that I attacked first, that I brought in the forks they used to tortured me, that I was attempting to raid the jailhouse. The lone dissenter, Chief Justice Brown, articulated the connection between my physical beating in the Brandon jail and the black community's demands for equality in Mendenhall. But this was ignored in the final decision. How could we ever begin to see progress toward justice when the upper levels of our justice system were so corrupt? The following lawsuit I brought against the police officers was settled due to the undeniable truth of the torture we had suffered in the Brandon jail.

The last time I got arrested was outside the national Capitol, in December of 2005. I went there and spoke to a crowd about the proposed budget that was cutting the Medicaid and Medicare budget but strengthening the budget for military activities. I told the crowd that while we were making bombs and going to war, we were neglecting our call to help the poor. Given the wealth of our nation,

I wanted to support the poor and inspire others to do the same. As an old man, my conscience was driving me to be engaged in the fight. (I had to smile when a courageous young Christian named Nate Bacon rode in the cab with me to the Capitol protest. Nate works for InnerChange, a Christian order among the poor, and it was his first arrest for civil disobedience.)

A part of the Christian faith is to free one's conscience.[5] If our conscience condemns us, we're in bad shape—because God is greater than our conscience. If your conscience recognizes that a law is evil, it is your responsibility to use the free will you've been given to rise up against it. Uprising will satisfy your conscience.

To disobey, you have to discover a cause that is worth dying for. We have made living in pleasure one of the highest values. That poses a real problem in our day. We've got to really magnify the gospel— God's love for humanity. If we enter that pain with Him, then we begin to discover that commitment.

Jesus called His disciples and walked with them for three-and-a-half years. In His call to them, He invited them to learn from Him but also to witness His death. We're going to arrive at that if we make Jesus adequate enough for the problem. We need to teach that this is discipleship. Whatever I have become in life was because of Mr. Leitch. He discipled me and showed me the power of the Word of God. I learned from him that the Bible was an important book of guidance, and it did guide me toward the truth of what is worth fighting for.

Martin Luther King, Jr., said, "If one hasn't found something that isn't precious enough to die for, that person isn't fit to live." That idea needs to be taught within the church. It needs to be taught within a discipleship environment.

If we, along with all the other heroes of the civil rights movement, had just gone along and obeyed—the police, the parade permits, the "system"—we wouldn't be where we are today. What made it civil disobedience is that when the police asked us to leave three or four times, we didn't! If we had a permit to march in Mendenhall or in Washington and didn't do anything radical in the face of injustice, it wouldn't be disobedience. It takes going one step further. There are opportunities all around us to make a stand—an unjust law, a racist comment, an oppressive system. Shane is an example of someone who practices civil disobedience, or holy mischief, as he likes to say, as an essential part of his Christian life. I like that.

SHANE: I heard a great preacher not long ago give a fiery sermon around the theme: "Just because it's legal doesn't make it right." It was legal to kick black folks out of stores and buses because of the color of their skin. But that didn't make it right. It may have been legal to take slaves from Africa and treat them like property. But that didn't make it right. Maybe it was legal to take the land from natives, but that didn't make it right. And it may be legal to sell handguns in bulk to "straw" buyers who sell them on our streets, but that doesn't make it right. It may be legal to make weapons that can kill 100,000 in one blast, but that doesn't make it right. It may have been legal to kill our lover Jesus on that cross . . . but that didn't make it right.

Oh yes, just because something is legal doesn't make it right. The great irony is that Lockheed Martin was allowed to stay open that Good Friday and those of us that gathered on their property to pray went to jail. I recall an old proverb: *In an age of injustice, the true place for just men and women is in prison.* As we look at history, we see that we are in pretty good company behind those bars.

Notes
1. See 1 Samuel 8.
2. "Demands of the Black Community," December 23, 1969, Perkins vs. State of Mississippi, 1972.
3. John Perkins, Let Justice Roll Down (Ventura, CA: Regal Books, 1976), p. 150
4. John Perkins, Let Justice Roll Down (Ventura, CA: Regal Books, 1976), p. 164.
5. Romans 13:1-5 makes it clear that every Christian "must submit himself to the governing authorities, for there is no authority except that which God has established." Scripture teaches us to make every effort to live at peace with everyone, to return good for evil, to turn the other cheek and, as a rule, to follow the laws laid down by governmental authorities (see Prov. 24:21; Rom. 12:9-21; Matt. 5:39). Even though many Roman emperors were despotic and evil rulers, in Titus 3:1-2 and 1 Peter 2:13-14 the apostles Paul and Peter still instructed Christians to submit to the Roman government.
   Jesus never advised or encouraged His followers to initiate physical violence or deliberate destruction of the property of others—even against despotic rulers, unjust laws or the evil actions of governments. For example, when Peter drew his sword to strike the centurions that had come with the Jewish leaders to arrest Jesus, the Lord admonished him, "Put your sword into the sheath. Shall I not drink the cup which My Father has given Me?" (John 18:11). This admonition of the Lord to the apostle emphasized that the weapons of Christian warfare are not physical in nature but spiritual (see 2 Cor. 10:3-5; Eph. 6:10-18). The conclusion appears

to be plain: Christians who are oppressed should first fight their battles in prayer, make every effort to overcome evil with good, strive to obey God first and foremost, and trust that He will deliver justice for them in due time (see 1 Pet. 5:10).

On the other hand, Scripture also shows that there are times when "we must obey God rather than men," as Peter said to the Jewish religious leaders in Acts 5:29. In an article for *Christianity Today* dated August 6, 1982, Kenneth Kantzer stated, "It is rarely good for a Christian to disobey even a bad law. That is why the Scripture so frequently urges Christians to obey even evil governments and laws that create trouble for them. Still, there are times when a Christian becomes thoroughly convinced that the total welfare of others would be significantly better if he disobeyed rather than obeyed a particular law. When that moment arrives, he must obey God rather than man." This departure from the rule of obeying governing authorities reflects God's commands in Scripture that rulers must govern with fairness and righteousness (see Jer. 22:3), deliver the poor and needy (see Ps. 82:4), rescue those being led away to death (see Prov. 24:11), judge impartially (see Deut. 1:17), and not pervert justice and take bribes (see Deut. 16:19).

Jesus knew that His followers would be in conflict with the governing authorities—to the point of physical violence, incarceration and death. In Mark 13:9,11, He told them, "You will be handed over to the local councils and flogged in the synagogues. . . . You will stand before governors and kings. . . . you [will be] arrested and brought to trial." These words from Jesus were not the gentle suggestion of a leader who expected His followers to be peaceably obeying every law and ordinance to the letter. Jesus knew the clashes and bloodshed that lay ahead when the ways of the world would begin pushing violently against Christians who were trying to serve God. He knew that for the sake of God's plan of salvation for mankind, His disciples would sometimes be led by God's Spirit to refuse to obey the governing authorities, and that those same authorities would not allow the words and the works of the disciples to proceed with ease. And yet, knowing this was going to happen, Jesus still instructed His followers to submit to every authority instituted among men.

This sounds like an impossible contradiction. On the one hand, Jesus tells His disciples to submit to the governing authorities because God Himself had placed such authority over them; but on the other hand, He tells them that they will be in mortal conflict with that same government. The key lies in the fact that, for the Christian, government is not the ultimate authority: God is. Christians are to obey the governing authorities as much as possible for God's sake, unless and until God's Spirit makes it clear to them that to obey the governing authorities would cause them to disobey God and His Word. In such cases, God calls us to peaceable resistance, as Jesus Himself modeled when He was persecuted.

Do not grant newcomers to the monastic life an easy entry, but as the apostle says, "Test the spirits to see if they are from God."
—St. Benedict of Nursia (480–547)

THE CRISIS

(Responding When Disaster Strikes)

John: Living in Jackson, Mississippi, we have seen our share of tornadoes; and of course there are hurricanes on the Gulf Coast just a couple of hours south of us. When a natural disaster hits, there is no time to decide who will lead and who will follow. Everyone must act. Any petty disagreement or difference has to be put aside immediately, or we risk muddling an opportunity to be God's hands and feet at the very moment of greatest pain and need.

At a moment of crisis, or when you need to act fast, you as a leader must synchronize everything you already know. My son Derek helped me understand this dynamic. Derek described a hypothetical football game that comes down to the last few seconds. When the team needs to score just one more time, the quarterback goes into the huddle. A play may be sent in, but usually he will already know the play, because he knows the situation and he knows his team. Derek said to me, "Everything that you've ever been taught about that play flashes through your head in that moment. You see why it is a good play, why it has worked in the past, what to avoid and why it will work now." This is what happens when a crisis occurs. Everything you have learned your whole life about the situation comes crashing through your head, and you act.

When Hurricane Katrina hit in August 2005, and New Orleans was flooded, people fled to Houston, Oklahoma City and Florida. On the television news I saw a report of how a local arena in Jackson was being used as a shelter for some who had come here.

I went down to the arena the next morning and started going there every day. It hurt to see the situation, especially to see older black men like me living out in an open space with so many others. They still had pride and dignity, but now they had to live collectively with the group, almost as migrants. It felt embarrassing, and I wanted to do something.

I knew that the Christians in Jackson had the means to help. Yes, especially the black churches. We could give the people in the emergency shelter better places to stay and give them more personalized care. But I was almost the only local church leader there in the arena.

One day, when I returned from visiting the arena, a television news crew was waiting for me. They had come to look at some of our projects that been damaged when Katrina cut inland and through Jackson. I was respectful and started off talking about our ministry, but I quickly switched the focus. With great passion, I described the horrific conditions at the arena, and right there on the television news I challenged the Christians in Jackson to go down to the arena, meet the people who had fled from areas hit much harder than our own and take them to the churches—bring them home! I was almost fuming, and I pretty much made it sound like I didn't expect the Christians to do anything even though they should. The television station aired my entire statement on the news that evening and then replayed it two or three times! The next morning, when I went to the arena, lo and behold, a dozen or so black pastors were already lined up to help. They were waiting until I arrived because they wanted to make sure that I saw them and that I knew they had heard my challenge.

It was moving to see the pastors there, and they came with passion. I was so broken up that I was ready to go back home when I saw the impact of the challenge. At that moment, I was a bit embarrassed.

Leadership usually emerges at moments of crisis. Because the leader is simply responding to pain, when followers, in turn, respond and share the pain, the leader has nothing to brag about. It wasn't the leadership that moved the pastors; it was the pain they felt when they realized how people were living in the shelter. What a leader brags about is the follower—that someone, in fact, did respond and did solve the problem.

In the situation in Jackson, pastors started taking people into their churches, and the over-crowded situation at the arena was eased. As often happens, solving one specific problem doesn't solve all of the problems, and there can be new ones. Most churches could put a roof over people's heads, but then the churches needed to feed and take care of them. I had sparked the compassion to help, so I could not smile and walk away, leaving the pastors to sort it out. We sent some money, more as a symbol to undergird them—to help them get started. I also had contacts at World Vision, Food for the Hungry and Feed the Children, so I shifted my attention. I picked up the phone and nudged these organizations to supply more of the resources the pastors in Jackson would need. They did.

WHAT A LEADER BRAGS ABOUT
IS THE FOLLOWER—THAT SOMEONE,
IN FACT, DID RESPOND AND DID
SOLVE THE PROBLEM.

I had asked the churches to respond, but I didn't ask and then run away. Rather, I asked and then tied our resources to their resources. When I realized what I had initiated and saw deep down that the pastors wanted to help, I could do no less. Together we were able to do a whole lot of development of a whole lot of people.

A few months later, Mississippi Governor Haley Barbour hosted a breakfast to thank people who had helped during the Katrina crisis. While I may not always agree with our governor on every issue, during Katrina, he, too, showed leadership. Immediately after Katrina moved further inland, Governor Barbour went to the hardest hit areas of the Mississippi coasts. There were whole towns that were wiped out. He didn't actually do much, but the very fact that he was present and entered into the pain of the people was an inspiration. In fact, when days passed before President Bush went to New Orleans, that inaction hurt those who were already hurting. He appeared to be aloof, which is the exact opposite of what was needed.

I know that Shane and I have already said this, but it is worth repeating: The key to real leadership is to enter into the pain of the people. Vicarious suffering is greater than our own suffering. Showing compassion means that you feel the pain because you reckon with the pain. It is one thing to suffer discrimination or go without food; it is another to feel the struggle of the oppressed person or the hungry person and then also walk with him to a place of freedom.

SHANE: What John didn't tell you is that his ministry buys and builds homes in Jackson, helping the poor get real housing. Two of those houses were damaged in Katrina.

John: Yes, but our houses were not as important to me as those people who were down in the arena, suffering. Nobody living in our houses got hurt, and everyone had a place to stay.

SHANE: I think what John has just shown us is that a good leader will look at the others' needs before he considers his own.

John: True, but it is also a little unnerving when reporters come. Usually Al Sharpton or Jesse Jackson represent blacks, so sometimes reporters come to me to get something different. They came to interview me because my house was damaged. That's nothing. It was the people's pain that helped me see that.

SHANE: We had a little situation in Philadelphia. There was a fire. In fact, it happened when I was working on the manuscript for another book, *Jesus for President*. In June 2007, a seven-alarm blaze started in a city-owned abandoned warehouse and spread into the neighborhood . . . *our neighborhood*. I have already said a little about this fire, but there is more to the story.

The fire destroyed a dozen houses on our block and displaced nearly 100 families. Cars exploded; it was nuts. It burned down our community center, our homes and the homes of some of the families we love so dearly. A priest said to us, "Those are the days when you wake up and say, 'It's a terrible day . . . but thanks be to God it is a day that the Lord has made.'" But here's the deal: Crises are moments that bring out the best or the worst in people—when you see people's true hearts come out. Within a matter of hours, we had neighbors bringing *us* food and clothes. Talk about leadership and people stepping up to the plate!

Everyone started organizing. We had no electricity anywhere, but my friend Brooke found a gas stove and started cooking for everyone and their brother (and their sister). People's gifts came to life. Michael set up a new website for the fire.[1] Jamie is a filmmaker, so he picked up his camera and started shooting. I even had an animal-loving friend who took in orphaned cats . . . now that's dedication! (God is still working on my attitude toward cats.) A neighborhood thrift store created emergency vouchers for victims so they could have a free credit of $500 to replace their lost things. My friend Tony Campolo established a system to receive emergency funds. Within hours, tens of thousands of dollars began pouring in, and over the following weeks we began to rise from the ashes.

Two years later, we are still in the middle of that rising. Even when we think we've made it, a new struggle emerges . . . like the one we are in right now. Check this out: After the fire—which, let me reiterate, started in an abandoned *city-owned* warehouse—had burned down our neighborhood, homes and community center, the city fined the families—the victims of the fire—around $10,000 each to demolish the remaining bricks of their houses! That's not the end of it. When some of those same families tried to find new housing, they were denied because the lien they "owed" the City had destroyed their credit. At moments like these, I start to understand better what Scripture means when it speaks about how our battle is not against flesh and blood but against the principalities and powers and authorities of *this dark world* and the spiritual realm.[2] There are real systems that we are up against, and I am not just talking about some people down at city hall.

After the fire, our insurance company—one of the largest insurers of congregations in the U.S.—dropped us . . . after years of no claims on our properties. The fire wasn't even our fault; it's not like someone fell asleep smoking or left a heater running too close to a blanket. Things like this could go unheard, but with good leaders on the ground and, yes, also in the systems of power, we are taking on the principalities! Amen.

We've had thousands of folks calling and writing, and it has made a huge difference. I finally got through to the mayor's office. After I introduced myself, they said, "We know who you all are . . . the whole world seems to be concerned about the fire in Kensington." As it should be . . . we should be just as concerned about a fire in the Kensington area of North Philly as a fire in Malibu or Santa Barbara.

Now, here's the best part: It wasn't just people from outside the neighborhood who were stepping up and leading things, but people from within it. The Red Cross set up a shelter nearby . . . that's what they do. But no one stayed there because the people in the neighborhood whose houses hadn't been destroyed had already opened up their homes and lives and made space for those who were displaced. That's community at it's best. It's a beautiful thing how that seems to come naturally to poor folks and to people who struggle . . . probably because they already know they need other people and don't live in the phantom illusion of independence and self-sufficiency.

Independence may be a cultural value, but it is not a gospel value and it does not work when the going gets tough. The gospel teaches us not independence but interdependence . . . community. Poor folks often know that best. Perhaps that's why Jesus says, "Blessed are the poor in spirit, for theirs is the kingdom of heaven" (Matt. 5:3). The poor know they need God and other people . . . it's the only way they are going to survive. Some of us fool ourselves into thinking we know better—until a crisis hits. Often that's when folks find God and community.

Granted, much of life does not exist in the moments of crisis but in the everyday relationships. Those aren't as spectacular, but they are just as necessary. After all, the gospel is not about doing great things but about doing small things with great love. Sometimes it's easier to respond to a Katrina or a seven-alarm fire in North Philly than it is to respond to the needs right next to us. But it's the small things, like a mustard seed, that change the world.

Notes
1. Check out http://www.thesimpleway.org/fire_index.html.
2. See Ephesians 6.

PRAYER

(Following Jesus' Example)

John: When Jesus prayed, the disciples listened. The Lord's Prayer is our model. We are to "pray like this."

The disciples observed Jesus when He prayed. They watched as He lifted up His hands and looked up to heaven. They saw Him go away to pray in solitude. We, too, should watch Jesus and pray as He prayed.

Shane warned you that I might include a list, so here goes. Here are seven things we can learn from watching how Jesus prayed, recorded in Matthew 6:5-16:

1. Prayer to God is very personal and intimate.
2. Prayer is a humbling exercise in itself.
3. We are to thank Him.
4. Our prayers are wasted if we cannot forgive others.
5. We are to ask for our own forgiveness.
6. We are to ask for His guidance.
7. We should always pray for His will to be done in the kingdom of God for the collective good.

Reconciliation is assumed within prayer. If we are not reconciled to our brothers and sisters, God won't hear our prayers. Unless we've forgiven those who have trespassed against us, how can He forgive us? The biggest deal with prayer is how we come before the throne. Do we come with pride? Do we bring our selfish desires? Do we bring a humble heart? Do we come for our individual needs and the collective needs at the same time?

In the Garden of Gethsemane, Jesus asked His father to let the cup pass from Him. This prayer comes out of His personal pain. "If it be possible let this cup pass from me." He yielded that personal desire to what He knew He was created for. He knew this was what He had come to the world to do, so His prayer was that His will might be aligned with God's.

This is good stuff, but tough stuff. If you are like me, your mind wanders when you pray. Sometimes when I pray, one minute I am talking with God about a particular need, the next minute I am writing down a plan to solve the problem. I have to stop myself and get back to God. Sometimes He will want me plotting out the answer; other times He will have something altogether different in mind. Sometimes, He just wants me to open my Bible and read. I find it amazing how many of my prayers are already answered right there in the Word.

God wants us to align our will with His will . . . one way we do this is through prayer. God wants to work out His will through us and to know His mind on a particular matter we need to be talking with Him about it . . . and listening. God wants to include us in His plans. He wants us to be workers together with Him to do His work. Prayer is not a substitution for action; rather, prayer is a preparation for an action through which God will use us. There are many prayers that God can only answer alone but He wants us to be the answer to our own prayers whenever possible.

As leaders, we have followers who naturally look to us for results or actions or solutions. This expectation can create a subtle pressure for us to move ahead of God with an answer, or sometimes it will freeze us and prevent us from moving forward. That's when we need to lean into God even more.

SHANE: Even the way Jesus teaches us to pray points us toward the path we are to follow—a path to freedom. Jesus teaches us to pray for the Kingdom to come, not just in heaven but also on earth. And we are to pray this day for "*our* daily bread." We are not to pray "*my* daily bread," as if I can separate my own sustenance from a brother's or sister's . . . "our" means "us." We are not to pray for our daily *steak*, but for the simple nourishment of bread. We are not to pray for tomorrow's bread or next week's bread . . . just today's.

We are also to pray that God would forgive us, as we forgive others. Our reconciliation with others is directly connected to our reconciliation with God. We cannot expect God to forgive us if we do not forgive others. Inasmuch as we judge, we, too, will be judged. It's beautiful, because Jesus' prayer demands something of us just as we are asking something of God. Prayer and action always need to kiss.

WHEN WE GIVE THANKS FOR
CREATION, LET'S PLANT A GARDEN AND
BUY LOCALLY GROWN FRUITS
AND VEGETABLES.

My friend Jonathan Wilson-Hartgrove and I wrote a book titled *Becoming the Answer to Our Prayers*. It is about how, as Christians, we need to be people who pray *and* act. Too often we use prayer as an excuse for inaction. When faced with the problems of our world, we have asked, "God, why don't You do something?" without realizing that God might be saying, "I did do something . . . I made you." When we pray for God to bless someone, we are challenged to see that we might be the hands of that blessing, for God has no hands but ours. When we pray, "Thy kingdom come, Thy will be done," we commit our whole lives to caring for the least among us—the unborn *and* the undocumented. If we Christians are praying by the model Jesus gave us, we cannot stop praying and acting until we see the restoration of all that is broken in our lives, and in our streets . . . broken political systems and broken families, polluted ecosystems and shattered lives.

When we pray for the hungry, let's remember to feed them. When we pray for the unborn, let's welcome single mothers and adopt abandoned children. When we give thanks for creation, let's plant a garden and buy locally grown fruits and veggies. When we remember the poor, let's reinvest our money in micro-lending programs. When we pray for peace, let's beat our swords into plowshares and turn military budgets into programs of social uplift. When we pray for an end to crime, let's visit those in prison. When we pray for lost souls, let's be gracious to the souls who've done us wrong. (Think about that one the next time some crazy gas-guzzling dude cuts you off on the freeway!)

To begin to act on our prayers with any seriousness is to remember why we pray in the first place—because anything worth doing is beyond our power to do alone. We cry out to God because we know we need help. But God chooses to work in and through us. We have a God that does not want to change the world without us.

A follower of Christ lives in reverence of him and does not take the credit for a good life but, believing that all the good we do comes from the Lord, gives him the credit and thanksgiving for what his gift brings about in our hearts. In that spirit our prayer from the psalm should be: not to us, O Lord, not to us give the glory but to your own name.

—St. Benedict of Nursia (480–547)

THE GIFT OF COMMUNITY

(Keeping Your Feet on the Ground)

SHANE: Part of John's strength as a leader is his consistency and longevity.

John: I think Shane is saying that I am getting old.

SHANE: Remember, we are as young as our dreams and as old as our cynicism. Ha-ha. John put roots in his neighborhood and stayed. He did it in Mississippi and in Pasadena, California, where he started the Harambee Christian Family Center. The place he made home was a tough corner where crack was a fundamental part of the neighborhood economy. When John settles in, he settles in for the long haul . . . because he knows that's how change happens. He spent 12 years developing Mendenhall Ministries in Mendenhall, Mississippi; 10 years developing Voice of Calvary in Jackson, Mississippi; 13 years in Pasadena, California, developing CCDA, the Christian Community Health Fellowship and the John M. Perkins Foundation; and he has spent the last 12 years back in Mississippi working in the Jackson community and strengthening the whole CCDA movement through the John M. Perkins Foundation.

"Stability" is a traditional monastic vow; it is to commit to a group of people and to be submitted to them. Stability is something poor neighborhoods are starved for. There are so many things that don't last—like landlords. And missionaries. Things come and go, and people are moving all the time—not far, but often. It's part of the culture of poverty that is so unhealthy. And it takes commitment—literally, a commitment to become a stable part of the neighborhood to change that.

I think back to those words John told me on our front steps of Potter House . . . "You'll see things begin to change . . . after about 10 years." Commitment is not a cultural value. Wanna be radical? Commit to a neighborhood for 10 years! Every generation has its good and every generation has its bad. One of the great things about my generation is our global awareness. With the Internet and all, the world has shrunk into a global neighborhood. Folks are aware of what's happening in Uganda and East Timor. Young folks care about who made their clothes and where their bananas come from and how much the folks who grew their coffee got paid. But there is also a sort of missional ADD. Young people want to do everything . . . for three months. They want to go to Africa. They want to do Mission Year, and City Year, AmeriCorps, Peace Corps, Jesuit Volunteer Corps. They want to do Teach for America and be an intern here and an apprentice there. But it can be very parasitical. They glean all this knowledge and experience but can end up doing internships until they're 40! Then they are ready to retire! Incidentally, these short-term experiences have to lead to long-term commitment. Otherwise, you end up running around from experience to experience and doing all sorts of little projects that are great for your own formation and sense of meaning, but they have very little lasting fruit or enduring impact on anyone else.

SHORT-TERM EXPERIENCES IN MISSIONS HAVE TO LEAD TO LONG-TERM COMMITMENTS FOR THEM TO HAVE LASTING FRUIT.

John: Young people go to college or start their careers in a big city. When you are 22, it is exciting and daring to live in San Francisco or Manhattan or Boston. When you get married, it can still be stimulating. But once children come along, most young couples that can afford to go to the suburbs, go. It is outward mobility. Then when the children go off to college, some parents move back to the city. This flow of young professionals and older empty nesters creates gentrification in some neighborhoods. We should see gentrification as an opportunity to reach these people and capture their hearts for the city during this move back.

SHANE: For the record, "gentrification" is the (often unintended) displacement of poor folks by young professionals who move into a blighted, usually historic block or section of the city and turn it into a trendy, upscale neighborhood. What often happens is that folks are able to get into houses cheaply and then fix them up. Sometimes they move into an old factory and turn it into studio space, or into an old general store and transform it into an art space or a café . . . but before long, what we see is that the neighborhood has not just "improved," it has changed. Many of the original or longtime residents can no longer afford to live in their homes.

In some areas here in Philly, these "empowerment zones" can end up creating a wall around the ghetto and force poor folks further into pockets of poverty while creating zones where newcomers move into beautiful new housing units. In fact, in Philadelphia, parts of West Philly around University City have been transformed by hipsters—where homes that once cost $50,000 now sell for $250,000 . . . they call it "Penntrification" out there.

It's tricky, which is why we need indigenous leadership and not just outside developers, and we need to live and grow roots in the neighborhoods and make sure the people that live there are at the table, or even leading the conversation. Certainly, it's great to see abandoned buildings come to life, but not if it means displacing the folks who already live there. As relocators, we have to be really careful, and sensitive about these patterns, and learn from great leaders . . . like our brother Bob Lupton who teaches a workshop on "Gentrification with Justice." He talks about how to renew neighborhoods with new jobs and missional neighbors and businesses, while simultaneously making sure that the current residents and most vulnerable folks reap the benefits of restoration.

John: We need the stability that comes from putting down roots. We get so many of these volunteers. We get so many people who are coming really just to look at you, to prepare to go look somewhere else. They're looking for God . . . this has taken them from place to place and eventually to us. Many of them give their lives for a few years and then move somewhere else. I don't blame them for moving on, but the fact of the matter is that it creates instability for us and the community—especially the children.

Sometimes we settle them down; and the ones that we help to settle down a little bit are the ones that do pretty well when they eventually do leave. H. Spees came to Mississippi for a long time—11 years—and did some great work in New Hebron. His footprints are all over the work we did in Jackson and New Hebron. I'm so thankful for him and for Dolphus Weary, Artis Fletcher, Jean Thomas, Dennis Adams, Phil and Marcia Reed and all of the hundreds of young people that have given years of their lives to our ministries. Two women, Lee Harper, from Mendenhall, and Alexis Spencer-Byers, from San Francisco, came to Jackson many years ago, and they have now started a beautiful little coffee house in an area of town where there was not one—just down the road from me. They are an example of putting down roots. They were intentional in selecting the location in a neighborhood that many have lost hope in and are making a statement both in ministry and business. It's called Koinonia Coffee House. It's located in the community, as a gathering place for the community—and it's beautiful. Next time you're in Jackson, drop on by . . . I hear they make a terrific latte.

Of course, God doesn't call everybody to Jackson, and so we want to be a teaching community. We want to train and inspire people who come here to turn some of their hope, excitement and mission intensity inward, into their own growth and discipleship. We want to help grow people who are looking to serve God and not just those looking for a spiritual adventure.

SHANE: We want to encourage this movement of people, this coming together of black, white, brown and every color. We want to see folks with gray hair and no hair hanging out with kids with cornrows and purple hair. What's so beautiful about CCDA and about being a part of God's Church is that it is not a forced or unnatural mingling of races or tokenism . . . Lord knows there is enough of that. It is about being born again, and recognizing that this family of Abraham and Sarah is a dysfunctional family. We have folks sleeping on the streets while others have an extra room in their house. We are people who want to figure out how to *be* the family God wants to see—young, old, formerly rich and formerly poor, all wrestling with the realities of this rebirth and the responsibilities that come with being born again. Now, when a 14-year-old gets pregnant, that is our daughter. When a kid on the block gets shot, that's our kid. When our neighbor doesn't have proper medical care, that's our mother.

John: Since its start, CCDA has been a group mostly made up of African-Americans and Caucasians. More recently, we have seen a growing number of Hispanics join us and some Asians and Native Americans. As CCDA has become more diverse, one might think the Caucasians (still the majority in the United States) would shrink away, fearing they would lose power. Yet we have seen just the opposite. More whites than ever come. In fact, more and more people who are in the majority reach out to minorities. Honestly, I never thought I would see this day, but now I'm seeing it in reality.

As I go around to colleges and universities, the behavior of this generation of young people—particularly this generation of young, white Christians—impresses me. You would think that this generation would be afraid of people, because white is no longer going to be the majority in America; you would think that would create fear. But this new young Christian generation is reaching out with love and compassion. What is thrilling me is how this generation is reaching their arms around each other. I'm seeing Hispanics, blacks, whites, Native Americans and even Indians (from India) joining together, without fear. We've got the possibility within our generation for the Church to witness this whole idea of one nation under God, with liberty and justice for all. This new generation of young people can take over this community development organization and move it forward over the next 15 years, keeping it relevant to the times.

I have lived most of my life, and I would like to think that I have accomplished some things; I give all the credit to Christ, of course. He is the one who gave me the vision. And I attribute so much of what has been done to the quality of the friends that God has given me. In a real way, my whole life is indebted to other people.

When it comes to friendships, I experience a curious combination of respect and fear. I respect people simply because they are human beings. But I also respect them for what God has done in them—who He has made them to be. If God cared enough to make that person, to have a call on their life, to weep when they weep, then who am I to not care? I have heard it prayed, "God, let me see people as You see them." That really has been my prayer. But be careful, God will answer that prayer and you will start loving people who in the natural you might not have thought were very lovable. You might end up with followers you never dreamed would listen to a word you say, let alone sit around the table with you for fellowship.

When I pray that prayer and realize that God wants to do something big through my friends, I actually fear them. It is a respectful fear. It is a fear that says I want to do everything I can to see God's plans for them come to fruition. When I look at the people on the CCDA board of directors and those in the civil rights movement of the 1960s, I see amazing men and women. Sometimes I wonder if I am even worthy of their friendship. I fear that if they knew me deeply, they would raise questions about whether or not they should be this loyal to me. I guess that brings me back to my need for acceptance.

Most of my friends have exploited me. But you need to realize that I told them to exploit me because I trust them so much. I want the CCDA board members to exploit me. We are in this together. My goal has been to see communities developed all over the country. I can't do that by myself, and I don't want to organize that. So they should take advantage of me if it helps them get into a church to speak or before a foundation that might give them money. If my name and reputation can help someone advance the vision, then I thank God. They are doing exactly what I wanted to see accomplished in life. I don't need a pat on the back or any credit. It is enough to know that the work is being done . . . I want to make sure the work continues on as well!

I pray the mission of Christian Community Development will impact the world long after I'm gone. As long as I am able, I want to continue speaking and traveling; but hopefully, more of my time will be spent in Jackson, Mississippi, at the John Perkins Retreat Center. Groups that want to learn more about CCDA can come down and spend a few days with me for an intimate retreat. Churches that want to help with our Zechariah 8 Community Project and get their hands dirty can come down for a full eight days.[1] I would die a happy man if I could live the rest of my life with Vera Mae, at our home in Jackson, while pouring into the next generation of leaders. I know Vera Mae would enjoy it!

It is true that I have not felt deeply worthy. Perhaps that is because the call wasn't mine. Sometimes I'd like to be religious and think that it had something to do with me. But it didn't. Sometimes I am tempted to think people follow me because they like me, but I know they follow me not because of anything I have done or said but because they saw Christ's call at work in me.

I respond to the apostle Paul when he said, "I have been crucified with Christ and I no longer live, but Christ lives in me. The life I live in the body I live by faith in the Son of God, who loved me and gave himself for me" (Gal. 2:20, NIV). I don't preach myself; I preach the call. The call comes from God, and I'm just responding to a call. That keeps you humble. It ought to be our human desire to do something for God and be able to say that He used me. A cult leader preaches himself. Am I going on too long?

SHANE: No, keep going. This is good, and I am taking notes.

John: Likewise, when I look at those who follow me, I look for Christ's call at work in them, and often I am humbled by what I see. We had a crisis at our CCDA board meeting in Miami. It was a crisis because of Barack Obama. We were meeting in Miami just weeks before the November 2008 presidential election. Obama was to hold a huge rally that day in an outdoor plaza, just blocks from our hotel. The rally shut down downtown Miami, and it almost shut down our board meeting.

Barbara Skinner is on our board, and she is one of Obama's close allies. She was kind enough to secure tickets to the rally for the board members—these were up-close seats, and many on our board also supported the Democratic nominee for president. The rally was scheduled for the same time as our afternoon board session, and we only get everyone together twice a year. But we were ready to adjourn early and head out to the plaza.

A couple of board members said, "Hold on, this is not quite a done deal. I came to the board meeting, we have business we need to discuss, and I've got to leave tomorrow." And it was also obvious that some board members were supporting McCain and not Obama. We talked about how attending the rally would take a side, and we as an organization have worked hard to be bipartisan.

Everyone grew very quiet, and I said, "I love you guys more than I love all the political rallies in the world. All that stuff is going to pass away. I've seen power and celebrity up close before, and really, all of it did not amount to much. You folks here are more important. If even one person's feelings would get hurt, we will not go to the Obama rally." If anything that we do ever causes one of my brothers or sisters to fall or to stumble, we have made a mistake and we carry the blame.

It was a crisis point. Either we went together, unified as a team, or we stayed to finish the meeting. And that's what we did: we stayed right there and took care of business.

I was more concerned about the friendships in the room and the gratitude I had for them. I would never put a condition on my friendship with anyone on the basis of what political candidate or party they supported. I wouldn't put that on my friends either—they can be as partisan as they want. That's not what my friendships are based on. I would sacrifice all of that for the sake of my friends.

SHANE: There's a lot to learn from that. We have to have the ability to not forget the little things, you know, of taking care of each other. Little things can become the big things. A problem can because a crisis, and a crisis can become a war. And you know what I think about wars!

How the board members came together over the Obama rally issue reflects the values that have been instilled in the group from the beginning—it grew out of a group of diverse leaders who knew they needed each other if they were going to be able to sustain their work. We bear each other's burdens. We advocate for each other. When there are disagreements, I have seen folks take the biblical idea of "honoring the needs of others above our own" so seriously that they end up championing someone else's perspective, even when they may see things differently, to make sure that person is honored and feels represented and heard, like in this situation with Obama. Some of the folks who didn't want to go to the rally were trying to make sure that some of those who did want to go were able to.

Dietrich Bonhoeffer once said, "The person who's just in love with their vision for community will destroy it. But the person who loves the people around them will create community." We cannot just be in love with the big vision; we have to love the people around us. I've seen enough people who are in love with a vision sit in church growth meetings or social justice circles and tear each other apart in pursuit of the vision or in trying to build a better world.

I am sure there are Catholic priests who love the church more than the people; and there are pastors who love their sermon outlines more than the people in the pews. There are leaders who love their vision more than the people around them and are going to run it into the ground. They end up tearing themselves (and others) apart, trying to build the Kingdom through their own expertise and willpower. One Christian community I visited talked about how they had all sorts of great ideas when they started, but it was the people that made it so difficult. They had a sign on the wall that said, "Everybody wants a revolution . . . but nobody wants to do the dishes." We can't forget the little things, like washing dishes or washing feet.

THERE ARE LEADERS WHO LOVE THEIR VISION MORE THAN THE PEOPLE AROUND THEM.

And we all know how easy it is for meetings to suck the life out of us. I sometimes think if the devil cannot steal our soul, he'll just keep us busy in meetings. I once heard someone say, "God so loved the world that He did not send a committee." God sent Jesus. God got personal, relational, set up His camp among us, became flesh, moved into the neighborhood. That's what we are called to follow—not just a vision but also a God who is personal and intimate and loves individuals just as much as the world.

When a group of leaders come together in a coalition like CCDA, we must ask ourselves, who are we together? Leaders and followers need to ask the same question: Who are we *together?* If we can't love each other and envision what God can do through us together, then how are we going to love the rest of the world? How are we going to change the world?

John: Loving each other within the Christian family of God might just be the greatest thing we can do. Greater love has no one than this. That might be the end we're seeking. That might just be our mission. That might just be what we were left here to do. God's love and the kingdom of God might just be the greatest reflection we have in the world. That might be what our work is directed toward. Our call is to carry the good news of God's love to the end of the world—wouldn't that change the world?

"Let us hear the conclusion of the whole matter: Fear God and keep His commandments [the great commission], for this is man's all. For God will bring every work into judgment, including every secret thing, whether good or evil" (Eccles. 12:13-14).

Everything you were taught can be put into a few words. Respect and obey God. This is what life is all about.

Fear Him—love Him with all your heart, soul and strength and know the terror of the Lord. Obey His commandment—to carry His wonderful love to all ethnic groups to the end of the world. We're not going to be able to obey all the time because of our selfish desires—our sin. But it is our desire that God will be honored. Our desire to obey God opens the door to all of God's graces. Is desiring to obey Him the focus of your life? I get energy from the idea that I might possibly get to be a part of God's plan—man, that feels good.

SHANE: Diversity is not easy. The more diversity—the more differences— you have, the more there is to argue about or see differently. We all gravitate to homogeneity. We are most comfortable around folks who are like us, who speak our language or our culture or economics. I worship in a congregation here in Philly that has all sorts of different people, and so we sing songs from all sorts of traditions—African spirituals and freedom songs, Taize, old hymns . . . and one day someone was complaining to me that they didn't like the worship that week. I said, "Well, praise God, I bet that means that someone else did!"

Maybe that is the "sacrifice" of worship—learning to appreciate that God's choir is a diverse bunch of people, so anytime a song isn't our style, that makes room for someone who has a different style. And there is the generational thing. I get so heartbroken when I speak at events that are filled with young people and not a single person over

60, and then the next week I speak to a Catholic order or a denominational event where I can't see a single person Twittering while I talk. Every person should have someone younger than they are in whom they are pouring their wisdom and life, and every person should have someone older doing the same for them.

John: Older people need hope too. It is difficult when you have lived your whole life one way, and then everything changes. As leaders, we must keep this in mind. We have several older people who have successful businesses, and they contribute a lot of money to our movement—to groups that work with community development. They get a lot of satisfaction when they see young people mobilized. These older people pray too. We need to not just take but also speak into their lives.

Part of what has held me up has been people who have prayed for me and who had hope for me. I don't think that my being able to persevere was based on my intelligence, my story or my charisma. I think it was because so many people prayed and hoped for me and with me. There are a lot of older folks out there who came out of the sixties, maybe they were part of the Jesus Movement, and they have always had a sense of justice, but the church has not been ready. Now we seem to be moving that way, so let's not forget the ones who have been praying and hoping all along.

Gratitude energy is the greatest kind of energy. The daughter of the treasurer for an oil company came to work with me for a week. Seeing the discrepancy between her family's wealth and the poverty in her own country made her angry. I helped settle her down and respond in love to her parents. She ended up getting her parents involved, and her father was part of the backbone of the national movement of CCDA. I helped her and her father focus their efforts toward the poor in gratitude for how they had been blessed.

Okay. I am going on and on about justice and friendship and prayer again (you get the idea as to how important they are). Shane will get us back on track about relationships.

SHANE: I've also had to learn that even as we are all trying to move closer to Jesus, that doesn't mean we are all coming from the same direction or have the same origin . . . it's always a good idea, when you are picking a friend up at the airport, not just to have the time they arrive but to know where they are coming from—you know, the flight details of where, origin city, airline. . . . It's the same for us as we try to lead folks toward Jesus and the gospel life.

Recently, I heard a woman named Shanique speak. She is part of a community in North Carolina that is connected to The Simple Way. She talked about her experience with white folks who see their spiritual journey as one of "downward mobility"—giving away possessions, moving to poor neighborhoods, living simply, giving up the American dream of suburbia, and so on. And then she said, that journey is real and true, but it is not everyone's journey. She went on to speak about her own life as an African-American woman in the South. Her family had been poor. Her family didn't choose community; their survival demanded it. She didn't need a vow of poverty; poverty chose her. She didn't see the redemptive side of suffering, only the stupid side. For her the last becoming first and the first becoming last had a different angle. God was rescuing her from the margins and from the suffering. Perhaps that's exactly why there is movement from the top to the bottom and from the bottom to the top—the last become first and the first become last; the mountains are lowered and the valleys lifted up; the hungry are filled with good things and the rich are sent away empty . . . this is the pattern of the gospel.

Shanique talked about how we have a God of mobility, a God that always keeps us moving. He is a God of exodus. For some of us the exodus is God rescuing us from our riches. For others it is God rescuing us from our poverty. For some, God is rescuing us from our power. And for others, God is rescuing them from their powerlessness. Shanique went on, "There is always a new chapter of the journey. Now I find myself having come out of the oppression and margins. I have had the chance, or *made* the chance, to go to school, get a good job . . . and now perhaps the path takes a new twist, and it is a path of downward mobility—back to my neighborhood, bringing my gifts back to others on the bottom, remembering where I came from and the suffering that still exists." We all have to be forever moving in this Kingdom. We have a God that doesn't let us settle into comfort, but keeps messing with us. As long as there is pain in the world it has to move us.

It seems that there is a place in the middle that is sort of a Kingdom space, like when you were playing tag or hide and seek as a kid and you finally made it to "base." There seems to be a space of reconciliation where rich and poor, oppressed and oppressors, are at the table together as a new creation. Proverbs 30:8 offers a vision where there is "neither poverty nor riches," where folks are not forced to steal out of desperation nor grow complacent in their excess, where there is no more rich and poor, just a family. After all, "reconciliation" is also an economic word. And the communion table is this vision of sharing the food of the poor (bread) and the luxuries of the rich (wine) in a new community where there is this day our daily bread . . . and I guess this day our daily wine. But no room for scarcity or excess.

John: There's something that aggravates me. I really don't like to be in charge of people. I will lead, but I really don't like to manage. I will dream with you, but don't ask me to help you put together your to-do list.

Ultimately, I don't believe that I have the total solution to your problem or anyone's particular predicament. Therefore, I don't really want to be in charge of you. I would rather that you make a contribution both to yourself and to our common task or mission because of who you are, not because I have given you directions. I try to hold in great esteem the dignity of each person. That means you have something valuable to contribute. Maybe your perspective, experience or solution will help me make a decision I need to make.

Humility is part of this equation too—and that is hard to talk about. Missions and church growth expert C. Peter Wagner asks a good question, "Once we declare we are humble, have we ceased being humble?" Nonetheless, I really don't want to over-exalt myself. Being in charge of someone is an exalted position. I don't want you to depend upon me. By nature, a person is exalted over someone who needs what he or she has. If I own the pond and you need the fish in the pond to survive, you are dependent upon me and I am exalted over you.

Of course, we need each other, so this question of exaltation and dependency needs to be worked out. And we need to always be moving to a place where each of us takes responsibility for ourselves. That is true leadership. Think about a baby. Parents are so happy when their baby walks for the first time. Of course it is cute, but think about it. When a child walks, he or she takes greater responsibility and is less dependent. Sure, the child will fall down a few times, but it only takes him a few days to be walking all over the place. When a child sees his or her parents excited, he takes more steps and learns fast. Soon enough, when the child falls, he doesn't even want you to pick him up. Once the child walks, the parents' relationship with that child changes. Rather than endlessly changing diapers and all of that other stuff, now they can also play together. Soon enough there's a certain amount of independence. (My great-grandson just started walking this summer— what a feeling that is!)

When we hire somebody, I'm anxious because he or she is going to be depending too much on me. Of course the person needs to be trained and get a clear job description. The tasks and goals must be communicated. We can't expect a person to know by osmosis what to do. Training is part of equipping, enabling and lifting a person to a place where we do not need to be in charge of him or her. I will help a person take the first baby steps, but soon enough he needs to be walking on his own. We all need to be in charge of ourselves and, ultimately, it is God who is in charge of all.

SHANE: That's good! I am going to write that one down. I think that I approach this in a similar way. I don't like to micromanage everybody, but I sure like delegating. The best leaders I know sure know how to work themselves out of a job and give it away. In fact, when somebody identifies a need or task that has to be done, I say, "Well, God must be calling you to do it." As the old saying goes, *Be the change you want to see.* So there's no room for complaining, groaning or murmuring.

St. Benedict talks about two things that destroy community— murmuring and idleness. We need to wake up to meaningful work and mission, and some people need structure for that. They don't just go out and find things that need to get done. And murmuring is lethal. There is no room for negativity and complaining. We either need to use every ounce of energy we have to change something that is wrong, or we need to stop complaining. Benedict even goes on to say that doesn't mean that when someone complains, their complaint is unjustified or untrue; it just means that nothing is going to change until they lead things in a different direction. As we said, the best critique of something that is wrong is the practice of something better. Living this way doesn't mean that your complaint is unjustified or that there's not a problem, it just means you should change it.

John: As leaders, we should love and nurture people into a place of self-responsibility. Sometimes a misperception of loyalty can get in the way of this nurturing and releasing of followers. It is not uncommon for managers, bosses and executives to grow nervous or even angry if they detect even the slightest hint of disloyalty among employees or followers. Sometimes this friction is our (the leader's) own fault because we have expected them to be just like us. Sometimes we are holding on to the person or employee when we should be letting go. Sometimes it is not disloyalty at all, but simply the baby eagle ready to fly, and we are holding them back—sometimes even in a stranglehold—because of our own selfish need for loyalty.

If we truly have in mind the best interests of those who follow us, then we will nurture them every day they are with us, no matter how short or long, then cheer them on to the next thing God has for them, whether that is in our group or cause, or someplace far away. Loyalty doesn't mean a person will be just like us, do only what we say or be on our team forever. Loyalty means a person contributes with who they are and what talents they have to make us all better.

SHANE: This is so important because we need people who complete our vision, and often that person will see things differently. If everybody just rallies behind us and shouts "Amen" to everything we say, then we're never going to move into the place of imagination, of reinventing and of rethinking.

We need people with the spiritual gift of frustration. Yes, the Church needs sanctified dissention. We need people who see what is wrong. But they can't just be naysayers; they need to be a part of the change and a part of leading us out of what's wrong to what's right. The best dissenters in the Roman Catholic Church become saints. Look at St. Francis. He left everything behind. Originally the pope said to Francis, "Go preach to pigs. Maybe they'll listen to you." But then the pope had a vision in which he saw the side of the church falling and Francis was holding it up. The pope called St. Francis back and eventually blessed the early Franciscan brothers. He said, "Keep repairing the Church."

Some of my best partners in community are people who are not necessarily my best buds. But they challenge me in the best sense of sharpening iron or refining gold; they purify my vision and motives. They'll say, "Why would we do that?" I can remember at one point there was a journalist who wanted to come visit The Simple Way. He was one of these big-time journalists and he wanted to do a story on our community. Sometimes we've been too quick to say yes.

SOME OF MY BEST PARTNERS IN COMMUNITY ARE PEOPLE WHO ARE NOT NECESSARILY MY BEST BUDS.

There are many journalists who want to do stories on "New Monasticism" or "The Simple Way," and we have become very sensitive to the dangers of this. Usually they want to portray the relocating white folks like myself as saints, saviors and sacrificial heroes moving into a poor neighborhood. *This is garbage and incredibly hurtful to the dignity of our neighbors.* We try to be "as shrewd as snakes and as innocent as doves" (Matt. 10:16). We do not allow cameras in the neighborhood. For instance, a network has wanted to do a story for two years now, and I have insisted that we will only do the story with them if it is in our New Jerusalem Community (40 people here in Philly), which is composed of and led by 90 percent people of color. The producer has insisted that they do it at our Potter Street Community (the original house, mostly white, where I live). So we will not do the story.

When this one reporter wanted to come, we all talked, and one of the people in the community said, "We need to be really careful with this." After thinking it over, we said, "Let's not commit to the story. Let's bring the reporter in and see if we can trust him to tell the real story."

So that journalist ended up coming to our community and he did a story on one of my neighbors, and he did a story on the old folks. We've got these seniors that make blankets for us to give out every winter. Those are the stories that made their headlines. Simple Way didn't even get mentioned. And I love it. That's the kind of creativity you can have when a group of people put their heads together and troubleshoot rather than simply going, "Bring in the journalist, whatever."

On another occasion, we had a major disagreement within our community about whether to have the Internet. Technology has always been tricky for us in our quest to live simply. There are decisions that have come really easy, like the decision to "kill our TV," so we got rid of the television. But the Internet was trickier. On the one hand, one of the folks in the community felt passionately that we should not have Internet access because most of our neighbors did not have this privilege, and this "digital divide" has contributed significantly to the economic inequities in the world. Folks who have access to technology continue to get exponentially more efficient, while those without technology are left miles behind. All that is true. And yet another person in the community felt strongly that for those very reasons we needed to have public Internet, and in fact was willing to run cable and transmitters throughout the neighborhood so everyone had wireless access, so our kids could use the Internet to do their homework the same as kids in the suburbs.

Well, it is times like that where we face a decision in communities that we need good leadership. We can reach a stalemate or split a community over a disagreement like this (and lest it seem ridiculous, all we need to do is look at a few church-splits to see that congregations have split over much more ridiculous things . . . like whether to have a heater in the baptistery). But community offers an opportunity to try and create a "third way," to think creatively and bring everybody's voice and vision to the table.

In this situation with the Internet question, we ended up doing both. Some members in our community lived without the Internet as a sort of act of solidarity or a technology "fast." Others spent their energy creating wireless access for neighbors. Likewise, we had folks that worked hard to live fuel-free lives and even went to the food bank with a bike and trailer (my buddy could haul 500 pounds of food on a bike). Others helped buy cars so we could run neighbors to appointments or take kids to the beach (my buddy couldn't pull that one off on a bike) . . . and others converted engines to run off waste veggie oil. That's the gift of community, different gifts in one Body, and how our vision can be made more complete.

One thing you notice as you look at communities in crisis or organizations that collapse is that the group often gets polarized by one or two people who have very strong opinions and hold the rest of the community hostage, in a stalemate of sorts. This can especially be true when leaders try to create horizontal rather than vertical power—by that I mean trying to lead by empowering and making room for every voice to influence decisions . . . making decisions by consensus.

We have experimented with a leadership style in our community called "consensus minus one." Consensus minus one means that everyone in the community agrees that they will not be a lone ranger, that no single person will block the community from moving forward on a decision everyone else feels good about. Some would argue it's also a good reason to get married, so your partner will have your back (or they may be the one standing in the way!). Ha-ha. And it is still a community-based, horizontal-power model of consensus decision making. Each of us essentially says, I will not stand alone; if what I feel is really coming from a place, not of self-interest, but of a concern for others and for the community, there should be others who agree (or at least one other person).

We really have to be creative as leaders if we are going to create alternative forms of governance and power to those in the world around us; if we are not going to "lord over each other the way the Gentiles do." Horizontal power . . . community . . . these things take work and imagination. Tyranny doesn't take any imagination. It's like violence—it's the way of Pharaoh and Caesar. We are to be different from the empire.

Not long ago, I was on my way to speak at a Quaker boarding school outside Philadelphia, and as I headed out, I got a phone call to inform me that there had been an incident on campus and several of the students had been caught with large amounts of marijuana. So the campus was quite emotionally charged. I sort of expected to come into the assembly that morning to face a student body that was ticked off at its administration. Little did I know that I was about to experience one of the most profound exercises in good leadership I had ever seen.

That morning, the dean of the school had sat down with the students and their families, and even with a group of other students sitting in as peers as they all simply tried to listen to the Spirit as to what to do (Quakers are good at that).

The official rules would have had the students automatically expelled, even arrested. If they were expelled, it would permanently mess up their future chances, and some of these kids already had the deck stacked against them for a lot of years. So this school was trying to do things differently. Without trivializing bad mistakes like this, they wanted mercy to triumph over judgment, as the Scriptures say.[2]

Lots of tears were shed. And then the administration made a beautiful gesture of grace. They decided not to contact the police, and they opted to allow the parents to withdraw their children from the school voluntarily, thereby avoiding expulsion. It was a moving thing to witness. One of the kids who had been caught with the drugs said, with tears in his eyes, that he was glad he had been caught, because he had a problem and was not able to control it on his own.

When the dean recounted the events during the assembly, she began to cry. You could tell that she hurt with those kids. And when she had finished the announcement, the entire school rose to their feet in a gentle applause. That's the sort of brokenness we need, not an iron fist, but the heart that breaks for the people we love. I went ahead and preached that morning, but the dean had given the only sermon needed that day.

Community has also taught me how much I often act out of my own white man-ness . . . even when I don't know it. Jesus had a way of really challenging the powerful and empowering the women and the marginalized. We have a lot to learn about that in our world that is still so dominated by white guys and testosterone.

We had a woman who was coming out of a situation of domestic violence move in to the intentional community house here with her two kids. The kids' dad found out where they were and started threatening our house, saying he was going to burn it down. Those are times when you think to yourself, *Maybe we should have thought this through a little bit.* So there was a restraining order and she had to go meet him at the police station to deliver her kids (we were still working on that part).

Every time she would go to meet him, he knew where she was walking from and would cut her off and do horrible things to her and the kids. So we sat down as a community to troubleshoot the situation. All the guys spoke up and decided that we needed to escort her. So we did. As soon as he saw us, his defenses went up. He started yelling and cussing, instinctively threatening to kill us. It was terrible. Here we are, a bunch of Christ-following peacemakers, facing off with a dude who was anything but a pacifist . . . he was about to pass-a-fist through our faces.

After that we regrouped as a community. What did we learn? The women spoke up. They pointed out gently but without trepidation that we were thinking out of our masculinity, trying to use the same tools of intimidation and coercion as he was. The next day they went with the woman and her children. And it was magical. This guy was totally disarmed, even stunned. He didn't know what to do. He wasn't about to try to fight four women. That's another one of those times when we see the gift of different people working together to solve a problem, making mistakes together and listening to each other . . . learning as we go.

That's one of those places where we need to listen, and learn, and make sure those most affected by the problems are leading us. You know, I actually don't understand domestic violence. Imagine a bunch of white folks trying to lead the civil rights movement.

EVERYONE HAS A PART TO PLAY,
BUT WE HAVE TO MAKE SURE
THERE IS SPACE FOR OTHERS
TO PLAY THEIR PART.

Imagine a movement of well-intentioned men trying to lead the fight for women's rights. These might be good ideas, but they're not going to work that way. We have to work together. Everyone has a part to play, including white guys, but we also have to make sure there is space for others to play their part.

John: As people like Shane and so many others have come around me, hoped for me and believed in me, I have come to realize how privileged I am. At the start of my ministry, I didn't see this. Like many young folks, I took for granted people's time and didn't appreciate how much it would mean to have some of the same people stand with me through the years. When we are young and the whole world is ahead of us, we don't see these things so well. As I have grown older, I have tried to live that hoping for others, as so many have hoped for me.

As a leader, I have felt a sense of being responsible for those who follow, and passing along this hope. I had a feeling that my mentors, those I had followed, had entrusted something beautiful in me. It was my obligation to do the same.

The biggest part of being trusted as a leader comes through prayer, hope and just staying with a person over the long haul. Of course, it can include financial support. There was an old couple in California, a white couple, who became my friends. They would give Vera Mae and me $400 a month, which for them was a lot of money. When he died, we found out that he had named us in his will.

There was an older black lady; she didn't have much money, but she named us in her will. These people had helped me when they were alive and then remembered me in their deaths. I felt a responsibility to press forward with the hope they had seen in me and hoped for me. I feel a responsibility not only to those who have gone before me, but also for the next generation. Part of being faithful is not only what we do now but also what others will do later. I try not to think about that too much because it can become overwhelming, but I do think about it. It is almost a burden.

My friends mean well, and many try to help me with this burden. Some nudge me to simply live out my life in simplicity and faithfulness; others want me to do something to secure a legacy. I do not worry so much about legacy. Vera Mae is quick to remind me that I have enough significance in this life. I try to help people find significance. There is a great amount of need for significance in the lives of successful people. The reason people have supported my mission over the past 50 years is that they want personal significance and fulfillment. Everyone has three basic needs: the need to be loved, the need to belong and the need for significance.

I'm living out my life hoping that indigenous people everywhere can emerge and find significance. I think so much about that and probably need to relax more.

I have some great friends who tell me they want to help me finish well. One of them is a businessman from Texas. Malcolm Street recently said, "For you to finish well, all you have to do is think about just being faithful and keep nurturing your relationship with your children and your family. Don't overburden yourself by thinking about all these other things. Just focus on those." The thought of simply being faithful has given me a sense of relief. I always think that I've got to help fix everything, but of course, I cannot. However, I can be faithful. It is a good lesson.

Our CCDA board talked about being faithful to future generations by bringing in young folks. That is good, but I think I would go on to identifying the gifts and strengths of individuals and then try to match them with needs. And that's when it becomes burdensome. I am seeing more and more that I can be faithful without actually carrying the burden.

Jesus tells us to take His burden. Knowing that there are thousands of other people around the country involved with CCDA who share my burden for the poor and oppressed makes it easier to carry.

SHANE: As followers of Christ and as leaders of others we need the character of Jesus poured into us. What a precious thing it is to be part of a cloud of witnesses—to find ourselves in a story that is big and ancient, to have a faith that has been passed on for generations and generations.

There's a place where Paul says to his young disciple Timothy, "I thank God, whom I serve, as my forefathers did . . . recalling your tears. I long to see you. . . . *I have been reminded of your sincere faith, which first lived in your grandmother Lois and in your mother Eunice and, I am persuaded, now lives in you also"* (2 Tim. 1:3-5, *NIV*, emphasis added). I love that. The faith that lived in someone else lives in us, and then it gets passed on to a new generation through us. In this passage in 2 Timothy, Paul makes sure Timothy gets that. He tells Timothy to take the things that he has learned and entrust them to a few reliable disciples. He is to pass on the things he has learned to a few others, and each of them to a few. And that's how this thing seems to happen. It's worked pretty well for the last few thousand years.

John: I have a quote for you: "Leadership is known by the personalities it enriches. It is not a matter of hypnosis, blandishment or 'salesmanship.' It is a matter of leading out from within individuals those impulses, motives and efforts which they discover to represent themselves most truly."[3] Most people create organizations for themselves so that they can do something for the people. More effective organizations and leaders will get the people they're helping involved. It drives me crazy when I talk to a person and they tell me their plans haven't included anyone else! They think they can be the thinker and the doer. We need other people involved!

That's the ingenuity of the church model. We are the Body of Christ, and everyone within the Body has gifts to share. We surround ourselves with a diverse Body that will fill in the holes we leave because of our own humanity. God made us weak so that we are forced to rely on the support of each other and, of course, God.

Notes

1. Check out www.jmpf.org for more information.
2. See James 2:13.
3. Harold W. Reed, *Dynamics of Leadership: Open the Door to Your Leadership Potential* (Vero Media, Inc., 1982).

EXCELLENCE

(Leading with Pizzazz)

SHANE: I want to say a little something about excellence. One of the things that happens when we work in poor communities in the midst of crises, scrambling for resources, is that we end up cutting corners and doing things with mediocrity. This is tricky when we talk about leadership. On the one hand, I heard a veteran inner city pastor talk about how we have to make room for people to fail, to make mistakes and try new things. He laughed and said one of their mottos is, "If it's worth doing, it's worth doing poorly." By that he meant, before you can do something well, like walk or ride a bike, you have to fall down a few times. And that is true. On the other hand, one of the things poor communities suffer deeply from is mediocrity. Our thrift stores only have other people's scraps, and the soup kitchens aren't always known for the quality of their food. The neighborhoods and schools are often run very poorly, with trash, graffiti and ugliness everywhere. It starts to wear on your dignity.

I sort of feel strange saying it, but one of the things I learned about working at both Willow Creek in Chicago and with Mother Teresa in Calcutta—is this idea of "excellence unto God." Now it looked very different in those two contexts. At Willow Creek, there is a conviction that Christian art should not be a "D" version of secular art with Christian language. Dramas done in worship should not be corny skits that you cannot really hear. Christian music shouldn't be so terrible. I remember hearing Rich Mullins talk about how folks will come up to him and say, "God gave me this song and I want to share it with you," and he would listen to the song and understand why God gave it away!

It seems that there is something to say about this sort of excellence—that we should use our gifts and we should lead others in ways that we end up spreading beauty. Our sermons, our music, our art should be beautiful—like that of the great composers; like that of a symphony or opera. On the other hand, if we aren't careful, there are holes in this commitment to excellence. There is a degree of so-called privilege with being able to pull off a beautiful event or worship service—a privilege of time and resources that make it possible, and even some bias on what is beauty (for instance I've been to some really beautiful hip-hop services . . . and to some ugly ones). In our quest for excellence, we can end up obsessing with some of the outward stuff and neglecting the inward, like the Pharisees, where we end up looking good on the outside but don't have any soul. We end up ripping each other apart every time a microphone squeaks or something goes wrong in the service. So there has to be some balance in this excellence thing.

MOTHER TERESA HAD A
DEEP CONVICTION THAT WHEN YOU
GIVE TO THE POOR, YOU SHOULD
GIVE YOUR VERY BEST.

Now, there is another dimension of this that I learned in Calcutta. Mother Teresa spoke of doing things with excellence unto Jesus, and she did not settle for mediocrity, especially when it came to caring for the poor. It was a great irony, because the sisters were so poor and had very little resources—oftentimes they didn't even have basic medications—but that didn't matter. She said that everything they really needed was given by God. On the one hand, I saw people reprimanded (nicely) for using too much soap and wasting resources; and on the other hand, I saw volunteers get scolded for not putting enough gravy on the rice they were giving to the poor.

Mother Teresa had this deep conviction that when you give to the poor you should give your very best, because you are doing it to Jesus. Don't give your scrap clothing; give your best pair of pants or shoes to the homeless. Don't feed them rice with a skimpy amount of gravy and no vegetables—you are feeding a king . . . so do it with excellence. It seems this, too, has something to teach us as leaders.

I have a friend here in Philadelphia who lives in a really tough neighborhood, and he throws the most fantastic block parties on the planet. He's got this radical philosophy of excellence unto God and unto the poor. He combines the best of Willow with the best of Mother Teresa. When he throws a block party he will have some of the best musicians—jazz players, harpists, rappers—and some of the finest circus performers (I performed once but have since been replaced by better performers . . . no hard feelings, though I did remove him from our Board of Directors . . . just kidding). He knows how to throw a party. At Christmas he sets up a candlelight banquet, free of course, where families and their kids come and are served a top-notch four-course meal, and listen to live music.

It seems that the banquet of God is exactly this kind of excellence—but it is critical that it is a feast of, with, and for the most marginalized. That's what the Jubilee festivals were about, and why the prophet Amos scolded the people for making it simply a feast for the rich. And that's what the early Christian agape meals were, and why Paul scolded the Corinthian church for desecrating the Lord's table when some people indulged while others went hungry.[1] So as leaders we need to wrestle with this idea of excellence. Excellence should never be an idol or privilege or something we tear people apart over, or a reason we do not let people learn to use their gifts and make mistakes. And yet we can never settle for mediocrity and ugly art and bad food for the homeless. As leaders, we need to make excellence available to the poor. Small things done with great love—that means trying to welcome the poor as if we were welcoming Jesus . . . because we are.

John: I was the youngest of six children, and my mother died when I was seven months old. My father dropped the five of us off at his mother's home and went off to find another woman—another life. We lived in rural Mississippi as sharecroppers.[2] Growing up in this system, I learned how to work hard. When I left Mississippi and went to California I started out as a janitor, and worked very hard. I learned to take great pride in making sure things were spotless and neat. Excellence, even in cleaning the bathroom, was a driving force in my work.

For me, coming to know God was coming to know the creator. I didn't have to look far to see that God is a God of excellence. Genesis 1 records God's response to what He had created each day: "It was good." I liked that about God, but didn't always find excellence in the church, particularly when it came to education. While the people in California churches sought excellence in their work, their family lives and their schools, when I came back to Mississippi the leaders weren't quite that way. Many preachers assumed that their black congregants couldn't read or write and therefore needed animated, expressive, passionate preaching. They relied on emotion to communicate the gospel and depended on emotional responses from their followers. At times I have been critical of this approach, but as I grow older I have begun to see the value in it. When I look back at how much of the white church's resources went toward upholding a racist system— encouraging and institutionalizing discrimination for two centuries— it's amazing the black race didn't go insane. I would have assumed that we would have become Quakers . . . that would have been the natural reaction! Instead, we adopted the Protestant faith of our oppressors. That proves the demonic nature of racism.

As blacks gained education and economic opportunities during the civil rights movement, I was both delighted and discouraged. Of course, I was encouraged by positive changes in society at large, but I saw that Christian thinkers and leaders oftentimes were less prepared for the changes than they should have been. While they preached Jesus as the Savior of the world and did a fabulous job at it, they didn't give much thought, study or conversation to how the world Jesus was saving was changing. To be ready for change and really connect with people, we must not only study Greek and Hebrew and topical application but also the hearts and dreams and hurts and voids of the people.

That has been a driving force in my life. I'm a third-grade drop out and I've never had higher education, per se. (Though I am self-educated and have never stopped learning.) So I don't set out to deliver a polished, intellectual or bookish sermon that dazzles people with big words, a rocket-science-type analysis or a poetic cadence. I simply want to communicate the word of God and His love in a way that is un-derstandable. This type of excellence is what I desire.

When I candidly troubleshoot problems I see (especially in the Church), sometimes people think that I'm putting them down or that

I am too negative. I don't see it that way. I'm trying to fix problems. Particularly Christians don't have enough gumption to accept criticism. Without proper criticism, there is no understanding of problems. Without understanding the predicament, there is no solving it . . . I hate to see good people waste their lives.

TO CONNECT WITH PEOPLE, WE MUST STUDY THE HEARTS, DREAMS, HURTS AND VOIDS OF THE PEOPLE.

When I was a teen, there were some good young folks in my town who were over-praised for natural abilities. Because of this their self-discipline didn't develop. This often happens with athletes, but can happen with anyone. An athlete might be able to throw a baseball 90 miles an hour, but talent alone isn't going to get him to the big leagues. He has to have discipline. I come from the era when people tied hard work, discipline and excellence together. I played ball with guys who were later drafted into the big leagues. Those guys had discipline to work at their baseball skills harder, train longer and play until they won.

Athletes place high expectations on themselves as a motivator to push them through to the next level. Sometimes I see kids playing basketball. They don't want to lose; they want to be the next Kobe. But even the stars know that no one can always win. Sometimes Lance Armstrong loses. The Yankees lose. Even Tiger Woods loses. This possibility of not making the cut is always there and must be part of what drives athletes to constantly improve on their game. Jackie Robinson, for instance, could never have broken down the color barrier in baseball without his competitive spirit and his drive toward excellence. He didn't simply open the door—he blew the hinges off. When you are the best at what you do, color barriers suddenly disappear. Muhammad Ali was excellent in and out of the ring. He was the greatest. Tony Dungy is the best at coaching. He won the Super Bowl with dignity and poise . . . then he gave God the credit. I like that.

I don't just fault the kids when they do not work hard or pursue excellence; I also fault the leaders. As leaders, we have to pull the best out of the people. We have to instill in them this idea of purpose and show them what quality means. This has to be part of our philosophy of ministry. Last year, I had a problem when I called out some kids who I didn't feel were being excellent. They got broken up about it and their feelings were hurt. The problem was that their leader hadn't established an expectation of excellence. It was my fault that I had called for a standard of excellence but failed to nurture my leaders so that they could transfer that expectation of excellence to our students. It goes down the chain. A standard of excellence is not enough. We also must have a system to build up an expectation of excellence.

As a society—and as a church—we have become so individualistic that our communal expectations have been lowered. The community is so weak that we have lost the authority to establish expectations. There's more to being poor than poverty. Poor people can pick up trash, not park cars on their lawns and take care of their homes. There can be expectations, but we can't communicate high expectations without authority. The church once had authority to set the standard of the "village"—for whites and for blacks. Then, with integration, many black church leaders left for better neighborhoods and rented out their old houses. As absentee landlords, they lost interest in their former neighborhood. Not only did urban and poor areas lose their best models of excellence when these leaders moved on, but they also lost the practical motivator of home ownership. It doesn't take a rocket scientist to figure out that, in general, renters will not keep their homes up as well as home owners. Renters don't have a stake in the property; owners do.

We're in the mega-church era, and I think we need to challenge that. The mega-church model will probably outlast me, maybe for another couple more generations. Now the mega-church does have some excellence . . . high-end sound systems, big-screen overhead projections and air conditioning that always works. Of course, this is not always bad. But there is a cost. Just because we have some pizzazz doesn't mean we are excellent on all fronts. For decades now we have broadcast our sermons, and now we have them on the Internet (podcasting). Yes, we reach lots of people through television and radio, but we lack touch. Yet that's what we crave as humans. We need a hug. We need a kiss. We need to be loved. We have to continue to challenge the Church to touch people at the community level. Just the touch is not enough though—there also needs to be nurturing. We can't lose our mission for each others. Actually touching and nurturing the people we want to reach is part of being excellent.

Notes

1. Scholars say that one of the things happening in Corinth was that the Early Christians would have these feasts with communion and dinner in their homes, but often the wealthier folks who could afford to miss work would show up first and already have eaten and busted open the wine . . . before the poor even made it to the meal!
2. Sharecropping is a system whereby a landowner allows a third party to use his land in return for a share of the crops produced on the land. It was widespread in the South during the first half of the twentieth century.

POWER

(Separating God's and Ours)

John: There is no denying it: as leaders, we have power. As public figures, we have power. As people who have a purpose, we have power. As believers who read the Bible, we have real power. How do we use this power?

I'm primarily a Bible teacher from Mississippi, so I may get to preaching a little here. This wonderful gospel *is* the power of God to bring about salvation and deliverance for God's people. That's us. His Word leads us to freedom. It worked for Moses and the Jewish people when they were freed from bondage in Egypt, and it works today. But sometimes I fear that we have taken God's powerful Word and have mixed it into our culture in such a way that the gospel has lost its power . . . and sometimes we have tried to claim the power as our own, thus contaminating it and, in essence, rendering it powerless. That's not the way it is supposed to be. So it is up to us as leaders to tap real power if we want to lead people anywhere, let alone to freedom.

I want to be a doer of the Word, not just a hearer. Of course, we need to hear the Word. But if we only listen and maybe talk about it a little, we fool ourselves into thinking that we are doing a good deed for God. If we have a way with words or can preach with charisma, we can repeat God's words and have followers, but they actually will just be hearers—like the leader, the followers will only hear the Word. When we hear the Word but don't do the Word, we deceive ourselves and risk misleading others.

I'm a third-grade dropout, but once I came to know Jesus Christ, I earnestly wanted to study the Bible. I wanted to go to theological school, too. I thought I could enroll, but of course somebody informed me that a guy without a high school diploma—and not even a GED—couldn't get through seminary. Not to be dissuaded, I accepted an invitation from Mr. Leitch, a man in my church, to study under him. For three years, two days a week, I would spend two hours or so examining Scripture and learning the great truths that would guide my life. This was in California, and I was working full-time in the business world at the time. So I do not have much patience for people who tell me they have no time to study God's Word.

This man discipled me around two basic passages of Scripture: Acts 1:8 and 2 Timothy 2:2. The Acts text is key, because it includes the last words of Jesus after His Resurrection and before He returned to heaven. Jesus had been here. He had dwelt among us, walking with His disciples for three and a half years. Then He walked with them for another 40 days after the Resurrection. During that time, He taught about the kingdom of God. Finally, He was ready to send His followers into the world to become what He called "salt and light." They were to be His messengers, His voice. Today we talk a lot about being the voice of the voiceless, which is good, but we are also to be Jesus' "voice." Jesus' last words to His disciples were: "But you shall receive *power*" (Acts 1:8, emphasis added). He had already told Pontius Pilate that there was no power other than the power ordained of God.[1] So to move forward in real power, we must be Jesus' voice and proclaim the gospel in word and in deeds.

When Jesus started His ministry, He said, "The Spirit of the LORD is upon Me, because He has anointed Me to preach the gospel to the poor" (Luke 4:18). Paul said, "I am not ashamed of the gospel of Christ, for it is the *power* of God to salvation" (Rom. 1:16, emphasis added). God transfers His power through the gospel, for the preaching of the cross is to them that perish foolishness, but unto us who are saved, it is the *power* of God.[2]

As God's people, we are supposed to be the ones who transform and transfer that power . . . specifically among the poor and oppressed. A primary way we show evidence of that power is through our attitude toward the poor. Do we visit the fatherless and the widows? Do we remember the least of those among us? Do we feed the hungry? Do we clothe the naked? That's preaching the gospel to the poor, and that's why we are here.

How do we move from hearing this word to doing it? Jesus said, "All authority has been given to Me in heaven and on earth" (Matt. 28:18). How does He transfer that power to us? Jesus said to the disciples, "You shall receive power when the Holy Spirit has come upon you; and you shall be witnesses to Me in Jerusalem, and in all Judea and in Samaria, and to the end of the earth" (Acts 1:8). It's clear that the gospel was supposed to burn through racial, cultural and economic barriers and rescue people. The gospel is two sides of one coin: it is both hearing it and acting upon it. It is both faith and works.

THE GOSPEL IS SUPPOSED TO BURN THROUGH RACIAL, CULTURAL AND ECONOMIC BARRIERS AND RESCUE PEOPLE.

An example of transferring His power is found in the life and the ministry of a guy named Nehemiah. In his day, Jerusalem looked like the Los Angeles riots; its gates are burned with fire. Nehemiah says, "Come and let us build the wall of Jerusalem, that we may no longer be a reproach" (Neh. 2:17). That's a message for all of us. Let's form the big coalition together. Come, let us, the Christians, rebuild the walls of America so that we, the Christians, may no longer be a reproach. I say this because the Church as it exists today is somewhat of a reproach. We don't have a strong witness in our culture or to people in places of power.

The children of Israel had been held captive in Babylon because they did not practice God's pattern of justice based upon Jubilee . . . which mandated that every 50 years the people would go free. There is no record that the Jewish community ever kept this Sabbatical year of Jubilee. And because they did not keep it, God sent them into captivity for 70 years. After the 70 years, God freed them to go back home. That's when Nehemiah came along—after they had been back in their country for about 40 years . . . trying to rebuild the city.

The children of Israel had the best Bible teachers they had ever produced when they returned from captivity. We call these teachers the Minor Prophets. During captivity, Zerubbabel, Ezra and others had spent day after day soaking up the Word, studying God's ways. But good, solid teaching was not enough to turn things around. That's where Nehemiah came in. Nehemiah was the kind of guy who I would like to be. He knew how power was transferred from God to people and to the next generation.

There are three primary ways in which we connect with the power of God. The first way is through prayer (which is why Shane and I have devoted an entire conversation to it). When Nehemiah heard about the sad condition of his people, he went into prayer for about four months . . . and then he acted. Prayer comes before action. It is through prayer that we come to know that we know God. Prayer is the assurance that the power we seek is from God, and it is the way we begin the process of releasing the power of God. So Nehemiah prayed with humility, which is essential to authentic prayer, and in that humility God's power was released. Through prayer, he took responsibility for the pain he perceived and accepted responsibility for the vision God had given him.

Sometimes when we see big problems all around us, we feel overwhelmed or anxious. It might be reasonable for us to hesitate before jumping in to lead people out of their pain. Nehemiah no doubt had these same feelings as he looked around his city and at his people. But he didn't use prayer as an excuse for not acting immediately. Sometimes people say, "Ah, that is too bad about your surgery. I will pray for you." But then they don't pray, nor do they send a note, nor do they build a wheelchair ramp. For some, "I will pray for you" becomes a convenient excuse to *not* act.

Real prayer is this: "Lord, what would You have me to do?" Real prayer is that His kingdom would come, that His will would be done here on earth. That's how Nehemiah prayed, and that's how we must pray. So, if we want to have the power to lead people to freedom, we must first be people of prayer.

The second way in which we connect with the power of God is by understanding and managing our time. Nehemiah prayed for four months, and then, when the time was right, he acted. The Bible says that now is the time to act—in fact, Romans 13:11 adds some urgency: "And that, knowing the time, that now it is high time to awake out of sleep: for now is our salvation nearer than when we believed" (*KJV*).

This is the moment for the Church to act because our problems are bigger than our economic system can carry, bigger than our political system can solve, bigger than our educational system can resolve. So now, we need God involved. What did Nehemiah do? He prayed. He went directly to the divine power source, and once he was connected with God's power, he went directly to the earthly place of power . . . the king. Without flinching or stuttering, he asked the king to let him go back to Jerusalem and rebuild the wall. Nehemiah knew his assignment. He had vision. Now was the time to carry out that vision.

> THIS IS THE MOMENT FOR THE CHURCH
> TO ACT BECAUSE OUR PROBLEMS
> ARE BIGGER THAN OUR ECONOMIC
> SYSTEMS CAN CARRY.

The third way we connect with the power of God is by counting the cost. Nehemiah counted the cost. He understood the materials, the labor and the time he would need in order to rebuild the wall. Likewise, as leaders we cannot jump into a vision blindly; we have to count the cost. If the vision is for reconciliation in the Inner City and among the poor, we have to understand that one cost will be moving back into that community. We've got to relocate. We've got to use the power of God to get reconciled and cut out the fears of gangs, racial stereotyping and other worries. Racism, for one, ought to be obsolete. This is the first time in the history of the world that all the walls of racism can fall.

But that's a wickedness in this country: it accommodated slavery and, in some places, it still accommodates racism. We have not repudiated that. We have not repented of that. Barack Obama offered an apology, but is that enough? Or do we need to use Solomon's words: "If My people who are called by My name will humble themselves, and pray and seek My face, and turn from their wicked ways, then I will hear from heaven, and will forgive their sin and heal their land" (2 Chron. 7:14).

Nehemiah refused to let his enemies distract him from the task at hand. The naysayers tried to do so from the time he got there, just like Shane experienced in Philadelphia. Nehemiah's enemies tried to deflect his eyes from the task that he had agreed with the king to perform. His foes tried to get him to break his word, but he wouldn't talk with them. He kept his eyes on the task. And after about 12 years, he finished the wall.

That sounds about right. In my experience, most good things take about 10 to 12 years to build. We have found in Christian community development that leadership doesn't begin to emerge from the community until we've been there for at least a decade. That means we have to commit ourselves—no fly-by-night leaders allowed. Most real problems will not be solved with a two-year or three-year plan. We've got to be present with the idea of giving our lives over time.

We all see how urban communities of America lie in waste. The gates are burned with fire. So I'm asking you to join with me to demonstrate God's power in the Mississippi Delta and everywhere. Henry Ford said, "Coming together is the beginning. Working together is progress. Staying together is success." Now that's power!

Notes
1. See John 19:8-15.
2. See 1 Corinthians 1:18.

NOTORIETY

(Squinting in the Limelight)

SHANE: Let's talk about fame, or notoriety, for a moment. One of the things I've seen in some people who start to become leaders or think they want to be leaders—especially young folks who rise pretty quickly into some sort of influence—is that their tendency is either to get infatuated with themselves or to do the opposite and sabotage themselves. They undermine their own influence. Both ways of handling notoriety are dangerous and reactionary. And neither one is rooted in the Spirit.

If God should choose to use us, then that'awesome. He can use any one of us; after all, we have a God who uses the weak things to shame the strong and the foolish to confound the wise.[1] Look in the New Testament at the sorts of leaders Jesus raised up. They weren't even good fishermen . . . always "mending their nets." He didn't go after the cream of the crop, the powerful, the capable. He went after the willing, the empty, the desperate folks who had nothing to lose. The late singer-songwriter Rich Mullins used to talk about how much we can learn from the story of Balaam and his donkey, referring to that old story in the Hebrew Scriptures where God literally spoke to Balaam through his donkey.[2] Rich said, "What I learned from that is God spoke to Balaam through his ass and God's been speaking through asses ever since."

So if God should choose to use us, then great, we shouldn't think too highly of ourselves. God can speak through donkeys and rocks. And if, on meeting someone, we think to ourselves, *God could never use them*, we should think again.

In the basement of our building, I have a prayer room. I hang different prayers on the walls. One of them is "Dear God, forgive me for thinking too highly of myself." And then it says, "Dear God, forgive me for thinking too lowly of myself." And then it says, "Dear God, forgive me for thinking of myself so much." That's the journey. Let's remember God, and let's remember who we are.

John: Sometimes leaders get infatuated with their own success. They start believing their own press. They get caught up with their own words, rhetoric and self-importance. And they think that gives them some kind of a mandate to lead some people. It's sort of a second point. I meet people who can put a few words together, put little things together, and they think because they can do that they have the right to be in charge. They think that once they get in charge they're going to impress people into following them. Some actually believe that the 501c gives them the authority to lead.

Usually, the person with the strongest muscles and the strongest willpower leads the weak. You know, that's the way it is in the black community, and it's a big deal. Many pastors run over people. They are bullies, and they end up with the power. I try to tell young politicians that if you listen to the people, you become a leader who almost can't be beat. In the black community, for good or for bad, if that person will listen to the people, this person can never be beat.

In Jackson, Mississippi, we had a man named Henry Kirksey who worked with the federal government to redistrict, to get black folks enfranchised to vote. That's what he was—a mapmaker. And then he ended up getting elected. He was first elected as a state representative and then elected as a senator, which is another form of state representative. But in those people's districts where blacks were, he could never be beaten. I don't know if he ever did anything for people, for anybody, but the people knew that he was for them and he didn't care nothing about money. All he did was just listen to the people's interests; and all he did was lobby. All he did was talk about the interests of the people. And they couldn't buy him off, because he didn't care nothing about money. He didn't care about clothes. He was just fantastic.

I guess I would say that I know so much of my own personal limitations that when I think of any achievement that I think highly of, they almost seem . . . mysterious. I'm still fascinated with those many miracles. All of my honorary doctorates have been miracles. If those colleges and universities knew me like I know myself, they would never have given me those honorary degrees. I see that as a miracle. Recognizing my sin and knowing my limitations have been important.

Vera Mae also lets me know my limitations. She keeps me humble.

Now, because this was a short chapter, and because we have not had a list for a while, we'll include three lists here.

First, list three influential leaders:

1. _____
2. _____
3. _____

Now list three people who have had an impact on your life, either positive or negative:

1. _____
2. _____
3. _____

(SHANE: For extra credit, write them a little letter this month and let them know you are thankful for them . . . for the positive ones . . . and praying for them . . . for the negative ones.)

Finally, list three people you have done something meaningful for this month:

1. _____
2. _____
3. _____

(SHANE: For extra credit, think of three more meaningful things you can do for someone.)

Notes
1. See 1 Corinthians 1:27.
2. See Numbers 22:21-35.

THE JOURNEY

(Traveling to Tomorrow)

SHANE: Leadership is about taking folks on a journey. It's about traveling along a winding road rather than just arriving at some destination. Think about Moses and what it must have been like for him as he led the Jewish people out of Egypt. The actual escape didn't take too long, but then they were in the desert for 40 years! Wandering. Eating manna. Complaining. Getting sidetracked with all those stinking idols. I wonder which was the most challenging part of leading for Moses . . . the moment of crisis when they were getting chased by Pharaoh's army as they crossed the Red Sea . . . or the day-after-day plodding along with all those people in tow . . . or their issues and their bickering and their fragility?

Sometimes, the moments of crisis are easier to navigate than the mundane routine of going on from day to day. At the least, a threat or disaster pulls people together in the urgency of survival. It's not as easy to rally people when today's tasks look just like yesterday's.

Despite how it looks and feels, the daily routine does not have be dull; and, come to think of it, that is where most of life happens. Moses did not just have a vision for the Promised Land. He had Aaron. He had community. He had God tabernacling with them. He had the journey.

John: Moses listened to the people. There were times when they probably drove him crazy, but he listened. So go to the people; live among them. That's the journey.

The first step is to learn from the people . . . to love them and start with what they know. (Jot that down, it is one of my big principles: *Start with what they know.*) The best leader is the one who listens to the people and sticks with a task until it is done. The people in the community will say, "We did this ourselves. The leader freed us up." You hear that a lot in community, and it's good. The people will give the leader a little credit for inspiring them, but they'll take the credit for the work themselves, as they should.

There was a pastor at a church in Pittsburgh. He was an older man and for 19 years did a good job, but then he died. The church didn't name a replacement right away; they just went on for five or six years without a pastor. And they did not miss a beat. How could they thrive for so long without leadership? The pastor who died had told the people that he had never felt he was *in charge*. He led the church, but he was not the one in change. Profound. He raised up people in the church who became football chaplains, Sunday School teachers and shelter workers. He raised up elders, ushers and role models. The pastor influenced a lot of people not by being in charge and not by being over them, but by living among them.

SHANE: Yeah, and this gets at why, when we start Christian communities in neighborhoods in which we aren't indigenous, we do not consider ourselves a "church" plant. We go in to join what God is already doing there, to submit to the local leadership of the Church in the neighborhood. We may eventually start some stuff or help lead Bible studies, worship nights or after-school programs or help plant community gardens . . . but as much as possible, the folks that are connected to the local congregations, and other great folks, are doing God's work before and around us. Sometimes it starts by just offering to do dishes after the potluck lunch on Sunday afternoon. It's funny, but in some of the old-school religious orders, newbie monks and nuns always did the grunt work of doing dishes and cleaning toilets . . . that's what novices did as sort of a rite of passage into the community. So it's a good place to start.

The inner city doesn't need more "churches"; it needs a Church, a Body, a people serving and working together as one family—Christ's body. We don't need a bunch of renegade folks moving in and starting "postmodern" church plants that are disconnected with the existing neighborhood congregations and the larger Body of Christ. We don't need folks to be sloppily calling everyone an elder or pastor without any accountability outside themselves . . . that's the stuff cults are made of. We don't baptize people in our bathtubs; we connect them to the local parish or a local congregation. We aren't para-church; we're pro-church.

One of the things we have nearly lost is the simple idea of a neighborhood parish. Every neighborhood should have a congregation or parish they can walk to, worship with and learn from. But we can't get sloppy with our language. We don't call services or meetings on Sunday "church." We call them "public meetings." Weekly services are great things to do—gathering publicly for worship, sharing prayers and needs and upcoming events, putting our money together, reading Scripture, sharing Communion. But that is not church; that's just the Church gathering together in a building. We don't call a building "Church." Rather, we are the Church. It is who we are—the Body, the Bride, the living incarnation of Jesus in His people.

IT SEEMS THAT WE ARE IN
THE MIDST OF ANOTHER ECCLESIAL
RUMMAGE SALE, WHICH MEANS
WE NEED GOOD LEADERS.

My Catholic friends get this better than some of my Protestant friends. They talk about the Church in a broad sense of the Body of Christ, but they *go to Mass*. And they don't shop around for a good parish. Worship is about liturgy; it's about remembering the story of where we come from and what we are here for. It's about reading Scripture and singing beautiful old songs and a few new ones—and connecting this ancient Story with the time and place in which we live. So the idea of a "commuter church" or "church shopping" becomes quite senseless, especially if the center of our public meetings is not the sermon or soloist but Jesus, taking Communion together, sharing needs and upcoming activities and seeking ways to find community. We can do these things anywhere, and they don't need to be fancy or take lots of money. They make a lot more sense when grounded within walking distance or when they take place close to where we live.

One of the congregations we are connected to here in Philly is growing rapidly. The Spirit is just doing beautiful stuff among us. But every time we grow beyond 200 people in the services, we start up a new location for public meetings. We don't need them to be big; in fact, they work much better when they are small. The Mennonites are on to something when they simply name their congregations after their neighborhood or street—it doesn't need to be anything clever; it's just about place and a gathering of Christ's Body in the neighborhood.

Most of life happens outside the meetings—just like huddles in a football game. Huddles are important parts of the game; critical in fact. We need to pull together the team, look each other in the eyes, strategize a bit, drink some water, get some good coaching, bow our heads and get back in the game. But it is silly to think of a football game that only consists of huddles.[1]

Let me address something here that I feel is necessary to add to the bigger "conversation" about Catholicism: We need to sift through the dirt of history to find the gems, no matter what tradition we come from. Part of my frustration with the Methodist tradition I was raised in was that I began to read John Wesley and to fall in love with his life, writing and teaching . . . and it put me at odds with many of the things I saw in Methodism today. I mean, Methodism had a fiery beginning; that's why there is fire wrapped around the cross in the Methodist symbol. Fire and cross—if we're not careful, the only place the fire will remain is on the cover of the hymnal and the pages of the past. We can't forget our histories and the men and women who made it. I'm not talking about war heroes, but church heroes, heroes of the cross. Talk about John Wesley—there's a radical leader. We cannot forget these folks from the past. Methodists need to read Wesley again. They need to take the best that their little part of Church history has.

We need the fire of the Pentecostals. We need the roots of the Catholics and the Orthodox. We need the sharp thinking of the Episcopalians and other mainliners. We need the politics of the Anabaptists and the grace of the Quakers. And we need to confess the dark sides of Church history, where our denominations justified slavery with the Bible, where we baptized the Crusades and militaries, where we killed each other over theology. True leaders are able to see the good and the bad . . . to confess the bad and try not to repeat it, and to celebrate the good and try to reproduce it.

In the same way we hold a photo negative up to light to see it clearly (note: negatives were the way people used to make photographs before digital cameras . . . wink), we need to hold our history up to Jesus to see how His light comes through; to see where the dark spots and the beauty are. If we don't look closely at history, we are doomed to repeat it. The future of the Church rests in not forgetting her past—both the good and the bad.

We play a game with the kids where we sit in a circle and whisper a story into the ear of the first kid. He or she can only hear it once, and he or she has to try hard to remember all the details. Then that kid whispers it to the next kid, and then the next. The last kid shares the story as he or she heard it, and usually it's hilarious to see what was lost in translation and what other things worked their way in. It's the same way with the story of the Church. It seems that every few hundred years we start to get confused. We forget the story. And every few hundred years there seems to be a pattern in history that the Spirit stirs up a renewal. Folks go to the wilderness, to the desert; they go to the margins and to the abandoned places of the empire in which they live. And they rethink what it means to be Christian. They retell the story.

My friend Phyllis Tickle has done a beautiful job studying Church history, and she says that every few hundred years the Church needs a rummage sale. We need to clear house and get rid of the clutter . . . and hold on to the things of eternal value, the treasures of our faith. It seems that we are in the midst of another ecclesial rummage sale now. And that means that we need good leadership. We need to make sure we don't throw out the family photo album by accident. But we also need to make sure that we get rid of that old bike in the basement with two flats and no chain. And, even though the TV works, it may need to go, too, along with grandpa's old revolver (as cool as it is). Okay, you get the idea.

We need leadership to make sure we don't accept everything as truth and that we don't spin our wheels thinking there is no truth. There are important truths—some are Christian doctrines like the Atonement and bodily resurrection and the Trinity, and others are Christian practices like nonviolence and enemy love and compassion for the poor and hospitality to the stranger—these are things we cannot lose or else we lose the essence of Christianity. Christianity is not just a set of doctrines or practices, but it is these actions and practices that ensure we remember the Story, that we remember Jesus, literally, so that we can continue to embody the Spirit of Jesus and be the fragrance of Christ in the world so that folks come to know God's saving grace.

We have a lot to learn about leading and following from the Catholic model of monasticism and how they do spiritual formation. By the way, monasticism begins with "mono," meaning one, and at its core it means the single-minded pursuit of Jesus—that is the one thing to which we devote our lives; like the pearl that we leave everything else to pursue.[2] That is why traditional monastic folks, monks and nuns, leave everything else that seduces them and competes for their love and attention, all other loves, to say yes to Jesus—hence the decision not to own many possessions and to live in celibacy rather than marriage.

THE WORK OF DISCIPLESHIP IS
ABOUT FORMING DISCIPLES WHO
FOLLOW JESUS, NOT JUST BELIEVERS
WHO BELIEVE IN JESUS.

Let's go back to formation. Each of us has a spiritual director walking with us to whom we are accountable and with whom we listen to the Spirit; again, there's that idea that we don't just hear the Spirit in a vacuum but that we have others to help us hear (where two or three of us gather in Christ's name, God is with us).[3] That's the model of mentorship; the model that says we should have somebody wiser than us that we are learning from. And then we should have some folks that we're pouring into as well. Then the work of discipleship is about formation; it is about forming disciples who follow Jesus, not just believers who believe in Jesus or worshipers who worship Jesus. As disciples, we certainly believe, and we certainly worship, but we are not sent into the world to make believers but disciples. A person can certainly believe in Jesus without actually following, and he or she can worship Jesus without doing the things He said. Making disciples takes time, discipline and grace. In most monastic orders, it takes years, even up to 10 years, to become a full member, a fully devoted follower of Jesus.

In our community, we compare the journey to an onion with many layers. There are different layers and stages of commitment, both beliefs and practices, and the degree to which we are entrusted with leadership correlates to how deep our journey has led us. You can see this even within Jesus' community—there are folks that are deep in the inner circle and folks that are way out on the edges, and Jesus is radically inclusive of the edges while radically strict on those in the middle . . . it keeps the momentum moving toward God.

It's not just about how long a person has been around; it's about how deeply he or she has embraced the practices and beliefs at the core of our faith. It is very helpful for folks to see themselves as part of this community with many layers of commitment, and even to celebrate that no matter whether they are in the middle or way out, they are still a part of this thing—although we do sometimes joke that the outer layers of the onion get a little flaky.

John: I have been around long enough to see people—leaders and followers—at all layers of the onion. Yet no matter the "onion" level, leaders need to believe strongly in the people they lead and see to it that they are discipled. While our vision will become the disciples' vision, they will never look exactly like we look, nor will their part of the vision look like ours. So, in this way, we must see our disciples as the people who are going to carry out the task. That's Jesus' model. He depended on others, and so must we. Jesus didn't write a book or start a Christian television network; He just modeled life to a few, who in turn modeled it to others.

As I mentioned previously, fame can destroy leadership. A leader can become so full of himself that he loses sight of the original vision— the image he sees in the mirror *becomes* the vision. Some people believe their image is important in leadership; however, it's that person's character traits (like honestly and humility) that are what's really important. We should model good character and expect our disciples to live the same way.

Sometimes what we see as positive character traits can appear to conflict with one another. Take the trait of consistency and the trait of flexibility. Leaders who want to be seen as consistent often take a "no compromise" stand and refuse to bend regardless of the facts or changing circumstances . . . or they refuse to recognize that they have simply changed their mind. I change my mind. I've changed it in the process of making a decision or during a project when I've received more information. Sometimes people don't like that . . . they call it "flip-flopping." Some people, once they have received a direction or opinion, want it to be written in stone, like the tablets Moses got from God. But most of life does not work that way. Some people want to go on in ignorance and maintain a certain status no matter what the truth. They would rather me not say to them, "I thought of this yesterday, and I found out it isn't right, so I've changed my mind today."

SHANE: We've had that happen, too. I think it's part of the journey. People will say, "But you said this," and I'll say, "Well, I thought about it more, and I changed my mind." Or, "I listened to what you had to say and decided you were right." That's not a sign of weakness, but of strength. Being willing to change and confessing when you are wrong are not only characteristics of good leadership but are also gospel values . . . and they are very countercultural as well. Think about some of the government leaders out there. They don't usually confess or admit wrong unless they are caught on tape or are about to lose an election. Being able to say we're sorry when we really do make a mistake is a gift, and there is something healing about confession. It's when we are struggling and not willing to admit it that we need to make it known. In the long run, voluntary confession is a lot easier than a forced confession. But our culture tends to beat up on people who change their mind (calling the flip-flop a mistake) *and* on those who really do make mistakes. No wonder no one wants to appear as if we have changed our mind, yet alone come clean.

As a leader, it's okay to change your mind. In fact, if you know that you're in the wrong, it's a bad idea not to do so. Sometimes, changing your mind means that you have listened to other people who had more insight. I told you about the fire that we had a few years back. Our whole block burned down. So we started thinking, *Well, we're going to need to build back.* We got all this money so that we could begin, and we developed this whole plan, including a full-on green building. We had these folks create an architectural plan and everything. Then we put down some sod as just a temporary thing, and the grass started growing and the kids started playing football on it. They loved just seeing the grass. That's when we started to realize that we didn't have any grass in our neighborhood. It was an endangered thing. And there are abandoned buildings everywhere. So we decided to hold on to what we had and build a little playground, put out some grills and have a neighborhood green space. We still planned to do all the stuff we were going to do in the community, but we were now going to do it out of abandoned houses; we'd fix them up. I think that's a good sign—the ability to change or rethink things.

John: There are so many beautiful things about going on this journey with other folks. We get to nurture each other. In the Church, we call each other "brothers" and "sisters" for a reason. We become family.

SHANE: Jesus' teaching on family is really interesting. On the one hand, He was saying things like honor your mother and father, and I think one of the real witnesses in the work that we do is having healthy families.[4] But on the other hand, Jesus had some really harsh things to say about family, such as if you don't hate your own family and son or mother and father, you're not ready to be a disciple.[5] So I think there are times when our biological family becomes a detriment, like when it becomes an idol. We justify comforts and luxuries that we could never justify for ourselves all in the name of family . . . "it was for the kids." But we have to extend beyond biological family.

I met one suburban couple that was so haunted by the inequities of the education system that for every biological child they sent to college, they create a scholarship for a kid in poverty whose only obstacle to college was economics. They felt that this was the only way to truly love their neighbor as themselves, so they were doing that. That is the responsibility that rebirth demands of us. The worst tribalism comes out of the myopia of the shortsighted vision of family. There's nothing that we'll kill quicker for than for our own family—whether that's "the fam" of a gang, or our own biological family, or our national family, or whatever. So, by extension, I think that when Jesus says "hate your family," He's not saying that we should stop loving our family. Jesus loved His mama, and when He was dying on the cross He said to His disciple, "John, you take care of her. This is now your mom."[6] He just had a different definition of it.

So, I think that the same love you've got for your own baby you should have for the children in Iraq, in Palestine, in North Philly, in Mississippi. That's where we really have to have that sense of being "born again," not of the flesh, but of the Spirit. That changes the way we think of things. Our "our" is no longer like "our nation"; we have a different "our." You know, we are transnational; we are "born again."

John: I appreciate the "our" part of community, but sometimes I wonder if we have lost that passion that Jesus had for all people to come into the family of God. I think the apostle John had a sense of that idea—the passion was to bring everybody in through the process of the new birth and the glory of this family. I think Paul had a sense of this as well—that now he was in this new family, the family of God. He counted his church family as gain, though his biological family, the tribe of Benjamin, was lost. Nothing measured up to the excellence of the knowledge of Christ.[7] He was talking about being in the family of God and his knowledge of what it meant to be a child of God. Once he had knowledge of the glory of what it meant to be in the family, he had great passion for those people outside of the family. So it was Paul's mission to bring others into the family; it was his desire and his joy.

I think that's what gave Paul power . . . that he recognized this change in his life and the passion stirred within him because of that change. It's a zeal we should all carry. The sticking point is that we should have this kind of passion for the *whole* world, because Jesus sent us not only to our neighbor but also to the ends of the earth.[8] We are all children of God . . . all of us, whether we're lost or not lost. This passion for everyone doesn't lessen my desire to be with my biological family. And the sheer magnitude of "the ends of the earth" doesn't weaken my passion for individuals. As Christians, we ought to be loving and showing compassion to every person.

SHANE: Yes, we need to love everyone. But how do we go about this within the context of family? John and I are really different in our current living situations and this whole family deal. When we talk about how we sustain ourselves, we have very different answers. He talks about Vera Mae and his children, and I think that's beautiful. But it's real different for the world I'm in. I'm 33, and I'm not married. I haven't ruled out getting married, but I have come to see that there are all sorts of ways to create community and intimacy for this work, and marriage is just one way.

Two of my mentors are celibate monks. One of them once said to me, "We should choose that which allows us to pursue Jesus with the most singlemindedness. For some of us that is singleness; for others of us it's marriage." What I see in John is that having Vera Mae and his family has allowed him to pursue Jesus with the most single-mindedness. There are plenty of people that I see today and that I see in Church history whose singleness has freed them up to pursue Jesus with the most singlemindedness and pursue their vision and the poor. Just look at Mother Teresa. We don't look at her and say, "Boy, if she had only met her husband!" We have to value singleness and know that we're called to Jesus.

WE HAVE TO HAVE LOVE, BUT A
BIOLOGICAL NUCLEAR FAMILY IS
NOT THE ONLY PLACE TO
EXPERIENCE THAT.

Our deepest longing is to love and be loved. As my monk friend says, "You can live without sex, but you can't live without love." So we have to have love, but biological nuclear family is not the only place to experience that. In a conversation on leadership it's so important to figure that out, because there are plenty of leaders who have destroyed their families in pursuit of their vision, their ministry and all these other things. And likewise, there are people who have committed terrible sins because they have been placed in a position of power or fame or notoriety or whatever and they haven't had community around them to support them, be watchful with them and correct them when they saw danger ahead. So they end up with cover-up—the bishops and the people who have committed sexual sins. When we say "follow me to freedom"—for some that freedom will be marriage, for others singleness. But no one is called to be alone.

John: Whether in a biological family or on a ministry board, we need each other as we go along in this journey. I was on the World Vision board for almost 20 years. During that time, two of our great leaders stumbled and left the organization—for different reasons, but nonetheless neither was good. What we discovered when we looked into why this had happened was that we as a board had created an environment *that had allowed it to happen.*

We did a lot to combat the problem; in fact, we did everything we could do. But in the end we decided that we would turn World Vision into an organization in which people wouldn't know who the president was. We had to destroy that image we had created. And I don't know if you know who World Vision's president is today. They've done a good job or removing that image from the position and creating ways for the leader not to be alone and subject to all those temptations. There's a need for a team.

That was one thing I always liked about Chuck Colson. Chuck had some understanding of the power of a team, both negative and positive. You might see his name big, but boy, the board of directors . . . I was on the Prison Fellowship Ministries board for 16 years, and Chuck listened to me and everybody else on the board. We didn't vote on things for him not to do. He would form a consensus. If one or two people were against it, he would always say to himself, *You know, this team, or this family, is more important than . . .* [whatever we had cautioned against].

SHANE: That's the way Mother Teresa was, too. I remember reading in her writings about some of the times she was sent to speak. And it's real funny, because she hated speaking. She would ask not to go. She would . . . well, with Catholics it helps that you take a vow of obedience, and it's the same thing as submission. There was one time when she tried to cancel—I mean, it was for a huge gathering of

Catholics—and she cancelled or tried to cancel, but her spiritual director said (and I think even just the fact that Mother Teresa had a spiritual director is important), "No, we feel the Spirit is calling you to go." And she said, "I hope you know this is the biggest sacrifice I've ever made." It was to speak and stay in a hotel. I love it. But she did it. You know, she did it.

John: Listening to God is important, but we also need to be sensitive to hearing the people around us—especially those who have some oversight over us or with us. No one person on a board is more important than another. We need to really listen. There are people in my life who have exercised that influence.

Some of my friends have even challenged things I have published in my newsletter, saying, "Don't do that again." Usually it had to do with going through certain fundraising motions—motions that went against the grain of who I am. My friends would reassure me that I did not have to follow other models but that I could do it the way I felt God had given me to do it. I didn't need to succumb to the pressure and press others. They said, "Wait until you don't have any money, and then ask people for it." That may be counterintuitive for some, but that is how I have always done it since. The summer is coming, and it's going to be tough for us. Well, we wait for the summer to come, and when we need the money, we ask people for it.

I used to tell my board of directors, "You guys can manage money better than I can. You all keep your money until we need it. Let's don't just lie and pretend that we need it." A good board member will help you with those kinds of things. They're there to help you to not do things the way the world does things. And God will help you, too . . . if you depend on Him.

SHANE: Bill Hybels and Willow Creek have been a good example recently of humility and confession. The leadership at Willow conducted a study of the congregation to try to get a sense of how the peoples' lives were being transformed. What they found was actually quite disturbing (and, unfortunately is probably true in many congregations, but they just haven't had the courage to conduct a study like this). The study at Willow showed that they had done a really good job at reaching people and getting folks to come to services, and even in seeing folks become believers in Jesus. But the disturbing part was that the study also showed that many of their members did not end up living much differently than they had before . . . their efforts were not having the fruit they had anticipated. They were good at making believers, but not as good at making disciples. So Willow released this study called "Reveal" as a sort of communal confession from the leadership to be transparent and honest about the places they needed work. That's beautiful. They certainly could have kept the results on the down low or tried to sugarcoat it a bit; after all, they are one of the most influential megachurch congregations in the United States. But they decided to be transparent, not only with their strengths but also with their weaknesses.

I worked at Willow for a year, and it was one of those places where if you complained you had just volunteered to lead. At one point I said, "No one's going into the city. No one's hanging out with folks that are poor and homeless." Promptly, one of the leaders at Willow said, "Let's start doing it then. Will you organize it?" So, before long, we were doing some urban plunge trips into the city.

Years later Willow began their $50 million building expansion, and I wrote a letter to Bill Hybels stating my concerns about the new building. He wrote me a handwritten letter back, page after page. One of the things he said was, "Don't tear down without building up." He went on to talk about how he had wrestled over the building expansion for 10 years. In the end, I did propose an alternative plan (not just tearing down), which was to start a Jubilee Campaign that would match every dollar spent on the new building with money that would go toward building wells overseas . . . they didn't take me up on it.

One of my major concerns was not Bill's leadership, but Willow's influence. I worried about the other pastors that would not wrestle for 10 years over their building projects. And I thought to myself, *What if Willow Creek helped provide water for an entire country (which they could do with a portion of their building fund) . . . what kind of ripples would that have throughout the rest of the evangelical world?!* That is the tricky thing whenever you lead. Other folks will try to arrive at the destination without taking the journey. It's the same way people say they are going to start a Willow Creek-type megachurch, and they copy the "drums and drama"—meaning they try to switch up the music and add a skit or two into the service—but not the journey.

Willow Creek started with a bunch of folks going door to door in the neighborhood selling tomatoes, getting to know neighbors, and listening to folks share their scars from the church. That's how you start a congregation like Willow Creek—go door to door sharing vegetables and getting to know the neighbors, not by getting a JumboTron.

A few years ago, Bill Hybels and Rick Warren really got going on responding to HIV. The first thing they did was to confess, "We're 15, 20 years late. We should have been on this." It's sad that the leaders in a lot of important social issues have been Hollywood actors and rock stars. I always joke that the Scriptures say somewhere that if the Church is silent, then, yeah, the very rock stars will cry out. Because that's what's happened. As the Church has fallen silent, other folks have begun to take the lead. But I'm excited, because I think that's changing. And, obviously, there are legendary leaders like John out there. But I also see a whole new generation ready to pave the way.

THE TRAGEDY TODAY IS NOT THAT RICH FOLKS DON'T CARE ABOUT POOR FOLKS, BUT THAT RICH FOLKS DON'T *KNOW* POOR FOLKS.

The tragedy in the Church today is not that rich folks don't care about poor folks, but that rich folks don't *know* poor folks. Pastors and leaders lose touch, too. And you reproduce who you are. So as long as there are leaders who no longer have relationships with poor or hurting folks, that begins to trickle down. We're never going to have a church of people who care about the poor unless there are leaders who know the poor. Mother Teresa was in the forefront of that. She never lost touch. Even when I was in Calcutta, she'd be out jumping rope with the kids or she'd be hanging out on the streets. That's one of the things that I admire about John and why I think CCDA is still a community of people who are practitioners. You ask them who are poor folks and they can name you a dozen names. There's nothing that can replace that.

Mother Teresa said it's very fashionable to talk about the poor but not as fashionable to talk to the poor. If we really care about the poor, we can name them; they're our friends. They're people that we're with. So I think that in some ways we have a Church that cares about the poor and justice in some general sense, but the place that we've really been missing is that we've lost our feet being on the ground. That's part of what I think CCDA calls itself to, to never lose that. John has modeled that. But it's always a temptation. For me, too . . . it's part of why I have a very strict amount of time that I'm allowed to be away from my community. And it doesn't matter if it's Harvard calling me. I am committed to stay in the neighborhood. Leaders are role models. They will not raise up a congregation that is committed to the poor until folks see them caring for the poor. We will not see congregations committed to racial reconciliation until they see it lived out in the homes and dinner tables, not just preached about from the pulpit.

John: It's easy to not stay at home. It can become a pattern—the pattern of your own staff, the pattern around you . . . and not staying at home isolates you from the very people you need to talk to, the people you need to be with. When people are away from home, they tend to become "important." At home, you become unimportant, or at least not the same kind of important. I am particularly talking about self-importance. When you are right there in the midst of the people all the time, you become one with them. God and what He is stirring up becomes all important, and self becomes less important.

SHANE: There are so many signs of the Spirit stirring things up, even in places we would least expect it. I was speaking in Texas when a fellow came up to me. He confessed, "I gotta tell ya, brother, I am a redneck. I'm a textbook gun-totin', pickup-truck-drivin' redneck. But I've been readin' your stuff, and it has messed me up. Now I'm a recovering redneck." Part of why people identify with my own story is that they can see themselves in my journey. They can see some of the stages of my own transformation down in East Tennessee. It happens because I am transparent with that stuff—I share with folks that I, too, am a recovering sexist, racist, homophobic redneck. God can make something out of anybody.

That awareness gives us grace with others, too, because it allows us to see how easily a person can get stuck in those patches of homogeneity, comfort and complacency. We remember how seductive the entanglements of our culture are, how pervasive the myth of redemptive violence is, how convincing the advertisements are as they tell us that if we don't buy this new lawn tool we will never be completely happy. What's exciting about the current movement in the Church is that there is a surge of momentum around issues that really matter, not just hot-button political debates. People are convinced that our faith has to connect to this world. And as young Christians have looked at the fragile world they've been handed from their parents, they are really asking what it means to not conform to the patterns of this world but to be transformed by the renewing of our minds.[9]

One of the exciting projects I helped launch with other young Christians is called the Two Futures Project. It's an ambitious campaign to abolish nuclear weapons that suggests we are at a crossroads right now: one future without nuclear weapons, and the other ruined by them. It is so refreshing to see Christians in the forefront of movements like this saying we cannot justify violence in the name of Jesus. We cannot simultaneously love our enemies and prepare to kill them en masse. A new generation in the Church is saying that our God does not bless bombs. Our God is the One who lived in Jesus and said that if we pick up the sword we will die by the sword . . . if we trust in the bomb we will die by it.[10] It was one more sign of the changing face of evangelicalism in post-religious Right America, where young Christians are not limited to the hot-button issues and stale debates of the past but are convinced that their faith has to connect to the world they live in . . . that they have to read the Bible in one hand and the newspaper in the other.

Some of the champions of this movement have been young evangelicals like Tyler Wigg-Stevenson, Rob Bell, Lynne Hybels and myself. There is also a spectacular list of endorsers like Noel Castellanos (CEO of CCDA!), Tony Campolo, Jim Wallis, Richard Cizik, Brian McLaren, Margaret Feinberg, Richard Rohr, Sam Rodriguez, Rod

Sider, and Miroslav Volf. But what's been really fun to see is how this movement is not just the "usual suspects" of Christian liberals and progressive folks. Check out some of the other endorsers: George Shultz (former Secretary of State for Ronald Reagan), Bill Hybels (pastor of Willow Creek), Chuck Colson (founder of Prison Fellowship Ministries), David Neff (editor of *Christianity Today*), Jonathan Merritt (of the Southern Baptist Convention), Tony Hall (ambassador and congressman), John Stott (author and theologian), Cameron Strang (CEO of *Relevant* magazine) and Leith Anderson (president of NAE—National Association of Evangelicals). I mean, it's an eclectic bunch! There is even a retired colonel of the U.S. Army signed on.

This sort of project does not just happen; it comes from good leadership and people who are willing to work together even though they may not agree on every theological or ideological point. It takes humility to allow folks to change and to collaborate, especially when it's with folks you've debated on panels! But that is what brings change—when we don't just preach to the choir but get out of the choir loft and into the streets to work together.

I see young leaders doing that everywhere. One school I was speaking at had a Young Republicans club as well as a Social Justice Club. As you can imagine, they were often at odds, and any time they got together to discuss issues or try to talk, things got ugly. But then they spent some time in prayer and reflection and tried to identify some of the things they could agree on. One thing they could agree on was that God did not want people to be cold on the streets. So they started making quilts and blankets together, and then they would hit the streets to deliver t folks living in the alleys and parks. It was beautiful, and it was in the context of action together—not just talking about it—that they found common ground. They're on the journey, and they're dancing and living and loving and following and leading.

Notes

1. This "ecclesiology," or way of thinking about what it means to be the Church, is one of the things that distinguishes those of us who identify as "new monastics" from some other contemporary movements and renewals within the Church today, such as some of the circles that identify as "emerging" or "Emergent.™" If you are unfamiliar with the term "emerging church," it has become a very confusing trend within the contemporary renewal happening in the Church. A decade or so ago, a bunch of young, mostly white evangelicals started seeing similar conversations beginning to spark all over the place about the reshaping of evangelicalism, the rethinking of missions, and the re-imagining of what it really means to be the Church (in history and today). Language of "the emerging church" connected many of the dots, which remained primarily white evangelical men, many of whom had great ideas and led vibrant communities and organizations.

   Nonetheless, it has always been evident that this is not the only conversation or renewal happening in the Church. Entire movements of hip-hop church youth and missional communities overseas and indigenous movements were also stirring, though they did not get the same airtime or book deals. Eventually, books and brands began identifying as "emerging church" or "emergent." So it got a little messy. In my opinion, "the movement" became a bit narcissistic. Much of the theology became sloppy within the movement, with folks who have repeated some of the mistakes of fundamentalism (only with more tattoos) and folks who have repeated the mistakes of liberalism (only with more wit).

   Meanwhile, there are many, many folks who seem to know exactly what "emerging church" is and think it is the antichrist. While there are many voices who self-identify as "emerging" or "emergent" and whom I consider close friends and refreshing voices in the Church, there are also folks who identify as emergent whose beliefs and practices, or lack thereof, I find very problematic. I also have many friends who deliberately do not identify as emergent or have never heard of emergent and whom I find to be beautiful, refreshing voices in the Church . . . and, likewise, there are those same non-emergent figures whose beliefs and practices I find deeply problematic.

   All that to say, I find the "emerging church" language, at least the Emergent™ brand, utterly unhelpful. There does not seem to be any real grain or DNA or any distinctive marks and practices (or even beliefs for that matter) that distinguish it. I once heard someone say that all you need to start an "emerging church" is a Bible, a candle and a copy of the *Matrix* movie (and some would say the first two are optional). It seems that "emerging church" has become little more than a box where you can put anyone who is under 40 and has fresh ideas—and not have to listen to them.

   So I will not spend any energy, other than this footnote, to try and defend a brand. It seems that it has became little more than a naming, with a proper noun, the current renewal in the Church. Rather than giving it a name, I find it helpful to locate ourselves within the monastic renewals and other reformations throughout history. There is a renewal . . . and just as the Jews did not write the name of G-D, I find it much more helpful to celebrate the renewal and join it, and to recognize that this is a pattern throughout Church history—renewals and reformations—but that there is no need for it to have a name, just like the artist formerly known as Prince. The minute we name the movement, we kill the movement.
2. See Matthew 13:44-46.
3. See Matthew 18:20.
4. See Matthew 19:19.
5. See Luke 14:26.
6. See John 19:27.
7. See Philippians 3:8.

8. See Mark 16:15.
9. See Romans 12:2.
10. See Matthew 26:52.

[The abbot or abbess] must be well-grounded in the law of God so that they may have the resources to bring forth what is new and what is old in their teaching. . . . While they must hate all vice, they must love their brothers or sisters. In correcting faults they must act with prudence being conscious of the danger of breaking the vessel itself by attacking the rust too vigorously.

—St. Benedict of Nursia (480–547)

FREEDOM
(Imagining a Different World)

John: God sets us free. Here's how it works: He disciples us into a place of obedience. Our obedience comes out of His love for us. Then it is our gift to understand and move into our freedom in His Lordship. Once we are fully submitted to His Lordship, we become free. It is the understanding of God's love for us that sets us free.

There is no record of the Hebrew people singing until after they crossed the Red Sea. Once they had been delivered from bondage, they could sing joyful thanksgiving out of gratitude. Paul carried that out a little further. When he was set free from his racism and bigotry, God called him to a mission—far away to the Gentiles. He obeyed that call. In his state of freedom, he became the Lord's bondservant. He delighted in being God's bondservant because he knew that he was loved and that in that capacity he could find real freedom. The ones we lead must have the assurance that we love them. That's where powerful leadership and followership comes from.

We always need to start with reconciliation. We can oversimplify it, but it's not simple. In fact, I think it almost takes somewhat of a supernatural act for true reconciliation to occur. Reconciliation begins with seeing the value of the person with whom you want to be reconciled. I don't think reconciliation is open-ended, vague or, as they say today, "whatever." I think reconciliation comes about in how we perceive every human being: the person who serves us at the Piccadilly restaurant down the road, the elderly man driving slowly on the freeway, the student who asks too many questions, the president—everyone. Do we reckon with this, or do we skip over it because it is too hard or because we don't want to face or change our real feelings? How we reckon with others is important in the sense that every person is created in the image of God. If we dare not reconcile, then we risk devaluing something God chose to create and that God Himself values. *What does it say about our attitude toward God when in our eyes we lessen the value of something He created?*

When I say there is value in everyone, I include inmates at the local prison. Can I identify with the pain of those criminals when some people think they deserve the pit they are in? Yes. How? For one, I go back to the simple truth that we all sin and fall way short.[1] I can have compassion for those who suffer . . . and I have compassion for those prisoners. I visit them regularly. I have empathy for the men there. Yes, they are criminals. They once were kids who have changed and who have now become something their mothers would never have imagined. I reckon these kids' backgrounds deprived them of the opportunity of the information they needed and the nurture they needed and the community they should have been raised in. As a community, we should have been more thoughtful and watchful.

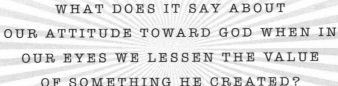

WHAT DOES IT SAY ABOUT
OUR ATTITUDE TOWARD GOD WHEN IN
OUR EYES WE LESSEN THE VALUE
OF SOMETHING HE CREATED?

I will be honest: Sometimes it's difficult for me to empathize with inmates, but I go to them nonetheless. The first thing I tell them is that they've got to take responsibility for their actions. I also give them hope, telling them that they're going to get out of there one day and that they can change if they will take responsibility. Freedom comes with responsibility.

When free people make excuses for bad behavior, they risk their freedom. Children are good at coming up with reason after reason for bad behavior. Some of my kids, when caught in a bad act, would even try to blame me or my parenting skills. They would say, "Daddy, you are the cause of it!" They wanted me to take responsibility for their mistake. Certainly we all fail each other at some point, but when we are old enough to recognize that someone has failed us, we are old enough to solve the problem with the help of Jesus Christ and extend love to that person. So when my children said, "Daddy, you are the cause of it!" I responded, "Okay, since you were smart enough to see that in my stupidity I caused your misery, then you are smart enough to take responsibility to help fix it." Scripture says, "Whoever commits sin is a slave of sin" (John 8:34). It is our responsibility to seek God so we can break free from that sin. Responsibility is not only chiming up when we have made a mistake but also the proactive breaking free from whatever enslaves us, no matter the cause. It also means taking positive steps toward freedom.

Leaders need to communicate not only the message of freedom with responsibility but also the action that follows. That's how I felt when Barack Obama was elected president of the United States. The election of the first black president was an important breakthrough for our freedom, but it also meant that as blacks, we would have more responsibility.

What did Obama's being elected president mean to me? Let me go back to election day . . . November 4, 2008. It was the fifty-sixth time Americans would go to the polls to choose a national leader, and the first time we could vote for a black man as part of a major ticket. Obama was ahead in the polls, but history proves that you never know for sure until all of the ballots are cast and counted.

I knew that the media would not announce the election results until after 10 P.M. my time . . . when the polls would be closed on the West Coast. I am not a night person, so I drifted off to sleep. At about three minutes after 10, my daughter Priscilla came running into the room shouting that Obama had won. I opened my eyes, and James Weldon Johnson's "Black National Anthem" came to my mind:

> Lift every voice and sing
> Till earth and heaven ring,
> Ring with the harmonies of Liberty;
> Let our rejoicing rise
> High as the listening skies,
> Let it resound loud as the rolling sea.
> Sing a song full of the faith that the dark past has taught us,
> Sing a song full of the hope that the present has brought us,

Facing the rising sun of our new day begun
Let us march on till victory is won.

Stony the road we trod,
Bitter the chastening rod,
Felt in the days when hope unborn had died;
Yet with a steady beat,
Have not our weary feet
Come to the place for which our fathers sighed?
We have come over a way that with tears have been watered,
We have come, treading our path through the blood of the
        slaughtered,
Out from the gloomy past,
Till now we stand at last
Where the white gleam of our bright star is cast.

God of our weary years,
God of our silent tears,
Thou who has brought us thus far on the way;
Thou who has by Thy might
Led us into the light,
Keep us forever in the path, we pray.
Lest our feet stray from the places, Our God, where we met Thee;
Lest, our hearts drunk with the wine of the world, we forget Thee;
Shadowed beneath Thy hand,
May we forever stand.
True to our GOD,
True to our native land.

The next morning, walking out onto my porch, I thought I could sing another song, in the loudest voice that I could raise:

My country, 'tis of thee,
sweet land of liberty, of thee I sing;
land where my father's died,
land of the pilgrims' pride,
from every mountainside let freedom ring!

I remember Martin Luther King, Jr. echoing the spirit of this anthem when he said, "I have a dream." It was King's message of having a dream of freedom that inspired my family and me in 1963. In a way, King's "I have a dream" speech is what started it all for us. The now legendary message was not some historic platitude for us. It was alive. Dr. King took all of our longing, all of our hope, and he put it into a dream . . . a dream we could also carry. What really stuck with me then was how I could have a dream that my four little children (we only had four at that time) would one day live in a land where they would not be judged by the color of their skin but by the content of their character.

I HAD THE PRIVILEGE OF LIVING TO SEE A BLACK MAN BECOME PRESIDENT OF THE UNITED STATES. HUMBLING.

When I saw Obama come out and accept the choice of the people . . . his election as President of the United States . . . I had a little grief. Mr. Rubin, Mr. Newsome and Mr. Hayes and so many of the people who walked with me in Mendenhall and those who bailed me out of jail . . . they didn't get to see this. Most of them were older than me, and they are no longer with us. My son, Spencer . . . he will never see it. And yet I had the privilege of living to see a black man become president of the United States. Humbling.

We celebrated during the campaign, on Election Day and on Inauguration Day. Obama's election goes beyond parties, politics and platforms. It is a symbol that gives us hope. He might not achieve all the hopes and the dreams that we have—he is human, after all, so he will make mistakes. He will not be able to do everything he says he will do, and he might even create some messes. I hope that Obama is a good president and accomplishes much for our nation, but no matter how effective his presidency, it will not erase the emotion and the hope that we now have. No one can take away what has been accomplished or what we now need to do.

The day after the election, as I sang my song, I had a hope that now is our time of action. But I also knew that it meant we had a part to play. Obama being elected meant the continuation of black people's liberation. But as blacks, we now have a responsibility to take control of our future. We can't sit back and expect Obama or the government or anyone else to do everything for us. Now we have to be more responsible. We're free, so now what can we do? That's what leading someone to freedom means—taking responsibility. Now is the time for action.

After Obama was elected, he invited me to a meeting of religious leaders that was held in December 2008. I had been in similar meetings with three other presidents, and I welcomed the opportunity. However, the date selected corresponded with surgery I had scheduled, and I was unable to go. Noel Castellanos of CCDA went, and he was an excellent voice for us. If I had attended, I wouldn't have gone with an agenda of telling Obama, "Now, you need to give us all of this, this and that." I think I would have said, "Obama, can you make a way for us to help you? Tell us your problems. Tell us the way you see it and let us tell you how we see it and how we can join with you in the responsibility of solving real problems." That's a whole different approach . . . hopefully an approach with a servant's attitude.

That's the attitude I try to take. That's a leadership concept, and it's also a followership concept. At this point, Obama's our leader. We elected him. He's the leader of the nation. Whether we agree with him or he agrees with what we want is not all that important . . . we will not agree on everything. That's a given. But he's our leader, and we'll ask of him, "How can we follow you into this situation? How can we help you?"

Yes, let's celebrate. Yes, let's have hope. Yes, let's take responsibility for the future.

SHANE: Now, how do I follow that? What a journey! What John couldn't tell you is that when he was telling the story of the first black president being elected . . . when he got to the point about his son Spencer not being here to see it . . . tears came to John's eyes. All I could do was sit back, with a lump forming in my throat, and appreciate the moment.

I remember watching the election with my African-American friends and seeing them literally weep as it unfolded. Even some of my peers who have significant anarchistic tendencies and very meager hope in politicians and government stared at the television, mesmerized, with tears rolling down their cheeks. I remember sitting in my neighborhood as a minority listening to the screaming streets, car horns and pots banging on election night, like the Phillies had won the World Series (again). I remember my homeless friends the day after the election looking into my eyes and saying, "Hope is in the air." It was a lot to take in.

It was not just an election. It was a moment in history.

I have to admit that I found myself pretty torn trying to figure out how to process the election. I remember seeing the headline in the satirical newspaper *The Onion* that read: "Black Man Given Worst Job in America." In some ways, it tried to capture the contradictions of the first black President cleaning up the messes made, primarily by white folks. And how much could he really change? How many hopes would he fulfill? How much hope should rest on one mortal man's shoulders?

Without a doubt, it was worth celebrating the historic moment. But I also wanted to be careful to hope appropriately . . . after all, Christian hope has always been a peculiar thing.

Part of me winced when I saw posters plastered in my neighborhood with Obama's face and the word "hope." Don't get me wrong: I like the brother, I think he's going to make some good changes, and some mistakes. In fact, "change" would make a much better poster.

John shared his song. The song on my lips the day after the election was a happy song.

My hope is built on nothing less
than Jesus' blood and righteousness. . . .
On Christ the solid Rock I stand,
All other ground is sinking sand.
All other ground is sinking sand . . .

This is why we can rejoice even as the world around us seems to fall apart. When kings fail, the poor can still rejoice because they never had much faith in a Caesar or a President. The poor can laugh when

Babylon falls because they know God still stands. They can laugh when markets collapse because they know God is their only reliable Providence. They can laugh because they never trusted in a 401k—they have been too busy trying to get this day their daily bread.

It is with this freedom that we must challenge the idea of America being the "messianic hope"—a positioning offered by political pundit and former U.S. Secretary of Education William J. Bennett and others. Heck, Barack even reiterated Bennett when he told some Chicagoland politicos, "America is the last best hope of earth."[2] That's bad theology. Our hope does not lie in Wall Street. Our hope does not rest in the American dream. Our hope does not come from a new Caesar or a new President (even a good one) . . . our hope is built on nothing less than Jesus' blood and righteousness . . . on Christ the solid rock I stand, and all other ground is sinking sand.

John: I liked Kennedy's 1961 inauguration speech: "Ask not what your country can do for you, but what you can do for your country." Freedom gives us the opportunity. Freedom says that we are no longer working for ourselves or for our own addiction. Freedom says that we are not longer working for the slave master. We were working to further somebody else's agenda . . . or to further our own agenda . . . but now we are free to do God's agenda. We are now free to work hard to do all that we can, to get up as early as we can, to go to bed as late as we can, in order to do that which God has given us to do . . . and it is good and wholesome. That's what freedom is for. Freedom is not doing whatever we want. It is doing all that He wants. Freedom is building our hope on nothing less than Christ our solid rock . . .

SHANE: . . . all other ground is sinking sand.

Notes

1. See Romans 3:23.
2. Barack Obama, speaking to the Chicago Council on Global Affairs, Chicago, Illinois, April 23, 2007. http://my.barackobama.com/page/content/fpccga.

THE END...MORE OR LESS

(Some Closing Thoughts)

SHANE: So this is where we end our conversation . . . or at least interrupt it for now.

John: We repeated ourselves way too often, but then we are both preachers, so what do you expect? We talked a lot about the inner city, the economy, racial reconciliation, being good stewards of the earth, community and having passion for the poor—but those are our callings. When you write your own book, you should emphasize what God has given you—and Shane and I will read all about it!

SHANE: We hope that what we have written will stir you to think, talk, follow and lead. We hope that it will stir up some holy mischief and cause you to find some folks you can plot goodness with. We know there is a lot we left out, and we sure didn't solve all the world's problems or tell how we can find peace in the Middle East . . . but the stuff we have pondered is the stuff that leads to real peace. As we promised, there is no recipe for success, no doctorate degree, no failproof strategy for leadership at the end of this book. Not even another list.

John: Just dreams of the young and young at heart . . .

SHANE: . . . and wisdom and vision of those we have followed. Every generation has its own exodus. And every generation needs its own Moses . . . its own Mother Teresa . . . its own John Perkins.

John: Yes, there are going to be a lot of John Perkinses in future generations. In fact, my grandson's name is John P. Perkins! Okay. And my great-grandson's name is John P. Perkins as well. So there will be a lot of us. It's time for you to join in, too.

SHANE: Come along with us as we live out this conversation . . . but know that there are many obstacles—so much suffering and poverty and violence. But our God is familiar with suffering. Our God can swallow up armies and pour out bread from the heavens. Wall Street may fail us, but the God who takes care of the lilies and the sparrows will never let us down. Certainly, there is evil in the world. But our Savior has stared evil in the face and overcome it with love. The world may be in chaos . . . but our God has overcome the world. And now we are invited to join the triumph of the cross . . . and to lead others on the narrow, rugged road to freedom.

Above all else I urge that there should be no murmuring in the community.
—St. Benedict of Nursia (480–547)

NINE MONTHS LATER...

(adapted from a conference call, July 20, 2009, and a few subsequent emails)

STEVE (the book's editor): Is everyone on the line?

SHANE: I'm here. Hi, John.

John: Hey, Shane, good to hear your voice. Andrew is here, too. He has been working with us in Jackson.

ANDREW: Hi, Shane.

STEVE: Well, we go to press in a few days. It's been quite a journey since John and I first talked about this book with our president at Regal, Bill Greig III, nearly four years ago.

John: I remember that day. After the memorial service for Bill III's father, I was telling how Mr. Greig (Bill Jr.) had been not only a wise businessman but also such a great friend, even supporting me at a time when not many believers were talking about helping the poor and reconciling the races. When he was with us, Mr. Greig would say, "It's the right thing to do." He and I would shake hands and roll up our sleeves and start writing. Bill III followed his father as president at Regal and is now a good friend, too.

STEVE: If I remember correctly, Bill III asked what your passions were today and if there was anything else you wanted to write.

John: I wanted to write about passing along this vision, this promise, this blessing of leading people to freedom. I pass it along to my children and to those in the CCDA movement. But Shane, for one, has shown me that it needs to go further. So who better to co-write with than someone I respect and someone who can carry on the "going further" part?

SHANE: The moment I heard the idea of writing with John, I knew I had to do it. And then we sat down in Miami to record our first conversations for this book. There was a convention going on down-stairs, but I wanted to stay for hours, just listening as you oozed out wisdom.

STEVE: I remember traveling to Mississippi and walking the streets of Mendenhall with John and Andrew . . . the place where this all started.

ANDREW: And later sitting on the front porch in Jackson reviewing the manuscript.

STEVE: We've had some people read the manuscript to give us feed-back. A pastor in Hawaii said our format was "creative" (we knew that), but he said it just might create a new paradigm in leadership books. And that he and everyone on his staff should read it.

John: I will vote for the new paradigm!

STEVE: Shane, you will be curious to hear about this one: Rebecca (who served an internship with Freeset in Calcutta) is part of an in-tentional community that a bunch of Azusa Pacific grads have formed in a struggling part of Pomona, California. They follow The Simple Way model. I asked Rebecca to check out the manuscript. She emailed back that it had started a dialogue in their community. Here's part of her conversation:

> Every day, as we take on the yoke of our Rabbi, we aren't promised a life of certainty and control but lives of a new free-dom—one found in Christ. Our newfound freedom is one that dares us as leaders and followers to wander into new grounds. These are grounds outside the imagination of the world and outside the parameters of certainty where some-

times we may learn of great failure, but if we journey long enough, we will follow the footsteps of the slaughtered Lamb to lives of tremendous beauty and truth.

SHANE: Good dialogue. Give Rebecca a shout out for me. Hey, Andrew, you are just out of college, too. What do you think about our ideas about following and leading?

ANDREW: Well, for my generation (and I am 24), we are bombarded with issues every day. There are conflicts in the Middle East, genocide, global warming, child slavery, the sex trade, the spreading pandemic of AIDS . . . the list goes on and on. There are also domestic issues like immigration, healthcare, the wealth-gap, education disparities, a broken justice system, lingering residue of racism, urban violence . . . where do I stop? Because the world is "flat" and we've got fingertip access to almost every corner of every nation, we are exposed to every issue.

"Issues" . . . that's how they're presented to my generation, and that's how we interact with them. We get to pick and choose what we want to get involved with—even going along with what might be trendy. After we've joined a Facebook group, forwarded an email or even taken a short-term mission trip, we might move on to the next "issue." Of course, the bouncing from one issue to the next runs counter to what both of you say, and it's counter to what God asks of us.

So there will always be "issues," but do we recognize them as "pains"?

John: Good question. But how does the pain of racism or the poor translate to you today?

ANDREW: In 1960, the pain you saw and experienced in Mississippi was clear . . . a hardened structure of personal bigotry, institutional racism and palpable hate. There were thousands of black Mississippians who lived with the pain of fear, humiliation, inequality and death every day. With the help of God and an army of ordinary radicals, you have stayed faithful, and while today Mississippi isn't perfect, it has come a long way.

The challenge for my generation is to take one of these "pains" we're constantly confronted with and find someone (yes, a real human being) who is living in this pain. We have to get to know that someone for the person God made him or her to be. Meet his or her families. Hear his or her struggle. I've had the privilege of knowing a number of Hispanic immigrants, and now immigration isn't simply an "issue" for me; it's become the pain of the people I know—there are faces and families and joy and suffering and hope. While I'll never know the fear of deportation or the alienation of being an outsider in the only country I know, it's now a "pain" I can speak to.

SHANE: Good word, Andrew. We should have made that point! But that's what this conversation is all about. Each of us will have our own "issue" that needs to become a pain, a cause, a vision, a promise of the hope of freedom that we carry. Maybe you're already living it. Maybe the people around you are living it. Maybe you have to find it. Listen to God, travel around the world, learn a new language, hang out in weird places and meet strange people. Find someone in pain to love. When those types of relationships are built and you commit to the people that feel the pain—not just the "issue"—it becomes contagious. That's when people want to follow. That's when you become a leader. That's when they will follow you to freedom.

John: I am so enjoying this conversation . . . now let's get some more voices in on this.

I will pour out of My Spirit on all flesh;
Your sons and your daughters shall prophesy,
Your young men shall see visions,
Your old men shall dream dreams.

JOEL 2:28; ACTS 2:17

THANKS

To our forefathers and foremothers . . . you made it possible for us to lead those who will follow us.

John: Thank you, Vera Mae, my beloved wife of 58 years. I thought of dedicating this book to you, but you deserve so much more than a simple dedication. Without you, I would not be who I am. Thanks also to all of my children, Spencer (deceased), Joanie, Phillip, Derek, Deborah, Wayne, Priscilla and Elizabeth. Thanks to my friends and to my supporters within the Christian Community Development Association who have caught the vision of serving God by serving the poor. And thanks to Bill Greig III for initiating this conversation.

SHANE: I suggested you write a thank-you note to some of those you follow, so it is only appropriate that I give thanks to those whom I have followed. Thank you, Mom. You taught me so much more than just how to sew. Thanks also to Tony Campolo, Mother Teresa, Shanique, Manuel, Miss Sunshine, everyone at The Simple Way, everyone on Potter Street in North Philly and . . . so many others.

ABOUT THE AUTHORS

SHANE CLAIBORNE

With tears and laughter, Shane Claiborne unveils the tragic messes we've made of our world and the tangible hope that another world is possible. Shane graduated from Eastern University and did graduate work at Princeton Seminary. His ministry experience is varied, from a 10-week stint working alongside Mother Teresa in Calcutta to a year spent serving a wealthy mega-congregation at Willow Creek Community Church outside of Chicago. During the recent war in Iraq, Shane spent three weeks in Baghdad with the Iraq Peace Team. Shane is also a founding partner of The Simple Way, a faith community in inner-city Philadelphia that has helped to birth and connect radical faith communities around the world.

Shane writes and travels extensively, speaking about peacemaking, social justice and Jesus. He is featured in the DVD series *Another World Is Possible* and is the author of several books, including *The Irresistible Revolution, Jesus for President* and *Becoming the Answer to Our Prayers.* Shane speaks more than 100 times each year in a dozen or so countries and nearly every state in the U.S.

John M. Perkins

John Perkins grew up a sharecropper's son in New Hebron, Mississippi, amidst dire poverty. After converting to Christianity in 1960, he moved to Mendenhall, Mississippi, where he and his wife, Vera Mae, launched the Voice of Calvary Ministries and became leaders in the civil rights movmement. As a result of non-violent demonstrations for racial equality, John was repeatedly harassed, beaten and imprisoned.

In Mendenhall, the Voice of Calvary started a church, health center, leadership development program, thrift store, low-income housing development and training center. In 1982, the Perkins family founded

Harambee Christian Family Center in Northwest Pasadena, a neighborhood that had one of the highest daytime crime rates in California. John is also founder and president emeritus of the John M. and Vera Mae Perkins Foundation for Reconciliation and Development, founder and president emeritus of the Christian Community Development Association, and has served on the board of directors of numerous nonprofit organizations. He has written several books, including *Let Justice Roll Down, With Justice for All* and *Beyond Charity*.

Today, the Perkins family lives in Jackson, Mississippi.

CONTACT

SHANE CLAIBORNE

The Simple Way
P.O. Box 14751
Philadelphia, PA 19134
www.thesimpleway.org

(*Note:* Shane's speaking schedule is listed on The Simple Way website.)

John M. Perkins

Visit the Perkins Leadership Retreat at the
John and Vera Mae Perkins Foundation
1831 Robinson St., Jackson, MS 39209
Email: info@jmpf.org
Phone: 601-354-1563
www.jmpf.org
facebook.com/pages/John-M-Perkins-Foundation/40947699914

(*Note:* Check out the latest happenings at Seattle Pacific University's
John Perkins Center at www.spu.edu/depts/perkins/.)